THE EUCHARISTIC FAITH

THE EUCHARISTIC FAITH

Ralph McMichael

scm press

© Ralph McMichael 2019

Published in 2019 by SCM Press
Editorial office
3rd Floor, Invicta House,
108–114 Golden Lane,
London EC1Y 0TG, UK
www.scmpress.co.uk

SCM Press is an imprint of Hymns Ancient & Modern Ltd
(a registered charity)

Hymns Ancient & Modern® is a registered trademark of
Hymns Ancient & Modern Ltd
13A Hellesdon Park Road, Norwich,
Norfolk NR6 5DR, UK

Scripture quotations are from New Revised Standard Version Bible:
Anglicized Edition, copyright 1989, 1995 National Council of the Churches
of Christ in the United States of America. Used by permission. All rights
reserved worldwide.

ISBN 978-0-334-05659-1

British Library Cataloguing in Publication data

A catalogue record for this book is available
from the British Library

Printed and bound by CPI Group (UK) Ltd

Contents

For Louis

Teacher, Mentor and Friend

Acknowledgements

Theology in its proper existence is the thinking and reflecting that takes place within the Body of Christ. I am one member of the Body of Christ, and we know and confess that each member needs all the other members of this Body in order to become who they really are as that unique member. Individualism is a theological sin, the posture of inescapable error. Thus, I wish to acknowledge some members of the Body of Christ who have assisted my formation as a theologian as well as in the particular work of theology that you have before you. I am thankful first to David Shervington and the editorial staff of SCM Press for taking this project on, and especially for David's patience during multiple delays of receiving this manuscript and for his enthusiastic response once he did get to read this work. Likewise, I am grateful for those who read specific chapters and offered their reflections: Marshall Crossnoe, Andrew McGowan, Stephen Fowl, David Fagerberg and Nathan Jennings. It is a blessing to offer my gratitude to Allyne Smith for reading the whole manuscript with his keen editorial skill since we first met over 40 years ago at our first day of orientation for incoming seminarians. We have shared many theological conversations as well as a great deal of other talks and experiences that have nothing to do with theology. Thank you to Stanley Hauerwas for writing the foreword, which in his inimitable style tells the reader to do what any author would want, that is, actually read and focus on what is in this book.

Theology also takes place somewhere. While the abiding argument of this book is that the Eucharist is where and whereby theology truly and really takes place, I would like to offer my gratitude to a couple of priests who provided me with a particular place to pray, read, think and write. I speak of that Oxbridge looking office I have on the third floor of the 'old part' of Emmanuel Episcopal Church in Webster Groves, Missouri. The two priests who have allowed me to come to this office and to remain there are Doris Westfall and Jenny Hulen. While the concept of this book reaches back a couple of decades, its planning and initial writing occurred while I was priest-in-charge of St Andrew's Episcopal Church in Edwardsville, Illinois. For four years and four months I was blessed to serve this parish as priest, pastor and teacher. We shared the Eucharistic faith and life; we shared the kind of friendship and love that animates the Body of Christ. Thank you, my fellow members at St Andrew's for our life and time together.

Life within the Body of Christ is not an escape from 'real' life; it is the transformation and celebration of our human life. God's providence in my life led me to a somewhat eccentric Anglo-Catholic parish where I met someone whom I would marry and with whom we would have three children. For this gift of life and love I am grateful to God, and I thank Jan for sharing this life with me for 33 years and for our wonderful children Nelson, Anne Marie and Breck. And then there is our grandson Anthony Khai who blesses us in so many ways.

Forty-one years ago at the age of 22, I showed up on the campus of a seminary to begin my theological formation. On the day I arrived I entered a simple wooden chapel to attend an afternoon celebration of the Eucharist. There were a few people present and the professor of liturgy was the presider. Wearing an unadorned conical chasuble, standing at an austere wooden altar, he presided and prayed with the simplicity and sincerity that I came to learn was required if we were to take the Eucharist seriously as God's work and not ours. The Eucharistic faith is faith in the Father who gives the Son and pours out the Holy Spirit; it is faith bestowed and received. The Eucharist is not a display of personal piety, whether genuine

ACKNOWLEDGMENTS

or manufactured, and it is certainly not an arena for partisan posturing. We strive for Eucharistic competence; 'we rehearse because it is not important'. Those lessons, that example, is the witness and embodiment of the Eucharistic faith and of the priesthood that serves the Body of Christ that is Louis Weil. I dedicate this first volume of my Eucharistic systematic theology to Louis: Teacher, Mentor and Friend.

Foreword

Keep reading. I begin with that admonition because I worry that some readers of this extraordinary book may take what McMichael has done for granted in the same way the Eucharist is taken for granted. After all, is it not the case that for many Christians the Eucharist is celebrated every Sunday? Accordingly, some may wonder what is so special about McMichael's claim that Christians are constituted by Eucharist and that Christians make the Eucharist what it is.

Keep reading. What McMichael has done is not theology as usual. This is not just another academic theologian trying to gain notice by emphasizing one or another aspect of the Christian faith – for example eschatology – to try to convince their readers how such an emphasis helps us better understand every aspect of the Christian faith. By rethinking everything from the reality of the Eucharistic faith, McMichael recovers the Christological centre of our faith in a manner that helps us see the radical character of the everyday. Gratitude turns out to be not only a central virtue but a strong claim, indeed even a metaphysical claim, about the way things are.

Keep reading. But read slowly. This is a book that has been long in the making. His project is one that could only be undertaken by someone whose theological judgements have been honed by fundamental reconsiderations of the work of theology. That is but a way to say that McMichael's book is the work of a mature theological mind that should make the reader stop often to read and reread sentences that should change the way we live and think.

Keep reading. McMichael wants his readers to think with him. For example, McMichael begins his book by asking 'What is the essence of the Christian faith?' Yet he soon questions whether that is an appropriate way to begin because that question can tempt the theologian to a reductive theological method. Put polemically, McMichael worries that attempts to try to find an essence of the Christian faith is to fall into the hands of Protestant liberalism.

McMichael is anything but a theological liberal, but that is why you must keep reading. You must keep reading because, like Barth, every theological claim demands being read in relation to other theological claims. Much later in the book, McMichael will say that 'the Eucharist is the essence of the Christian faith', which means he must be saying something quite exact given his earlier worries about 'essence'. Some may think it useful to label McMichael as a 'postmodernist', but such labels fail to do justice to the theological substance that has shaped this book.

Keep reading. McMichael is obviously well versed in the ancient as well as more recent theological works, but he does not develop his account of the Eucharistic faith by entering into conversation with other theologians. I have no doubt he thought long and hard about whether or who he might discuss in an effort to make his position more recognizable. But as I have suggested he is not just making another theological proposal. He is trying to help us see what it means to live in a universe created and sustained by a Eucharistic God. It does not get more serious than that.

Keep reading. Let me give one example, though McMichael's book is one long example, of how a sustained reading of *The Eucharistic Faith* changes how we think about ourselves and the world. In his wonderful chapter on truth, he makes the obvious but seldom acknowledged observation that 'Truth is timeless, but we are not.' What a wonderful sentence. It is a sentence, moreover, that hopefully he will develop further in the volumes he plans to write after this book. That truth is timeless is but a way to remind us, as McMichael does throughout this book, that this is a book about a very particular truth because God is a very particular God, that is, God is a Eucharistic God.

I have tried to do no more than to entice the reader of McMichael's book to keep reading. But why me? Why should anyone think I am someone that has a standing to make that suggestion? After all I am not even a proper theologian. I am an ethicist. It would be counter-productive for me to try to respond to that worry. What I can say, however, is McMichael's observation that theology should change a theologian I take to be true. It is also true that reading a theologian as serious as McMichael will also invite changes but then that is the way it should be. Keep reading.

Stanley Hauerwas
Gilbert T. Rowe Professor Emeritus of Divinity and Law at Duke University

Introduction

What is the essence of the Christian faith? This has been an abiding question for Christian theology from at least the eighteenth century, and it has received a variety of positive answers as well as an array of objections and rejections. It would be fair to refer to this question as a characteristically modern one. It is only with the emergence of our critical capacities, expressly in the realms of history and reason, that we would pursue the question of essence. That is, applying our now honed critical perspectives and skills, we can begin to question the Christian faith from outside the confines of church and its authoritative teaching. We can locate ourselves in our own minds, in our guilds of professional scholars; we can claim the high ground of science with its perches of objectivity and method. From these perches we can look over there where Christianity is, and we can survey its forms and contents. When we look at Christianity, we do so with suspicious and critical eyes, because that is the way we are supposed to look at everything. We want to know what is being hidden from us, what has gone wrong, and if there is anything left over there that we can use, that is beneficial for us and for the world. No longer, even if we did at all, do we look for a vision of God, a vision that demands contemplation and not criticism, a vision and a reality that not only eludes our critical grasp but places us into question: 'Where were you when I created the universe?' Unlike Job, modern scholarship, even religious scholarship, did not repent of its scientific methods. Actually, the question of the essence of the Christian faith can be a way of avoiding God.

As we begin to pull away the layers of the various expressions and existences of Christianity, whether by demythologizing (modern) or deconstruction (postmodern), we can search for that essence lying underneath all the language and vestments that have clouded and clothed it so that we could no longer see it with our modern eyes. And once we have identified this essence, 'the pearl of great price' of our intellectual and ethical kingdoms, we can dust off its pre-modern debris, polish it and find something to do with it that will serve our purposes here and now. Thus, identifying the essence of Christianity, or of the Christian faith, and there is a potential material difference between these two as there is between what is religious and what is theological, is an act of dislocation and then relocation. Is the location of this essence 'essential'? Cannot this essence have a variety of existences? Is it not true that the content of Christian faith can take on various forms, be expressed in a variety of languages, philosophical idioms, and certainly must be appraised according to a diversity of contexts? And yet, are we not aware that the question of the essence of Christianity has been pursued both to identify this essence and to deny that it even exists? There is an argument that draws the connection between Ludwig Feuerbach, whose essence of Christianity is an infinite projection of a god that does not exist, to Adolf von Harnack, whose essence has to be rescued from its primitive and pre-modern distortions.[1] This search for an essence of Christian faith drove René Descartes to meditate and to look inward, and following him on this inward journey, Friedrich Schleiermacher was able to identity this essence as a feeling of dependency. We look for an essence by looking at ourselves, and we discovered it within us. Having done so, everything else that exists outside ourselves is put into question by us. By questioning ourselves, and discovering the answers within ourselves, we are now able to question everything around us in terms of the answer that we have already, the answer that is us. Even, and especially, God becomes a question that either receives a variety of answers or no answer at all.

What is the essence of the Christian faith? Instead of a question that leads us to a reduction of the Christian faith, is it possible that this question could lead us to an expansive perspective of the Christian faith, perhaps even to the abandonment of this question in order to inhabit the Christian faith as it is, and not as we wish it to be, to what we can use or to what can motivate us to do good things? That is, asking the question of essence could lead us to abandon this question for greener theological pastures.[2] If we are to remain with this question for a little longer, seeking to ask it as a proper theological pursuit, we can ask not only what is this essence, but where is it located, how does it exist as itself and not otherwise. That is, we do not seek to separate essence from its existence, from its potential normative location and from the how and why of what or who it is. We presume, we have faith, that the essence of the Christian faith is something that generates its own scope and depth, that calls for our being drawn to it rather than drawing it to ourselves. Instead of asking first how we see anything, we can begin to ask about what there is to see? Or, can we be transformed in our seeing, knowing, thinking and loving? 'Blessed are those who believe and have not seen.' Certainly, while Thomas suffered from a proleptic Cartesian anxiety, one cannot blame him for wanting to see certain signs before he was willing to believe that Jesus had been raised from the dead. His desire to see the scars left by the nails and the spear was indicative of all our desires to be able to recognize that Jesus shared our history, that we could locate the presence of Jesus in what we already know, in what has already happened. Thomas wanted signs that were given to him from his history, knowledge and experience. But what if these customary and domesticated signs are illusory, even perhaps, deceptive? Is there a theological *aporia* of wanting our own signs of the presence of Jesus, our own sacraments of faith?

The sixth chapter of the Gospel of John begins with an account of Jesus taking five barley loaves and two fish, giving thanks over it and giving it to a large crowd to eat. Not only did this crowd have enough to eat, but there was food left over. Later, Jesus and his disciples went to the other side of the lake from where this feeding took place. When the crowd realized that Jesus had left them, they crossed the lake to look for him. When they came to Jesus, he had this to say: 'Very truly, I tell you, you are looking for me, not because you saw signs, but because you ate your fill of the loaves. Do not work for the food that perishes, but for the food that endures for eternal life, which the Son of Man will give you' (John 6.26–27). It is possible that we not only see signs that point to ourselves, we can look past the signs of the presence of Jesus in order to seek our own intellectual, physical, ethical, spiritual, political, cultural and religious satiation. We already know what will satisfy us, and we want Jesus to give it to us. At this point, we do not share the request Philip makes to Jesus: 'Lord, show us the Father, and we will be satisfied' (John 14.8). This consideration of what kind of signs we seek, or wish to see, or whether it is not signs that have our attention, but our pre-existing needs, has begun to move us away from the question of our self-identification of the essence of the Christian faith to the presence of a person who himself is capable of asking questions of us. Jesus redirects the crowd from why they came to him in the first place to what he alone can give them. Bread that fills the stomach can be had in a variety of places, but only Jesus gives the bread that feeds us into eternal life. And since only Jesus gives us this bread, we can only receive it where he is, where he gives it to us. This presence of Jesus, this location of Jesus, can lead us to repent of our search for essence, and instead to seek him, to seek first the kingdom of God.

One such theologian who abandoned the modern quest for the essence of the Christian faith, who strove to seek what God is giving us as it is given and not otherwise, was Karl Barth. Barth's relentless pursuit and exposition of theology as faithful to God's address to us, to the Word of God, led him to reject the inheritance of modern theology, to turn away from our presence to ourselves towards the presence of Jesus as the Word of God. For him, theology, this 'church dogmatics', is the abiding effort to assess, and correct if needed, the church's proclamation of the Word of God, to make sure that the church was indeed proclaiming the Word of God and not some other word that we would prefer to hear and to know. For Barth, fidelity to the Word of God is rejection of the temptation to speak of an essence of Christianity, to pursue a method that would identify such an essence.

In a Church dogmatics the position usually occupied in dogmatic systems by an arbitrarily chosen basic view belongs by right to the Word of God, and the Word of God alone. It does not belong to a conception of the Word of God. It is another matter that in every dogmatics a conception accompanies and ought to accompany the confession both of the Church and also the individual. But in a Church dogmatics this conception must not assume the dignity and function of a positive principle. It must not usurp the position of the object of dogmatics. This object, which must dictate dogmatic method, is the Word of God itself. It is not a conception of it. It is not, therefore, a basic dogma, tenet, principle or definition of the essence of Christianity. It is not any kind of truth that can be controlled. But - and we must remember this point, especially when we are thinking of the autonomy of dogmatics - this centre is not something which is under our control, but something which exercises control over us. The autonomy in which dogmatics has to choose its method must consist solely in the recognition of its theonomy, i.e. in its free submission to the sovereignty of the Word of God alone.[3]

Any of our theological identifications of the essence of the Christian faith would lead to the displacement of what is the only appropriate centre and guiding principle of theology, which is the Word of God itself. We are not, according to Barth, to get in the way of this Word with our concepts or systems; we should allow the Word to speak for itself, to address the church without having to pass through our state of mind, through our societal, political or religious dispositions and predilections. Theology serves the Word of God alone as this Word is proclaimed in and by the church.

While Barth wishes to leave the question of the essence of the Christian faith behind, and does so by his unyielding engagement of, and exposition of, the Word of God, we can still ask whether this effort leads to an adequate presentation of the Christian faith. That is, does this focus on the Word of God as the object of theology, the controlling agent of theology, give us the scope of its fullness, the catholicity, of the Christian faith when we do focus on what it is that makes the Christian faith what it truly and really is. In a sense, we could say that Barth points us in the right direction, but he himself never fully inhabits the location where this address of the Word of God takes place, in the Eucharist. As the Word of God, this Word addresses us with the promise of a place prepared for us, of the Word becoming our flesh, of the astounding claim of the resurrection of the body, and of the creation of the Body of Christ in which we can become members by baptism. Yes, let us leave behind the modern question of the essence of Christianity, and let us also leave aside the postmodern apathy or antipathy towards the possibility of any normative and accountable centre of Christian faith. However, let us go to the Eucharist, to inhabit the place that is the Christian faith, that is where the Word of God addresses us within the life that this Word creates, the living Body of Christ. For the proclaimed Word of God is an arriving person who desires to share his life of communion with us, which is why this Word is spoken in the first and in the last place, the origin and destiny of life in Christ. Consider the following account of martyrdom in the early church:

> Then Saturninus, the priest, was arraigned for combat. The pro-consul asked, 'Did you, contrary to the orders of the emperors,

arrange for these persons to hold an assembly?' Saturninus replied, 'Certainly. We celebrated the Eucharist.' 'Why?' 'Because the Eucharist cannot be abandoned.' As soon as he said this, the proconsul ordered him to be put immediately on the rack … Then Felix, a son of Saturninus and a reader in the church, came forward to the contest. Whereupon the proconsul inquired of him, 'I am not asking you if you are a Christian. You can hold your peace about that! But were you one of the assembly; and do you possess any copies of the Scriptures?' 'As if a Christian could exist without the Eucharist, or the Eucharist be celebrated without a Christian!' answered Felix. 'Don't you know that a Christian is constituted by the Eucharist, and the Eucharist by a Christian? Neither avails without the other. We celebrated our assembly right gloriously. We always convene at the Eucharist for the reading of the Lord's Scriptures.[4]

The argument of this book, its guiding principle, is that the Christian faith is the Eucharistic faith. If we seek to understand the Christian faith in all its fullness, its catholicity as well as its apostolicity, we will have to inhabit the Eucharist and encounter the centre of the Christian faith there in its normative Eucharistic way: the arrival of Jesus to give us his life of communion. Furthermore, not only is this inhabiting of the Eucharist the way into the normative existence of the Christian faith, the place prepared for us to become faithful, this inhabitation serves the transformation of Christian theology, its Eucharistic renewal.[5] If we seek to understand the Eucharistic faith, we will need a Eucharistic theology to do so. Furthermore, if we wish to present an appropriate appreciation for the scope and depth of the Eucharistic faith, we will need to articulate and develop a Eucharistic systematic theology. Before proceeding with an introduction of what I mean by a Eucharistic systematic theology, it has to be acknowledged that the following argument and presentation for the Eucharistic faith, and for the Eucharistic renewal of theology, is the effort to go where we have been directed by the work of Alexander Schmemann.[6] While it has to be acknowledged that Schmemann was working within, and addressing, the theology and life of the Orthodox Church, I am not working within any specific ecclesial tradition or for any prior existing theological school or movement. Rather, I am calling for something that exists theologically as the celebration of the Eucharist, and yet does not exist as a full ecclesial expression and constitution of the faith, and hence its theological accompaniment, that takes place there and then. I am arguing for a faith and theology that exists already as the Eucharist, and that does not yet exist fully and faithfully as church and as theology.

The task I set before me is to reimagine all of theology from the Eucharist. As argued and explicated in this book, especially in its first two chapters, the 'essence' of the Christian faith is located in and as the Eucharist. This Eucharistic place for faith and theology is taken as God-given, the faithful and theological place prepared for us. Now, what do I mean by 'reimagine'? First, let us consider how we would imagine what is taking place in and as Eucharist. Imagine here does not mean fantasy, but an engagement with a presumed reality, even though we are not able to construct or know the fullness of this reality; analytical certainty and clarity are not at home in this imaginative engagement. Fantasy is the construction of a reality that we presume, actually claim, does not exist. The premise here is that there is an imaginative reality taking place within the Eucharist with or without our theological engagement with it. That is, there is this theological reality with or without our theological study or account of this reality. Thus, the theological task is to encounter, engage, really inhabit, what is already taking place in and as the Eucharist. While we are aware that more is going on 'than we can ask or imagine', this mystery is not an obstacle to theology but its invitation. Mystery is not-knowing; it is the inexhaustibility of knowing. We seek to inhabit the imaginative theology that is taking place within the Eucharist. We seek to be held within the present tense of theology, even though we recognize the formative role of the past tense as well as the renewal that comes from being placed before the horizon of the future tense; indeed, to be in the place where and whereby this future 'theology' becomes our reality. It is from within what is taking place that we can appropriately appreciate what has taken place and expect what might or can take place. It is only from within the imaginative place of the Eucharist that we can speak authentically of our theological past and our theological future.

The task of 'reimagining' is an exercise and discipline that would allow the imaginative theological reality that is the Eucharist to shape, direct and nurture our theology, our seeking to understand this faith. Reimagining is how we speak, think and understand what is happening in and as the Eucharist. One way we might put this premise is to say that God imagines a place and life for us, and we seek to inhabit, live and understand this God-given imagination. Of course, when we do reimagine the imaginative reality taking place within the Eucharist, we are thinking, speaking and understanding it outside this place. I am writing this introduction right now; I am not celebrating the Eucharist. This is how our theology seeks to understand the Eucharistic faith by being habitually nurtured and shaped by it, while also being aware of how this theology may or may not differ from other projects that have sought an account of the Christian faith. Therefore, while we are aware of other theological styles, systems, concerns and agendas, we cannot allow ourselves to be distracted from this reimaginative task; we cannot allow our theology to be dislocated from the Eucharist.

What do I mean by 'all of theology?' This phrase refers to the wholeness of the Eucharistic theological reality, which again, is the fullness of the Eucharistic faith. We could say, 'all of theology that is the Eucharist'. What this phrase does not mean is that we have to say something 'Eucharistic' about all that is considered theology in the church and in the academy; or, that we have to take whatever are the reigning issues and agendas of theology into our Eucharistic imagination. We are not striving to provide a Eucharistic gloss on theology nor a Eucharistic interpretation or critique of the state of theology. The task before us is to understand the wholeness of the Eucharistic faith, to present a Eucharistic systematic theology. Regard for the wholeness of the Eucharistic faith is what leads us to refer to this project as a 'systematic' theology. We desire a theology, a reimaginative enterprise, that is adequate as well as appropriate to the fullness of the Eucharistic faith. Thus, we are concerned with both the scope and the depth of this faith. The second reason we refer to this theological task as 'systematic' is the pursuit of the inherent coherence of this faith. This is why the task is to reimagine all of theology *from* the Eucharist. The Eucharist is the 'system' of this systematic theology. This project requires vigilance that it does not turn into a series of theologies of the Eucharist nor become a systematic theology with occasional, even ad hoc, references to the Eucharist. We will not remove the Eucharist from the customary subjects of systematic theology so that we can examine it with the typical questions of liturgy or of sacramental theology. Nor will we take some theological material from the Eucharist and use it for another non-Eucharistic systematic theology. The task is to present a theology that is both Eucharistic and systematic, that derives its 'system' from the Eucharist.

The book before you is the first volume of this Eucharistic systematic theology; its scope and imaginative content is the Eucharistic faith. It is an exploration and presentation of the faith that resides within the Eucharist and of the faith that is the movement into the Eucharist. Since we are exploring and presenting the Eucharistic faith, we are doing Eucharistic systematic theology.[7] This volume has four phases to this movement into the Eucharist and within the Eucharist. They are: Theology, Seeking, Understanding and Faith. We begin with a consideration of the questions of the origin and nature of theology as they are located within and as the Eucharist. That is, we first argue for and present the origin and nature of what we will pursue, and how we will do so. The second phase is to provide normative content and shape to the Eucharistic theological landscape that we surveyed in the first phase. The customary regard for content and shape of theology is the identification and explication of its sources. And while we do indeed seem to follow this custom by speaking of tradition and Scripture, we are not referring to them as sources but as spheres and modes of seeking. The second phase of our movement into the Eucharist is seeking the Eucharistic faith in and through tradition and Scripture. We place tradition before Scripture because we engage Scripture within the Eucharist, and thus, within the shape and structure, the theological economy, of the Eucharist. As seeking an understanding of the faith, our seeking an understanding of the Eucharistic faith will have to be a Eucharistic operation. The third phase of this Eucharistic theological movement will take up three arenas where understanding is held to take place, or how understanding takes place. These are the arenas of knowledge, language and truth. However, we are not entering these arenas of understanding as they exist outside the Eucharist. We are not developing an epistemology, linguistics and metaphysics so that we can *then* seek to understand the Eucharistic faith.[8] Instead, the three chapters constituting this phase of understanding will approach the questions of knowledge, language and truth from within the Eucharist. The fourth and last phase of this theological movement into and within the Eucharist will be an imaginative account of the faith that resides there, of the faith that is the movement within the place that has been theologically prepared for us.

Since the task set before us is to reimagine all of theology from the Eucharist, to do our theology from within the Eucharist, and to allow the structure and economy of the Eucharist to shape our seeking of an understanding of the faith that abides there, I have sought to engage the reader directly, to invite the reader to come along with me as we enter the Eucharist, as we seek to understand what, and primarily who, we find there; or, more appropriately, who we meet there, the one who arrives to give us his life of communion, for the life of the world. Therefore, I have not included very much scholarly apparatus. I seldom address specific theologians directly, although the reader will find some of this address in the endnotes. However, I do address many of the basic themes of theology that have directed much of the work of particular theologians. So, I invite you to accompany me as we go to the Eucharist, to enter its mysterious and imaginative reality, and to be renewed in our Eucharistic theology, in our Eucharistic faith.

Notes

1 This identification of modern atheism with modern theology, the argument that modern theology's employment of, search for, a common philosophical ground between theology and other 'scientific' pursuits of knowledge, paved the way for the emergence, and later philosophical hegemony, of modern atheism, is well exposited by Michael J. Buckley, *At the Origins of Modern Atheism* (New Haven: Yale University Press, 1987). Another work that is illuminative here is Louis Dupré, *Passage to Modernity: An Essay in the Hermeneutics of Nature and Culture* (New Haven: Yale University Press, 1993).

2 For how the question of the essence of Christian faith has been reductive of theology, but also how it can lead to the renewal of theology, I have been assisted by Stephen Sykes, *The Identity of Christianity: Theologians and the Essence of Christianity from Schleiermacher to Barth* (London: SPCK, 1994).

3 *Church Dogmatics* I/2, translated by G. T. Thomson and Harold Knight (Edinburgh: T&T Clark, 1980), p. 866.

4 As quoted by Alkiviadis C. Calivas, 'The Eucharist: The Sacrament of the Economy of Salvation', in *One Loaf, One Cup: Ecumenical Studies of 1 Cor 11 and Other Eucharistic Texts*, edited and introduced by Ben F. Meyer (Macon, GA: Mercer University Press, 1993), p. 117.

5 For a more sustained and comprehensive argument for the Eucharistic renewal of theology and for the development of a Eucharistic systematic theology, see the concluding chapter, 'Theology', in my *Eucharist: A Guide for the Perplexed* (London: T&T Clark, 2010).

6 A good place to begin with Schmemann's argument for the Eucharistic renewal of theology is his 'Theology and Eucharist', in *Liturgy and Tradition:*

Theological Reflections of Alexander Schmemann, edited by Thomas Fisch (Crestwood, NY: St Vladimir's Seminary Press, 1990), pp. 69–88. Of course, the reader is advised to engage Schmemann's final and major work, *Eucharist: Sacrament of the Kingdom*, translated by Paul Kachur (Crestwood, NY: St Vladimir's Seminary Press, 1988).

7 It needs to be acknowledged that the operation of theology seeking an understanding of the Eucharistic faith could be construed as liturgical theology. While it indeed is seeking to abide within the liturgical event and reality that is the Eucharist, and thus, to treat this liturgy as the primary theology of the Christian faith, it is not only an argument for such an enterprise nor is it the Eucharistic instantiation of a liturgical theology. That is, we are abiding within the particularity of the Eucharist as the event of faith, theology and salvation. We are not applying liturgical theology to our consideration of the Eucharist. However, any appreciation of liturgical theology would serve to illuminate this Eucharistic systematic theology. For a good introduction to the scope and nature of liturgical theology, see David W. Fagerberg, *Theologia Prima: What is Liturgical Theology?* second edition (Chicago: Hillenbrand Books, 2004).

8 This is why this volume is the first of a Eucharistic systematic theology and not a volume of what is called 'Fundamental Theology'. This distinction will be articulated and paramount in the three chapters of this phase 'Understanding'. It will also be stated in the fourth phase 'Faith'.

PART 1

Theology

1

The Eucharistic Origin of Theology

When did Christian theology begin? The answer to this question, if readily supplied, would involve a presumed definition or understanding of theology so that we could identify or locate its beginning. For it is possible that different versions of theology can and do have different beginnings. This is certainly the case if we are considering the genesis of confessional theologies or the proliferation of various theological 'movements'. If we regarded theology as a textual affair, we would then look for these initial texts for theology's beginning. So, in posing the question of the beginning of theology, we are already engaged in the question of the nature and purpose of theology. Also, the enquiry into the beginning of theology can become the starting point, the point of departure, for the sustained effort to present a history of theology, a trajectory for its developments over time. This would be primarily a descriptive task, while acknowledging that interpretation is never absent from any theological endeavour. One might even attempt to study theology without ever really doing it. The question of theology's beginning exists then among an array of answers and a variety of questioners. Not only *what* is the answer, but *who* wants to know, and *why*.

By posing the question of the beginning of theology, I wish to explore the origin of theology. When theology began is a dimension of a whole constituted by the other dimensions of why, where and how. Origin is not just a temporal beginning, but a teleological substance, 'the assurance of things hoped for, the substance of things not seen' (Heb. 11.1). In this way, the origin of theology is its origination. When theology happens becomes our entry into the place where and when theology begins. And it is possible or plausible that once an origin as origination of theology has been located and identified as such, we can then speak of an abiding normative origin, a place where and whereby theology is called from and towards its own proper origination. Could it be the case that theology is properly approached not as something constructed but generated? Thus, my engagement with the question of the beginning of theology is my entry into a reflection on the nature and purpose of theology, the possibility of its abiding origination and normative generation. However, this is not another rendition of 'return to the sources', for my primary objective is not the historical analysis of primitive theological texts in order to achieve a contemporary application of their wisdom or to 'perform' some postmodern reiteration. To ask *when* theology began is to ask *where* theology began, how do we continually begin again, and why are we called from and towards this beginning. What lies ahead as assurance and substance? Where does theology take us? Asking the question of the omega of theology begins with a return to its alpha.

Christian theology began with the appearances of the risen Jesus, who was raised from the dead. That is, theology began when persons were confronted with a presence that could only be realized by an act of God. We might say that this presence was presented to persons who otherwise would not know it. Jesus is not located, he arrives, and because of this arrival, persons are compelled to say what this arrival means for their understanding of God's nature and will. Furthermore, persons must now come to terms with a presence that calls into question their own presence in the world. If there is a life (not just the extension of life) beyond death, a life that appears from the dead, then all our conceptual worlds or rational systems, all the ways in which we strive to make sense of ourselves, our presence in the world and to ourselves and to each other, have been disrupted. Do we try to fit the risen Jesus into what we

Does it not start with His birth?

His triumphal not cosmictly normal!

already know, already believe, or do we begin again to know, to believe, while abiding in the presence of the risen Jesus? The radical newness of the appearance of Jesus now raised from the dead compelled a renewal of understandings of God, self and world. Because Jesus has appeared to them from the dead, from their prior grasp of truth and reality, they are called to enter a place where and whereby Jesus will meet them, where and whereby they will now *see* him - in Galilee, in Jerusalem or on the road to Emmaus.

While Jesus appears from the dead, he arrives *from* the Father. The recognition of the return from the dead to arrival from the Father is the moment of theology's origin as well as its enduring movement of renewal. Jesus is here not because he shares our life ordered towards death, but because he arrives from the Father with the gift of life ordered towards living into the presence of God. The basic theological question - Who is God? - is now accompanied by the question: Why is Jesus here? Why he is here is inextricably bound up with the questions, how did he get here? and who is he really? The resurrection inaugurates the beginning of theology, while the ascension provokes the origin of theology.

The appearance of Jesus from the dead is the surprising event that happens in familiar places or in familiar ways. What is new is this appearance from the dead, but the risen Jesus seeks out those who have had a prior knowledge of him, those who have shared his history. He appears to the women who had accompanied him, to the disciples whom he had called to follow him; he meets them back in Galilee, or in Jerusalem where he had left them to their lives; he shows up when some of these disciples have gone back to fishing, or he joins a couple of disciples on their journey to teach them about the Scriptures and to share a meal with them. Jesus appears to his disciples in another upper room, this time not for a 'Last Supper' but for the conveying of his peace. For the disciples, all these places and activities have a history, a prior experience; they have been

19

there and done that before. And Jesus was with them then and there. Now they go to these places and back to these activities without Jesus. He is dead to them; he has departed their history. When Jesus appears to those who have known him previously, he confronts them with the possibility of knowing him in a new way because the old way of knowing him is dead. Theology begins with the possibility, really the necessity, of knowing Jesus as the one who appears from the dead. As such, due to this necessity, this confrontation with this new presence among the places and modalities of the old, indeed the unbridgeable divide between the old and the new that is death, those who are met by Jesus are forced towards a new understanding of him, invited into the possibility of a new history. They are not asked to deny their prior knowledge or history with him. Rather, they are now confronted with the possibility of *understanding* this knowledge and history in light of the appearance of Jesus from the dead, who appears where he was but not how he was. Put more directly into theological categories of the academic sort, the disciples cannot rely on a prior epistemology, ontology or study of history to locate Jesus. He appears from the dead; he has vacated all such localities. Jesus relocates himself, and the disciples' epistemology, ontology and study of history will have to be transformed to make room for this relocation. Theology begins when Jesus appears speaking his word of peace in that room where the disciples are gathered in fear behind locked doors. Banished from the Garden of Eden, humanity now finds itself in a place of fear, with the doors locked shutting out its future. Might there be another kind of future than the one they expected to happen? Might there be another type of gathering besides this one arising out of fear? Can these doors be opened to reveal a place of hope? Jesus said to Nathaniel, 'you will see greater things than these ... you will see heaven opened' (John 1.50–51).[1] Can there be a faith, hope and love that are not constituted by our human gatherings, projections and accustomed ways of making sense of this life? We will not know whether this is possible or not unless and until Jesus appears from the dead with this possibility, with our being forced to unlock the doors of our minds, hearts and bodies. Theology begins with the necessity of asking these kinds of questions; theology begins with the appearance of Jesus risen from the dead.

The beginning of theology is constituted with the beginning of the presence of Jesus from the dead. Theology is the possibility of a new and different life present in the world. Theology begins when God begins the new creation. As the firstborn of this new creation, the presence of the risen Jesus is always the beginning of theology. Theology begins with the risen Jesus, because this is the how, what, why, when and where God begins with us to place us within God's redemptive order. Theology begins where God makes this beginning. Therefore, theology is inherently the seeking to act and to understand before and towards this risen presence of Jesus. However, what are we then to make of the ascension of Jesus, his 'return' to the Father? Does this not place a stumbling block before any of our proper theological efforts? How are we to seek faithful acting and understanding in the presence of the risen Jesus when he is no longer here, no longer with us in the way he was? After the ascension, we cannot locate him where he once was; our historical locales of his presence are not places to meet him. Has Jesus left us to our own theological devices? Are we to turn the empty tomb into a theological classroom?

The turn from the beginning of theology towards its origination is the movement from the resurrection to the ascension, the movement from the risen presence of Jesus to his promised presence. While the beginning of theology is Jesus showing up from the dead where we are, the origination of theology is our going to where Jesus arrives from the Father. There are three possible places of theological endeavour: Jesus is where we belong; Jesus is where we are but does not belong there; and we are to become present where Jesus now belongs.

The first place is regularly occupied by all the efforts to locate Jesus within our reigning epistemology, philosophical trends, historical-critical reconstructions, comparative religious studies, due regard for our experiences of self or specified group, and within our cultural or societal contexts. While a caricature of the first place would be the effort to bring heaven to earth, or to see heaven in earthly terms, the second place would be the effort to escape the earth to get to heaven. The abiding presumption of this second place is the dialectic between God and humanity so that Jesus bridges this divide providing us 'the way [out] to the Father'. Jesus here is God's intervention in the world rather than the world's apotheosis, affirmation, explanation or strategy for progress of all sorts. Rather than some type of depth-dimension or a horizon of limitation (first place), the second place stresses discontinuity, the necessity of a disruptive presence, not so much the yearning for illumination but the demand of sacrifice. In this second place, Jesus shows up to take us somewhere else, to where he belongs. In the first place, we could say that Jesus is displaced so that he can be replaced where we are. For the second place, the theological movement is characterized by our displacement so that we can be replaced where Jesus would have us be.

The third theological place, as a place opened up by the ascension of Jesus and his promise to arrive from the Father, is a place where Jesus belongs and yet a place where we can go to in this life; it is a place that exists now for the sake of the arrival of Jesus. This third place subsumes Jesus' prior history of arriving when he would enter the towns and villages, when people would gather to hear him and to be touched by him. Fundamentally, this place recapitulates the incarnation but instead of rooting God's life in ours, now there is a place for us to become rooted in Christ: 'As you therefore have received Christ Jesus the Lord, continue to live your lives in him, rooted and built up in him and established in the faith, just as you were taught, abounding in thanksgiving' (Col. 2.6-7). The reality and history that Jesus has shared 'with us' now can stand before the place where he arrives to give us this reality and history as his, not ours. We move into this place by offering ourselves. The economy here is not displacement to replacement; it is the offering of all other places into the place of Jesus' arrival, which opens up the possibility of the transformation of any place as now his. He invites us to share this place with him, to receive his life.

The ascension of Jesus inaugurates the origin of theology. Since the risen Jesus does not continue to inhabit the places located within the co-ordinates of our history or experience – the tomb where we placed him is empty – the first Christian believers in Jesus were confronted with his absence. His presence before death and his presence from the dead now exist before the horizon of his absence and his promised arriving presence from the Father. How and what will these first Christians believe without any longer having Jesus sharing their presence? Has he left them to their own theological devices? Can we speak of a theological environment suspended between the presence and absence of Jesus? An environment inhabited by the arriving Jesus to encounter his offering believers? The first theological place emphasizes the proximity of Jesus; he is here with you as you are here. The second theological place stresses the distance of Jesus; he is there calling you away from here. This third theological place is characterized by Jesus arriving from there to here so that here may be where the believer receives what now belongs both there and here: 'may your will be done on earth as it is in heaven'. Faithful acting, thinking and speaking are now found and formed within the place created by both the absence and presence of Jesus.

Theology begins with the resurrection and originates with the ascension. In order to explore this assertion more deeply and with greater scope, we can take up Anselm's now classical definition of theology as faith seeking understanding. Within the theological environment created by the ascension of Jesus, how are we able to identify the origin of theology? Theology originated when, faced with the absence of Jesus as one who shared their presence as well as the disappearance of his immediate agency as teacher, preacher and healer, the early Christians had to seek an understanding of their faith in him in a way without him. Or, they would seek an understanding of their faith in him while aware of his beckoning and promised presence as the one who invites them to share his presence among them. How do we make sense of all this, of all that has happened, of everything we have been through with him, of our knowledge of him as the one who appears from the dead and yet promises to arrive from the Father by the outpouring of the Holy Spirit? These are good candidates for the initial and inaugurating questions of the early Christians; that is, of the origination of theology. Engaging these questions was not limited to the subject of Jesus; these questions are about God. The first theological endeavours of Christians presumed the God who was known already, who had a history of speaking and acting, and when the Christian faith moved out from its initial Palestinian locale, the seeking continued towards speaking and understanding this Jesus and this God in ways that proclaim a faith over against other forms of belief and religious practice. Theology originated when the early Christians took what they already knew about Jesus and about God prior to the ascension, and then sought to understand this knowing according to the trajectory of Pentecost: 'I still have many things to say to you, but you cannot bear them now. When the Spirit of truth comes, he will guide you into all the truth; for he will not speak on his own, but will speak whatever he hears, and he will declare to you the things that are to come' (John 16.12-13).

While the ascension opens the place where and whereby theology originates, this place is not a status quo to be maintained or a vacuum to be filled by our agency alone. The subjectivity of our presence is not the primary reality over against the presumed objectivity of Jesus' absence. The faith

24

of the early Christians was not a self-referential seeking of understanding; this faith sought the presence of Jesus and the understanding that takes place only in *his* presence. Theology is this faith seeking the presence of Jesus; the presence that he offers. Theology and its guiding questions of who this Jesus is and who this God is originate with the seeking of the *active* presence of Jesus as the presence of God who arrives for our understanding. This understanding again takes place within the gift of a living presence, our reception of the presence of Jesus for, with and now in us. Theology originates where and whereby Jesus' presence transforms our presence for, with and in him.

When faced with the ascended absence of Jesus and the promise of his arriving presence, the faith of the early Christians sought an understanding made possible within the place provided by the continuum of the prior, risen and ascended presence of Jesus. The early Christians did not then form a seminar to discuss and to articulate this understanding. The seminar room, classroom or discussion forum was not the place where theology originated. The early Christians did not do theology by writing texts or engaging in speculative adventures of cognition. They did their theology while seeking the presence of Jesus, gathering in the place of his arrival. The early Christians celebrated the Eucharist. Theology had a Eucharistic origin.

Eucharistic Origin(s)

If we are going to speak of the Eucharistic origin of theology as well as regard this origin as the proper theological generative place, then we are required to explore the question of the origin or origins of the Eucharist itself. The answer to this question is not as straightforward as might have been presumed; and in fact, a great deal of recent scholarship on this question has left its answer even more ambiguous than it once was.[2] Traditionally, the origin of the Eucharist has been assigned to Jesus' actions and words at the Last Supper as we have them in four different accounts (Matt. 26.20–29; Mark 14.17–25; Luke 22.14–20; 1 Cor. 11.23–26). Also, this traditional account of the origin of the Eucharist has focused on the so-called institution narrative: the words of Jesus over the bread and over the cup. However, recent scholarship has cast a wider net for its study of the possible origins of the Eucharist to include the other meals of Jesus with his disciples, the Jewish meals of the same period, and the formal meals or banquets existing then in the Greco-Roman social context. This pursuit of parallels for the early celebration of the Eucharist in the reigning ancient culture, including the Jewish one, has destabilized the role of the institution narrative as the original text of the Eucharistic liturgy. For when we ask about the place and role of the institution narrative in both the accounts of the Last Supper and in the primitive accounts of the Eucharist, what is it that we are asking? Are we pursuing the *why* question – why did the Christians begin to celebrate the Eucharist? – or, are we asking *how* the Christians enacted the Eucharist? Perhaps, we are asking a *what* question: What was the meaning of the Eucharist for these Christians? What does it mean to say that the bread and wine become the Body and Blood of Christ? We might have evidence that can lead to a firmer answer to one of these questions but not to the others. Indeed, the evidence could lead us to stop asking some questions and begin to ask new ones. And before going any further with this question of the origin(s) of the Eucharist, we need to acknowledge one fact and one crucial distinction. The one fact is that our evidence for the origin of the Eucharist is both varied and sparse. Some of these sources for the study of Eucharistic origins are the subject of scholarly debate on whether they are really about the early Eucharist or not, for example the *Didache*.[3] When we do study these documents, we are faced with evidence that belongs to a particular community and time (even when we cannot assign either of these exactly). That is, the evidence we do have for the early celebration of the

Eucharist does not allow for us to craft a narrative that can trace the development of the Eucharist in any linear fashion from the first into the fourth centuries. The crucial distinction to keep in mind is this: The scholarly study of the Last Supper accounts is not necessarily the same exercise as the study of the primitive Eucharist. While we would not study one without the other, they cannot be conflated into one textual and ritual entity. With these caveats as guides, we will consider the possible origins of the Eucharist and then turn directly to the more focused question of the place and role of the institution narrative.

When we study the origins of the Eucharist along with the Last Supper, we are working with the distinction between the historical events themselves and accounts of these events. That is, there is the Last Supper itself, and there are the four accounts of it. There are the celebrations of the Eucharist by the early church, and there are possible references to these celebrations in the New Testament and a few documents that refer to them either directly or indirectly. Regarding the origins of the Eucharist, recent scholarship has sought to place the accounts of the Last Supper, and thus the origins of these Eucharistic celebrations, within the broader context of the many meals that Jesus shared with his disciples as well as the meals described in the resurrection narratives. Furthermore, scholarly study of the origins of the Eucharist has broadened this context to include not only Jewish meals during this period but the formal banquets practised in the Greco-Roman world. Here, possible parallels of ritual or structure are sought and identified between pagan, Jewish and Christian meals of the first and second centuries AD.[4] When investigations of the origin of the Eucharist focused exclusively on the accounts of the Last Supper, there was the effort to find direct lines of development from Jewish ritual structures to Christian ones. The whole contested question of whether the Last Supper was a Passover meal or not set the stage for identifying developmental steps between a Jewish meal and the Last Supper into the early Eucharist. Was the Last Supper a Passover meal, or was it a formal Jewish fellowship meal, and how can we trace the words and actions with bread and cup from the Jewish context to the Christian church? Again, such a linear progression has been rejected, and this rejection is not only due to attending to a broader ritual context, but to the awareness that we do not know that much about first-century Jewish ritual or liturgy. Just like the Christian liturgical witnesses, the sources we do have emerged centuries later than the time of any purported enactment. We read back from the sources towards possible reconstructions. Therefore, our knowledge of the context of other meals with Jesus besides the Last Supper, of Greco-Roman banquets, and of Jewish meals, does not contain evidence for a clear assignment of the origin of the Eucharist.

The traditional identification of the Last Supper as the origin of the primitive Eucharist has focused on the so-called institution narrative: the accounts of Jesus' words over the bread and over the cup, especially with the command to 'do this in remembrance of me' found in two of the accounts (Luke and 1 Corinthians). The presumption of this origin would lead us to the use of these words in the early Eucharistic prayers. However, what if the function of these words, the institution narrative, was not originally liturgical? This question arises when we are confronted by the absence of these words in our first sources of Eucharistic praying or liturgy.[5] Two principal sources dated from the early to mid second century for Eucharistic liturgy do not contain the institution narrative. Both the *Didache* and the *First Apology* of Justin Martyr offer prayers and a description of the Eucharist without mentioning these words that do appear in the Eucharistic prayers of the fourth century.[6] The 'first' Eucharistic prayer that does have the institution narrative is found in the document known as *The Apostolic Tradition* of Hippolytus, which has been dated variously from the third century into the fourth century.[7] What are we to make of the absence of this narrative and then its later appearance? The answer or answers to this question can only be suggestive; we do not have the historical evidence to proffer any definitive conclusions. One enduring argument is whether the prayers of chapters 9 and 10 of the *Didache* are Eucharistic prayers or blessings of bread and wine used not at a Eucharist but at an *agape* meal also practised by the early Christians. However, much recent scholarship rejects this two meal or ritual typology, saying that even though a prayer text does not resemble the later ones of the fourth century, and hence more 'Eucharistic' looking, this does not mean it was not a Eucharistic text or prayer as such in the first, second or third century. Furthermore, the study of texts from this period cannot be treated as they would later because Jewish and Christian prayer was extemporaneous.[8] The presider at the Jewish meal or at the early Christian gathering, formally a Eucharist or not, would have prayed according to a pattern of traditional praying, but would not have been reciting a given text. Hence, Justin speaks of the presider praying 'as he is able', and Hippolytus gives an example of how a newly ordained bishop might pray over the bread and cup. While these sources do not provide all the relevant texts and actions of a primitive Eucharist – they are not prayer books as we have them – could it be that the institution narrative was not employed as a repetitive liturgical text, and certainly not as a 'formula for consecration'?

The possibility that the institution narrative was employed by the early Christians other than as a liturgical text is entertained by Andrew McGowan in his article 'Is There a Liturgical Text in this Gospel? The Institution Narratives and their Early Interpretive Communities'. Rather than follow the usual path of seeking to determine what Jesus actually said at the Last Supper and its attendant concern for authorial intent in each of the accounts of these sayings, McGowan draws on contemporary literary theory and the role of readers and communities in the interpretation of texts. That is, instead of focusing solely on how the text reached a community, the interpretative task is to reflect on how the community received the text: not how the text came to existence, but how the text can shape a community or reader. The meaning of a text is constituted by a dynamic interplay between author, text and community.[9] As to the question of the origin of the Eucharist, 'original' is appreciated not just by how this text originated, or even why it originated, but what did this text originate? Look at what originated as the way to take up the question of origin, rather than speculating to get behind what did originate. Thus, the 'origin' of the institution narrative belongs as well to the community of its use. Is this use liturgical, or might it be catechetical? Not what was said, but why it was done as an act of faith?

McGowan analyses three early references or uses of the institution narrative: 1 Corinthians 11.23-26; Justin Martyr's *First Apology* 65.3 and 66.2-3; and *The Apostolic Tradition* of Hippolytus. He notes that the meal at Corinth as depicted by Paul does not follow the template of the narrative. The institution narrative has been 'handed on' by Paul before writing this letter, and Paul refers to it here in order to remind the Corinthians of how they are to act when they gather for the 'Lord's Supper'. Thus, Paul's concern is more ethical than liturgical.[10] As for Justin, McGowan identifies how the institution narrative gives the basis for the Eucharist and does not offer a description or a prayer text. Instead of quoting the institution narrative within his account of the Eucharistic prayer, Justin conveys how the text allows his community to understand the Eucharist. McGowan writes:

> For Justin and his community, the institution narratives them-selves had not so much a strictly or narrowly liturgical function as a catechetical one with regard to liturgy; this is implicit in the way the narrative is set interpretatively over against the description of the eucharistic assembly, and explicit at the level of the apologetic account itself, in which Justin seeks to use the narrative to teach the meaning of Christian faith and life in etiological terms, rather than to describe it.[11]

When the institution narrative does appear within a direct example of a Eucharistic prayer, as it does in *The Apostolic Tradition*, its place and role serves as part of the recounting of God's redemptive acts and as a warrant for what follows. While it is spoken as part of a liturgical prayer, it retains its catechetical resonance.[12]

McGowan's assessment of the catechetical function of the institution narrative in primitive Christianity finds support in the work of Paul Bradshaw, which deals thoroughly and directly on the question of the origins of the Eucharist. Bradshaw as well observes the absence of this text in our early Eucharistic sources, and then its later appearance in the great Eucharistic liturgies of the fourth century. He asks why the institution narrative does not compare between the accounts of the Last Supper and the Eucharistic prayers of the fourth century. After his own analysis of these early sources, Bradshaw offers this summary conclusion regarding the role of this text in early Christian faith and worship.

they are etiological stories intended to furnish an explanation of the basis for particular beliefs rather than of the origin of certain liturgical patterns. The remembrance of the sayings of Jesus over the bread and over the cup provided the grounds for the conviction that the bread and the contents of the cup consumed at Christian meals were the body and blood of Christ. Thus, the institution narratives were neither liturgical texts to be recited at the celebration nor liturgical instructions to regulate it, but catechesis of a liturgical kind. It was their regular repetition for catechetical purposes ... that gave them their particular literary style and character ...[13]

According to Bradshaw, even when the institution narrative does appear in the fourth century within the Eucharistic prayers, it retains its catechetical role.[14]

This analysis of the original role played by the institution narrative in the early and developing Eucharistic liturgies insofar as our sources of them are indicative can serve to further illuminate the question of the Eucharistic origin of theology. The enactment of the Eucharist without the recitation of this narrative allows for the possibility that this event was not solely based on following a particular command to 'Do this'. Rather, the primitive celebrations were for the sake of being in the presence of the risen and ascended Jesus. The Eucharist is celebrated not because Jesus directly commanded it, with the focus on following this commandment as such, but because the Eucharist is for the church to be in his presence once again and in a renewed manner. The locus for the instigation of the Eucharist, its origin, is as an act of faith in and with the risen and ascended Jesus. The origin of the Eucharist does not reside in the church's past, but in its presence with Jesus and towards a promised future with him. The introduction of the institution narrative is as a statement of faith and not directly as a liturgical prescription. We do this because this is what we believe. We do this because we believe Jesus is present now in this way. The institution narrative is employed at first to justify the Eucharistic faith rather than the Eucharistic liturgies. Furthermore, the origin of the Eucharist is not rooted in the intention of Jesus as such, in the effort to somehow align the church with his mental state or original intent. This priority of the presence of Jesus to and for the church as the originating reality of its faith, instead of trying to ascertain his intentions obscured as they are by 'ancient texts', will guide the later exposition of the Eucharistic nature of theology.

While the institution narrative has been traditionally viewed as a narrative of liturgical performance, we can now view it as a narrative of primitive Christian faith, a faith whose normative place is the Eucharist, the event of this faith, the faith of this event. The Eucharist is celebrated as the performance of faith; this is why we do it more so than how we do it. The Eucharist has a primarily theological basis rather than a liturgical one.[15] (This has implications for any scholarly efforts to find liturgical or ritual parallels for the Christian Eucharist in pagan mystery cults or for any history of religions perspectives.) The Eucharist has a theological origin. The Eucharist is a liturgy because there is the desire to enact the Eucharistic faith. The Eucharist is the liturgical event of the Eucharistic faith. The question of Eucharistic origins brings us to the nature of theological origins. The Eucharistic faith is constituted by being in the Eucharistic presence of the arriving Jesus. Theology is seeking understanding of *this* faith.

Worshipping Jesus

The question of the Eucharistic origin, and its theological implications, cannot be pursued solely on the grounds of liturgical textual evidence, that is, the questions surrounding the compilation, employment and meaning of the various iterations of the institution narrative within the New Testament and early liturgical sources. That is, the theological question of origin does not only reside with the how and what of the Eucharist but with the why. While the Eucharist is a liturgy, it also is an act or event of worship and devotion: 'They devoted themselves to the apostles' teaching and fellowship, to the breaking of bread and the prayers' (Acts 2.42). This worship of the early Christians is the context of why they celebrated the Eucharist. As such, the answer to this question of why is not primarily regarded as self-referential, a question that might generate a variety of answers from the inherent diversity of worshippers. Rather, worship becomes a response to, a posture towards, the one worshipped. We worship him because of who he is, what he does, and this worship generates theological understanding; this is what it means to worship this God in this way. Therefore, the question of the Eucharistic origin of theology is the broader question of early Christian worship of God, of devotion to Jesus Christ.

One scholar who has written extensively on the question of devotion to Jesus as the major origination and development of

Christian theology is Larry W. Hurtado. Hurtado's principal thesis is that worship or devotion to Jesus arose within the earliest circles of Christians, and that this worship took on a binitarian shape. That is, the earliest Christians incorporated the worship of Jesus within their previous worship of the one God of Judaism. They did not so much abandon Jewish monotheism as transform it in light of their worship of Jesus. Thus, Hurtado argues that the attribution of divinity to Jesus was not a development of a second phase of Christology occurring when Christianity moved out from Palestine into a more Hellenistic world. Rather, the regard for the divinity of Jesus originates within the Palestinian Jewish Christians as witnessed by their worship of Jesus, their devotion to him within their worship of God. He writes:

> But evidence suggests strongly that, well before these later developments, within the first two decades of Christianity, Jewish Christians gathered in Jesus' name for worship, prayed to him and sang hymns to him, regarded him as exalted to a position of heavenly rule above all angelic orders, appropriated to him titles and Old Testament passages originally referring to God, sought to bring fellow Jews as well as Gentiles to embrace him as divinely appointed redeemer, and in general redefined their devotion to the God of their fathers so as to include the veneration of Jesus.[16]

The textual basis for Hurtado's argument is the authentic letters of Paul, which are the first documents we have reflecting early Christian patterns of devotion to Jesus. Also, Paul not only addresses questions of worship or cultic veneration of Jesus within the communities he founded, but his letters witness to a prior devotional practice and understanding, one which Paul had previously opposed as well as received upon his conversion.

According to Hurtado, it is the Jewish religious background of divine agency which becomes a resource for the earliest

Christians to understand and express their experience with the risen and exalted Jesus Christ. Furthermore, this Christian understanding of the reality of their experience fostered their worship of the one God through their worship of Jesus. This primitive binitarian worship is for Hurtado the basis for further Christian Christological developments through the employment of various titles and the formulation of doctrines. That is, the earliest understanding of Jesus, the origination of theology as the identification of who God is because of Jesus, is rooted in the worship and cultic veneration of Jesus, which informs and shapes the use of titles and the development of doctrines and not vice versa. Thus, we are not to look for the beginnings of Christology, and consequentially the origin of Christian theology proper, by focusing first on the use of titles or the development of doctrines, for example pre-existence, but by attending to the textual witnesses in the New Testament of devotional practices. For Hurtado, 'the cultic veneration of Jesus in early Christian circles is the most important context for the use of the Christological titles and concepts'.[17]

Instead of abandoning their Palestinian Judaism, the earliest Christians sought to draw upon this background to make sense of what they were experiencing, of what they came to know as the risen and exalted Christ. Hurtado examines several NewTestament'"" passages to demonstrate the connection made between the exalted Christ and the chief divine agency of this Jewish background. These texts are: Acts 2.33-36; Romans 1.1-4; 1 Thessalonians 1.9-10; 1 Corinthians 15.20-28; Philippians 2.5-11; and 1 Corinthians 8.1-6.[18] He identifies what he refers to as a mutation or innovation in Jewish monotheism by these worshipping Christians. There occurred 'an unprecedented reshaping of monotheistic piety to include a second object of devotion alongside God, a figure seen in the position of God's chief agent, happening among a group that continued to consider itself committed to "one God"'.[19] Hurtado delineates six features of this Christian mutation of Jewish monotheism: early Christian hymns, prayer to Christ, the name of Christ, confessing Jesus, prophecy and the risen Jesus, and the Lord's Supper. The Lord's Supper is an innovation because the Jewish religious background did not include meals for the purpose of 'celebrating and perhaps communing with God's heavenly "chief agent"'.[20] Addressing directly the Pauline Eucharistic texts of 1Corinthians 10.14-22 and 11.17-34, Hurtado states that 'Jesus is perceived as the living and powerful *Kyrios* who owns the meal and presides at it, and with whom believers have fellowship as with a god'.[21] The presence of the Risen Christ was not only the beginning of a distinctive Christian experience and understanding of God, but this 'revelatory' experience and understanding recurred within the corporate worship of the earliest Christians, for example 1 Corinthians 14.26.[22]

Following the work of Hurtado, we can not only place the question of the Eucharistic origin of theology within the broader context of worship of the risen and exalted Jesus Christ, we can locate the ongoing origination of theology within the worship setting and practices of the earliest Christians. Their worship of God includes their worship of Jesus, and it is directly this worship that compels them towards the understanding that the one God of their Jewish faith has now been distinctively and definitively revealed through the life, death, resurrection, ascension and promised second coming of this Jesus along with the outpouring of the Holy Spirit. Later formulations and developments of this understanding, of this theology, will be attempts not to stray from, or distort, this original and originating Eucharistic faith.

Location of Jesus: Location of Theology

Where is Jesus? This is the original and originating question of Christian theology. The original Christian life and faith was constituted by abiding in the presence of Jesus. Baptism joined persons to Christ making them members of the Body of Christ. All subsequent thought and behaviour were to make sense of, and within, this Body. Where Jesus is located is where Christians are found. This concern for location, or what could be rendered a spatial perspective, becomes a trajectory characterized more by the deepening of mystery than the pursuit of rational justification. Understanding where we are located, where Jesus is, requires discipline – indeed, the asceticism – of not wandering off into greener epistemological and ontological pastures. Hence, there is the theological effort of abiding *here* and not elsewhere. What makes sense within the Body of Christ is not required to make sense in other places. However, this does not mean that theology cannot incorporate knowledge and patterns of thought from outside this Body. All such efforts will be adaptive, the Body is not misshaped, theology is not misplaced. That is, the scandal of particularity abides. Theology, then, is not fundamentally located within our minds, our wills, our experiences, or in our respective cultures and histories. Theology *in* Christ; it happens where Jesus is *now*.

Where is Jesus now? The origin of theology belongs to the place where Jesus is, while the originating question for contemporary theology is where is Jesus now? Reflecting on the location of Jesus, the 'where' of his presence, does not exclude prior habitations, history is still *there*. However, as the originating question of theology, it faithfully reflects the origin of theology: abiding in the presence of Jesus. While theology has a history, theology is not history. History is what happens in the wake of abiding within the immediate presence of Jesus; being where he is. Jesus is not back in the first century wondering whether we will come and visit him. Rather, where Jesus has been is now here because Jesus is now here. The history of Jesus provides the background for his contemporary presence, and we regard this history from where he is now, where we are with and in him, the historical perspective of the Body of Christ.

Abiding in the presence of Jesus is the origin of theology. The implications and consequences of this assertion are manifold and far-reaching. The first Christians were characterized by being placed in Christ, becoming constitutive members of the Body of Christ. Prior to this placement, one passed through a period of repentance, self-examination, ascetical practices and teaching. That is, one began to learn how to live in this new place, what it means to live here and not live in the world. Baptism took someone from living in the world to living in Christ. After undergoing baptism, the new Christian was taken somewhere, to the place where the Body of Christ was alive and alert to the arriving presence of Jesus. This place is called the Eucharist. The newly made Christian was received into the church, the assembly whose existence embodied the expectation of this arrival. This was not primarily the place for their presence to be known and recognized; it was the place for knowing and recognizing the presence of Jesus. Indeed, the place to receive and share his life, the life he has before the Father, the life the Holy Spirit bestows. The origin of theology is here because this is where Jesus is with his Body. Whenever theology is removed from this place, located elsewhere, theology can become fragmented and distorted. Theology is attempted, or constructed, in places not primarily defined by the abiding presence of Jesus, where he is now for the exchange of life, for the realization of communion with God and with each other. Simply put, there is the temptation that the origin of theology is located where we are as we are. Once we have surveyed and understood where we are, then we can find a place for Jesus to be there with us, to know him the way we know ourselves. Theology becomes Jesus abiding in our presence. Or, we might be so captivated by our presence that we ignore the possible or promised presence of Jesus. We can construct theological worlds or worldviews that function quite well without Jesus, or we can incorporate him into these places as they already exist.

What is the crucial theological distinction between the place where Jesus is and the places where we are? The distinction between these places is one of movement. We go from our respective places into the place of Jesus' abiding and arriving presence. We move from the intellectual contours, historical memories and capacities for action of a place into the place occupied by the mind of Christ, the memory of the Body of Christ, and the arena of God's Triune agency. We may go to the place where Jesus is and still look for the signs of other places, putative sacraments of our own presence. However, this is not the movement of offering and sacrifice. Rather, this is going somewhere for the sake of other places, for places I can still call my own. The movement from where we are into where Jesus is places us at the bestowal of divine agency. The Eucharist is that place where God's agency is constitutive of its existence. Without God's presence and agency, the Eucharist does not exist. Jesus is here in the way that he is here because God makes it happen. Theology originates where God *happens to be*. That is, theology properly abides where there is the Triune nexus of ontology and history. Epistemology is formed and nurtured in this place. Knowledge of God takes on the Eucharistic shape and *telos*.

At the origin of theology there are no categories, subjects, theories or curricula. There are not different types of theology, or a variety of subdisciplines. 'Original' theology is reflection on abiding in the presence of Jesus, on being true to his person, his presence and agency. Theology originates from where this reflection emerges, where the truth of this presence takes place. Therefore, as will be argued throughout this volume, we will not be guided by the customary templates for either the existence or the study of theology, we will not strive to say something 'Eucharistic' about each of the usual subjects and disciplines of theology. Rather, we will strive to inhabit the Eucharist as the place where and whereby theology originates, and this will lead us to discover anew what are the appropriate disciplines, subjects and concepts of theology. They will be identified by belonging within the Eucharist in the way in which they are disciplines and dimensions of the theological reality that is the Eucharist. Thus, we turn from regarding the Eucharist from the question of its origin to an exploration of its inherent nature. We will inhabit the Eucharist, and from this abiding perspective, we will identify the disciplines and dimensions of the Eucharistic nature of theology.

Notes

1 All quotations from Scripture are from the New Revised Standard Version.

2 While the literature on this question of Eucharistic origins has become voluminous, here are some oft-cited representative works: Andrew McGowan, *Ascetic Eucharist: Food and Drink in Early Christian Ritual Meals* (Oxford: Oxford University Press, 1999); Xavier Leon-Dufour, *Sharing the Eucharistic Bread: The Witness of the New Testament* (New York: Paulist Press, 1987); Eugene LaVerdiere, *The Eucharist in the New Testament and the Early Church* (Collegeville, MN: The Liturgical Press, 1996); Martin Stringer, *Rethinking the Origins of the Eucharist* (London: SCM Press, 2011); and Paul Bradshaw, *Eucharistic Origins* (London: Oxford University Press, 2004).

3 All of the Eucharistic liturgies or texts referenced in this volume can be found in R. C. D. Jasper and G. J. Cuming, *Prayers of the Eucharist: Early and Reformed*, third revised edition (New York: Pueblo Publishing Company, 1987). Henceforth, *PEER*.

4 Paul F. Bradshaw and Maxwell F. Johnson, *The Eucharistic Liturgies: Their Evolution and Interpretation* (Collegeville, MN: Pueblo, 2012), p. 1f.

5 The following analysis of the role or lack thereof regarding the institution narrative in early Eucharistic documents relies on the work of Andrew McGowan, especially his "'Is There a Liturgical Text in this Gospel?" The Institution Narratives and their Early Interpretive Communities', *Journal of Biblical Literature* 118/1 (1999): 73–87.

6 *PEER*, pp. 20, 25.

7 *PEER*, p. 31.

8 See the classic study of this by Allan Bouley, *From Freedom to Formula: The Evolution of the Eucharistic Prayer from Oral Improvisation to Written Texts* (Washington, DC: Catholic University of America Press, 1981).

9 McGowan, 'Is There a Liturgical Text?', pp. 76–7.

10 McGowan, 'Is There a Liturgical Text?', pp. 79–80.

11 McGowan, 'Is There a Liturgical Text?', p. 83.

12 McGowan, 'Is There a Liturgical Text?', pp. 84–5.

13 Bradshaw, *Eucharistic Origins*, p. 14.

14 Bradshaw, *Eucharistic Origins*, p. 15.

15 This distinction between the theological and the liturgical has implications for other scholarly perspectives on the question of the origins of the Eucharist that involve looking for parallels with pagan mystery cults. Also,

scholarly efforts drawing on ritual studies or from the comparison of religions for study of Christian liturgy are not addressed here and are excluded from the 'theological' perspective propounded and developed in this volume.

16 Larry W. Hurtado, *One God, One Lord: Early Christian Devotion and Ancient Jewish Monotheism*, new edition (London: Bloomsbury, T&T Clark, 2003), p. 11. See also Hurtado's *Lord Jesus Christ: Devotion to Jesus in Earliest Christianity* (Grand Rapids, MI: Eerdmans, 2005).

17 Hurtado, *One God, One Lord*, p. 13.

18 Hurtado, *One God, One Lord*, pp. 94ff.

19 Hurtado, *One God, One Lord*, p. 100.

20 Hurtado, *One God, One Lord*, pp. 111–12.

21 Hurtado, *Lord Jesus Christ*, p. 146.

22 Hurtado, *Lord Jesus Christ*, pp. 71–4.

2

The Eucharistic Nature of Theology

What then is theology, really and truly? Who is capable of answering this question? What is our frame of reference when answering this question, and is there a place to which we are accountable for this answer? Theology is not the construction of God. Primarily, theology is not the study of how we have talked about God; it is not the exposition of the content of our prior speaking and presumed understanding of God. Theology is truly and really itself when it is directed towards God, when it takes shape within the place where and whereby God has provided for its essence and existence. The reality and truth of theology, its existence and essence, is contingent upon, accountable to, the real (existence) and true (essence) of God. Therefore, the question now is: How do we really and truly do theology?

If God is prior to theology, then how does theology exist as a consequence of this priority? It does so by not posing *a priori* the question of God. Our capacity to speak of God is inversely proportional to our posturing as a questioner of God. Before we can think or study anything, we find ourselves in a place or places always already provided by God, at least in any sense that God is Creator. Any entertaining of the venture to ask the question of God, begins in, if not at, the place where we are already. The proper theological question becomes: Where is God? Where is the place whereby we seek God's presence? Theology happens in the presence of God. Theology happens in the place where and whereby God has prepared for us to become theologians, those who speak of God with whom they are in

42

communion. The nature of theology is communion because this is the nature of God, the natural state of God with us, of our movement towards God's future for us. This communion is the bridegroom and bride – Christ and his church – the marital union of truth and reality, essence and existence, as both eternal and temporally gifted.

Being in the presence of God is not a neutral site, nor is it 'ground' on which to stand; it is rather a place of encounter. Communion with God is the precondition for theology realized by the movement of persons, both divine and human. Theology exists as reflection on the encounter of these movements, on the event of this communion. Thus, the nature of theology is not an enduring reality, a static essence that is always there for our study. As such, any proposed theological method that proceeds from a prior identified condition or desire of human existence will not serve appropriately or adequately as a faithful reflection on the dynamic existence of this communion always contingently constituted by the mutuality of the giving and receiving of sacrificial selves. Thus, the nature of theology is this movement of mutuality existing with the priority of God and for the consequences of abiding with this priority. The nature of theology does not exist in a place protected from the nature of God. Furthermore, since there are indeed faithful consequences of abiding with the priority of God, abiding in the presence of God, there are dimensions of this abiding. That is, our faithful abiding, our theology, comprises an array of dimensions. 'Dimensions' is employed here because, while we are focusing on one dimension, we are aware that what we are engaged in has many dimensions. We cannot dissect the dimensions from each other; they are the ways into the nature of what we are considering. The nature of theology has dimensions; the Eucharistic nature of theology has Eucharistic dimensions. These are dimensions of our abiding in the presence of God, and there are dimensions of God's presence to and for us.

As theologians, we are not to guard our self-assigned

and self-determined places from any intrusions from an unaccounted-for divine agency. However, if indeed the nature of God shapes and directs the nature of theology, and this nature is characterized not by status but by movement, then how are we able to do theology? What are the preconditions for our capacity as theologians, and for any faithful direction and shape that our theology might take? What are these Eucharistic dimensions of the Eucharistic nature of theology?

Scripture

Theology abides with the priority of God in faithful return and response to the ways in which God has abided with humanity, the ways in which God has returned to creation, to the people of Israel, and has returned definitively and eschatologically in the person of Jesus Christ. There is a narrative of this divine abiding, and of our response to it; it is called Holy Scripture. The nature of theology will be shaped by this narrative; it will expose the movement of mutuality that led to its scriptural consequences. Likewise, theology will develop its own scriptural consequences as it seeks to abide with the priority of God through the priority of Scripture. However, this abiding is occluded if not distorted by the exposition of a singular text by a singular theologian. The temptation here is for the theologian to choose a way or method to approach the text without this method really and truly becoming an approach to God, much less a sacrificial movement towards God. That is, the priority of God narrated by the text becomes the priority of the exegete over the text. How do we guard ourselves from this reversal of priority, from a text becoming the object of our study or from our self-generated response to it? As an abiding narrative of God's priority pregnant with the possibilities of faithful consequences, Scripture's normative role is within that place where God's priority is encountered as and always as the gift of divine communion for the possibility of our communion with God and with each other such that the scriptural narrative makes

44

THEOLOGY

sense of who we are now and here, those who have received what God gives for the life of the world. We are at home with Scripture within the Eucharist, and the normative role of Scripture as the faithful narrative of abiding with God's priority is found within the economy of the Eucharist. This is one dimension of the Eucharistic nature of theology, a dimension of God's priority.

Tradition

Tradition is the history of abiding with God's priority. Tradition is not the history of theology or the history of the church or churches. The distinction between tradition as a theological history and the history of theology is a reflection of the primary and presumptive distinction argued here between 'God's priority' and the 'priority of God'. Employing the phrase 'God's priority' rather than the 'priority of God' emphasizes the fundamental tenet that God possesses God's own priority. God chooses the how, why, when, what and where of this priority. Again, to speak of God's priority is not exclusively the assertion that God as Creator precedes the creation; there was God before there was a world or humanity. This is a priority ordered towards consequences. Thus, God's priority is conveyed in the idiom and mode of revelation, while its consequences are received as the idiom and within the mode of faith. God determines God's own way of being prior; God speaks as God. The 'priority of God' could resonate in the same way, but it can imply a postulate of our speculation. That is, our theological method, strategy or starting point can grant the priority of God without henceforth allowing this priority to shape and direct our theological work. The priority of God can be an abstraction first before we make any concrete theological claims. 'God's priority' projects the actuality of this priority and eschews the possible multiplicity of how we might render a priority of God. (Any negotiating between a theological *a priori* and *a posteriori* will be accountable to the economic framework of God's priority and its proper consequences.)

What is God saying?

45

Tradition is the consequential abiding with God's priority. Tradition is what happens as it happens when God's priority arrives in our midst realizing its own consequences through our faithful reception of this priority, of this arriving God. Tradition is not an object of our detached observance, a process given over to our analytical typologies. Tradition is the reception of what is being handed on; it is the consequence that transpires between God's arriving presence and our sacrificial availability to this arrival. This is the economy of receiving and handing on, and any working out of this economy will be transparent to God's 'handing on' and our receiving. God's handing on is the tradition of God's priority, and our reception is the tradition of its consequences. God's priority is fully and definitively revealed through the sending, arriving and giving of Jesus to us for the life of the world. God 'hands on' Jesus for our 'reception'. Abiding within this handing on and receiving, within this receiving and handing on, takes place in and as the Eucharist: 'For I received from the Lord what I also handed on to you' (1 Cor. 11.23a). The Eucharistic nature of theology retains and realizes tradition as the consequential abiding with God's priority.

Reason

How then do we actually do theology, while God's priority is arriving and presenting its own consequences? This is the question of generating theology from the place where it happens, the understanding of faith that the Eucharist makes possible. We seek this understanding from our place within the Eucharist, within the economy of communion as the mutuality of divine and human selves. As such, reason is never an autonomous faculty of the human mind. Reason is not a way to choose our objects and to determine our subjectivity. Reason is the medium through which what happens here lays hold of our imaginations, showing us what is possible to know and how we might *become* knowers of God. Thus, reason does not have its own standards for operation and for achievement. Reason operates within the dynamic of gift, the movement of who is present to know and what then is required of us who seek to know this presence. Within the Eucharist, we are never set over against any object. We allow ourselves to be comprehended by the multiple dimensions of God's Trinitarian presence. We are epistemologically surrounded by God's presence both by God's own arriving presence seeking for us to know God in this way, and by other knowers who share this epistemological vocation. There is no method of thinking here, no epistemological strategy or possibility derived from our potential as knowers. Likewise, any history of human rationality, any development of philosophy will stay outside the parameters of this enacted communion and will wait to be invited. If an invitation is issued, it will be for the directed purpose of analysis of a proper theological reality. The outsider is not ushered in to determine what can be known and to tell us what kind of knowers we are. Reason on the outside of the Eucharist will find a home within the Eucharist but will remain only as an invited guest. There is a tradition of Eucharistic rationality, but it will not confine our understanding to the dictates of the past. The arrival of Jesus will always be 'more than all we can ask or imagine' (Eph. 3.20b); the arriving of Jesus from the Father realized by the Holy Spirit will always be the greater than can be thought. The Eucharistic nature of theology includes the exercise of reason so that the creativity of God will be disclosed, enacted and placed before us as the horizon of our desires for the consummation of this communion.

Knowledge

The theological knowledge that takes place within the Eucharist - the knowledge of God and knowing ourselves as these knowers of God - will not be confined to the purported limits of human reason. As Eucharistic knowers, knowledge does not stop at the outer limits of our rationality because this knowledge is not a product of our capacity to know nor is it henceforth available to us to replicate under self-determined conditions. We know God because God first knows us in Christ. God's knowledge of us makes our knowledge of God possible. The arriving of Jesus is the invitation to share God's knowledge of us as the way to know God. And since this is always an arriving knowledge, we are always seeking it where and whereby Jesus arrives to be sought. However, we do not seek his arriving presence for the sake of producing a knowledge we can now call our own, to trumpet our capacity as knowers. The sacrificial mode of all faithful knowledge is never abandoned for the fleshpots of modern scientific objectivity nor for the postmodern delights of boutique profundities. We are truly held accountable for what we know by the Eucharistic shape of any adequate knowledge. Does our knowledge of God make Eucharistic sense? Can we say that what we know and how we know it emerges from the place where our hearts and minds are lifted up in thanksgiving for what and who we now know here?

Baptism or Natural Theology?

Do we as humans have a natural capacity for this knowledge of God, a natural course of reason that can reach where minds are lifted within the Eucharistic economy? Do we have a natural capacity for Eucharistic epistemology? Are these appropriate questions or concerns for a theology emerging from the Eucharist? Have we not already abandoned the category of natural or of human nature when we gather for the Eucharist? The Eucharist is celebrated by members of the Body of Christ, by those who have been baptized into the death and resurrection of Jesus Christ, receiving the gift of the Holy Spirit. Perhaps, then, any previous concern for a natural theology, or of any prior human capacity for knowledge of God, is left behind when we enter the waters of baptism. Of course, any debate on the nature of theology involving the enduring questions of whether it is a science, belongs in a university curriculum or must adapt to the demands of what is purported to be contemporary rationality will carry on in their respective habitats. But we are not asking these generic questions, these speculative forays into abstract possibilities; we are asking about the epistemological capacity of the baptized gathered for the celebration of the Eucharist. In so doing, two agendas are present: the degree to which these baptized have been formed as such, they strive for the mind of Christ; and the other is the agency of God towards the baptized. That is, the relationship between revelation and faith is realized within the economy of the Eucharist. While the Eucharist is the place and event where and whereby knowledge of God is given as the sharing in God's knowledge of us, we can ask whether there is knowledge of God outside this Eucharistic encounter. We could entertain the notion that there is a natural knowledge of God, a knowledge available exterior to the Eucharist, but this knowledge requires an authorization from the Eucharist. Natural theology will be gathered into the Eucharistic economy as an offering towards an epistemological communion of all kinds of knowledge that its knowers are willing and able to lift up to the promised arrival of all and absolute truth. Since the object of theological knowledge is God, and reason attends to this object, the knower will not be able to contain or control any genuine knowledge of God because God is known as the knower of us, as the God who seeks to understand us as we have understood ourselves. Here, we are dealing with an incarnated epistemology, which is always on the move between God and humanity. Our attempts at detached objectivity have no place in the Eucharist, have no place before the presence of God. Rather, we are called to an objective silence, a stillness that allows for the movement of God to make itself known: 'Be still, and know that I am God!' (Ps. 46.10). We do have the natural capacity for this stillness; we have the potential for silence.

Language and Experience

For the Eucharistic nature of theology, how do we understand the theological categories or realities of language and experience? Or, should we approach these concerns separately and then bring them into a conceptual relationship? We have the customary distinction between theological language as an expression of an experience of God and language that makes this experience possible. This distinction can be further refined by asking about what language and whose experience. Once again, our horizon is not generic or speculatively abstract; we are exploring the basic questions of theology within their proper and faithful venue: the celebration of the Holy Eucharist. Thus, we are asking about Eucharistic language and Eucharistic experience and the Eucharistic relationship between them.

The Eucharist is the enactment of a given structure, or grammar, that is linguistically performed. There is an economy of actions with accompanying language. The language itself then is an action, and we act with language. This Eucharistic language is primarily conceived from the scriptural and liturgical imagination. That is, we turn outside ourselves to take up the language that will place us in the Eucharistic presence of God. This language is inherently not self-referential; it is not an interior movement but an exterior one. The normative question before us when entering the Eucharistic event is what is the appropriate language here? What do we speak to and within the presence of God, a presence for us, the presence of God's Eucharistic action? The normative question is not then what is our experience prior to entering this Eucharistic event? We are not here to share our experience, but to share a common life as the Body of Christ. We might ask what is the normative experience of the Body of Christ, and what is the appropriate language to speak of this experience? Does this mean we cannot speak of a Eucharistic experience or that we should ignore any non-Eucharistic experience? It does not. The consideration here is of normativity and appropriate priority; it is not the exclusion of the totality of human existence. We are indeed gathered in the fullness of lives. We are not to leave our experience behind. Rather, this experience is offered in the Eucharist and can undergo a transformative interpretation through the performance of Eucharistic action and language. What do our lives mean within the Eucharistic interpretative dynamic of these actions and these words? We offer our non-Eucharistic experience into the movement characterized by the language of thanksgiving, praise, petition and remembrance that is shaped by the inviting presence of God. The Eucharist is its own hermeneutic.

Sources, Systems or Methods?

The Eucharistic nature of theology is reflected in the abiding regard for the priority and primacy of God's active presence within and as the event of the Eucharist. In this way, and only in this way, all our theological efforts and appeal to 'sources' cannot become self-enclosed intellectual, ecclesial or pious manoeuvres. Our theology cannot presume the absence of God. Rather, our theology is rooted in the Eucharistic presence and agency of God. We do theology for the sake of sharing in the Eucharistic life of God. Thus, our theological efforts have more to do with allowing God's active presence than with defining a disembodied aspect or attribute of God's nature, and certainly not with a more refined doctrinal pronouncement or one more reason to abandon doctrine altogether. The question then becomes not what theological method should we adopt or construct in order to be accountable to ourselves as theologians, but how do we continually and steadfastly encounter, discover and convey the reality of God who is here in this way for us (place, presence and agency)? The consequences of this mediated immediacy of God for any enterprise purporting to be 'systematic' theology are truly transformative.

Systematic theology is the effort to speak of, to address, all the basic questions and claims of theology in such a way that they are in relation to each other. Theology becomes a comprehensive and coherent narrative or vision, one that seeks to be faithful to the scope and promise of God's saving will and revealed nature. One profound argument against systematic theology is that God cannot be domesticated to any system as such. The reality of God cannot be circumscribed by our attempts at coherent depictions or descriptions of this reality. Likewise, another argument is that we as possible systematic theologians reside within our respective cultures, experiences, languages, each in our own 'worlds', such that it is impossible for a theologian to offer any sort of comprehensive theological narrative or vision. On one hand, God does not belong within a metanarrative, and on the other, neither do we. Having been given birth from a diversity of postmodern mothers, each theological life seeks its own proper understanding, while not straying into the difference of others. However, the Eucharistic nature of theology is not a reflection of our natures, whether they be construed as historical, existential or cultural. Rather, the nature of theology is contingent upon the nature of God as Eucharistically offered and received. Therefore, 'systematic' theology will be the abiding effort to know and speak of the relations between the various modes and witnesses of what God is doing in the Eucharist, and how we encounter and respond to this event. The system is not applied to the Eucharist; it is discovered, and it is not like any other system. This system represents the patterns of reciprocal movements between and among God and the gathering of the baptized. It is a system that is always broken and transformed by the communion of God for our communion in Christ and by the Holy Spirit. Eucharistic systematic theology is our theological way to stay here in the place of communion and to speak from this place, understanding this faith here, while seeking the understanding of all potential theological places from the perspective of this Eucharistic place.

The guiding presumption of this Eucharistic place is that God wills to be known here as the God who gives the Son's life to his Body gathered to receive him. Thus the presence and agency of God are always the primary realities of this place, and they enter it for the sake of this primacy. We go there for the sake of receiving this life, and then we reflect on what we have received and how we have done so. That is, we do not go into the Eucharist primarily to do theology but to share communion with God as God offers it. However, theology is generated by our willingness to be open to this gift, to render ourselves as sacrificial knowers and thinkers. Theology is generated by the desire to know more, to have a keener awareness of this gift, to understand the faith that has brought us here, that is indeed realized here. The nature of this theology, what is natural about it, is the realization that we do not start from our self-appointed or self-determined places with its other presumptions. We do not establish a theological method rooted in the concerns of non-Eucharistic places, presences and agencies. To do so would be to betray the theological place provided for us 'before the foundation of the world' (Matt. 13.35; Eph. 1.4). When it comes to abiding in this theological place where and whereby the gift of the Son's life is present and offered, we do well to be haunted by the question, 'So, could you not stay awake with me one hour?' (Matt. 26.40b) The Eucharistic nature of theology is maintained within the suspension between revelation and faith, between the offer of God's life of communion as the presence of Jesus conveyed by the Holy Spirit and our reception of this life, which we then seek to understand for the sake of knowing its abundance, its depth and scope, and hence, its systematic concerns and consequences. This Eucharistic nature of theology, this seeking of understanding, requires a form of vigilance, a keeping vigil, that we not fall from this place into other possible places of knowing and understanding that supposedly have more attractive or even practical fruit. To eat that fruit is to be once again driven out of the place, presence and agency of God's pleasure, and to hear the admonishment received by those wandering through their methodological deserts: 'Who told you that you were theologically naked?'

Eucharistic systematic theology is never confident in its

own system. The Eucharistic nature of theology is the natural condition of vigilance before the primacy of God's presence and agency in that one place where such a condition is required. We keep vigil for the arrival of Jesus, and therefore, we do not engage in ever more sophisticated accounts of the possibilities for our own presence, the structures and theoretical systems inherent in human nature and history. This is why one of the fundamental attributes of the Eucharistic nature of theology is asceticism.

Theological Asceticism

Knowledge is not just the question of how we know anything, but how we know one thing. What are we seeking to know and why? What is required of us to become knowers of this one thing? In addition to the question of how we form or educate ourselves to become this type of knower of this type of thing, we can ask not what we need to add to our lives, but what we need to remove. Not just what is the optic through which to see truly what something is, but what are the obstacles to such knowledge? What is the way to this knowledge, and what gets in the way? In order to discover the inherent systematic nature of theology residing within the Eucharist, the relational and revelatory mutuality available by God's presence for and as communion, we have to purge ourselves of any self-serving expectations or predetermined schemas of what we want or need to know, or even of what can we know. The primary question is not our capacity as knowers, or how we are knowers, but how we place ourselves before the presence of God. Placing ourselves before the presence of God is the movement of no longer living primarily in our own presence. The primary theological movement is neither the journey within or without; it is the journey towards, the self-offering movement towards God, to find ourselves before God as we are.

This journey is a practice, a set of disciplines, a true *askesis*. The epistemological question for theology is what is the correspondence between the presence of the known and the presence of the knower? Furthermore, this is a presence towards each other, a presence constituted by the movement towards each other to be in the presence of the other. That is, we do not engage in a mapping of our presence as such, but instead seek to discern the vectors of our potential movement towards God. These vectors become disciplines, a set of practices, the *askesis* of the movement that is the Eucharistic nature of theology. As such, the disciplines or practices of the Eucharist become the proper theological asceticism. What are these practices, how do they become the *askesis* of the Eucharistic nature of theology?

They are gathering, listening, interceding, confessing sin, receiving forgiveness, offering, remembering and invoking. These actions constitute the Eucharistic event, the seeking of an understanding that is possible only in the presence of God as communion offered and received by those who offer themselves for this purpose, indeed for this 'reason'. Thus, they are the ways that the Eucharistic nature of theology is practised. We will consider each them by briefly first identifying them as Eucharistic actions, and then more expansively as theological *askesis*.

Gathering

The Eucharist happens when members of the Body of Christ have gathered for this event. The gathering or assembly of these members indicates their willingness, their commitment, to perform all the subsequent actions. The gathering is for the sake of what happens here and now through this set of normative actions. One does not decide what to do next once this gathering takes place; we do what comes next. Our next action is given to us to perform. This is how the Eucharist happens, and in no other way does it do so. There are two theological practices that follow from this initial Eucharistic action: theology is done within the company of the members of the Body of Christ, and it is done through a set of normative actions or disciplines.

Theology is by its Eucharistic nature a corporate reality, a gathering of minds and wills to know the one Christ as present from and before the Father in the realization of the Holy Spirit. Thus, the theologian will practise the sacrifice of the individual mind, the *kenosis* of autonomous subjectivity. The theologian will yield to the movement of being brought into a reality rather than striving to construct or to represent one's own theological world. Does this theology express, witness to, what is going on with us more so than what is going on with me? The *us* here is the Body of Christ and not any self-identified or self-determined other body. It is the otherness of Christ that supersedes all possible iterations of otherness but is also the theological environment for the proper appreciation of the otherness of selves not identical to the theologian. For it is as the Body of Christ, within and from this Body, that we are able to see the face of Christ in others; knowledge of the one Christ in the variety of the members of his Body. Therefore, while the gathering of this Body is the place for theology, and not any other places identified through the autonomy of nature or will, there is not to be any exterior enforcement of a uniformity of theology, any artificial or alien metanarrative that truly does not belong within the Eucharistic living of this Body. The Eucharistic nature of theology has its own God-given mystery of the one and the many, the theological accountability to speak of the one Christ within the full catholic scope of the voices of all members of this Body.

The Eucharistic gathering as the entrance into a continuum of normative actions signifies that theology will not be pursued by any and all methodologies. The Eucharistic nature of theology does not contain nor construe any method. Theology can abandon the task of seeking to orient itself regarding other 'sciences', and it certainly can cast aside any anxieties about whether it belongs in the university, and if so, how. While indeed theology may exist in a variety of places and take up the concerns of other intellectual and moral discourses, it only belongs as and within the Eucharist.

'Belong' as in the place where we are addressed by, and offered, the Word made flesh ('belong' as in the dual sense of the German *gehoren*, a place and a hearing). This is where we hear and are heard. All questions that otherwise might become the linchpins of method are transformed into the self-questioning that characterize members of the Body of Christ. Not what is there to know rooted in my capacity as a human knower, but how do I become a more diligent knower of this presence of Christ, and how will this knowledge transform me, shape us, as this Body? The continuum of normative actions one commits to when being gathered into this presence of Christ, towards this gift of presence, is a way to knowledge and not a method of thought. This Eucharistic place, this theological nature, is always a gathering towards and into the presence of Christ, not the collapse of God's life under the weight of our epistemological limits, our moral predilections or our ontological fears.

Listening

The Eucharist is a gathering of listeners. Once gathered, having begun the Eucharist, entering into its economy, the stage is set to listen to what has been given as God's address to us, the proclamation of Scripture. Before this gathering employs language through its own address to God in prayer, it listens to the textual witness of God's historical and linguistic encounter with humanity. It listens to what God has done with other people, at other times, in other places. This listening that happens here and now within this celebration of the Eucharist is for the sake of a possible and expectant hearing. We listen to what God has done and said so that we might enter the imaginative sphere of what God can say and do here and now, of how God might receive and respond to our subsequent address to God in the idiom of liturgical prayer. Within the normative economy of the Eucharist, only those who listen to God are allowed to speak to and of God. Our language to and about God has listening as its pervasive and accountable companion.

Seeking to be faithful to the Eucharistic nature of theology, the theologian will nurture the attribute of listening. While this listening is primarily directed towards the proclamation of Scripture, it ought to become a comprehensive disposition. We listen before we speak or write, and when we do speak and write we do so as abiding listeners to and for the one about whom we are talking. In order to listen for God, to receive what God gives us to hear about God, we are to purge ourselves of always listening to and for ourselves. When I am dominated by my own speech, I am tempted to listen to only what God might say that sounds like me. I recognize the voice of God only when God speaks the way I do. However, listening is essentially receptivity. We receive the possibility of speaking about God in the way that God speaks or addresses us. This possibility of doing theology arising from our receptive listening does not lead to a monolithic or monotone theology. This is so for two reasons. First, the abundance of God's address, issuing as it does from God's own life, will always escape our attempts to define its existence. There is always the more of God's address than what we can say. Yet, because our listening for this address is the possibility for our speaking, when we do speak there is a reflection of, a witness to, what has been addressed to us and of the one so addressing. Secondly, each member of the Body of Christ speaks from their place in this Body. We hear the same address, but we do so as distinctive members of the one in whom, with whom and for whom we listen. This indicates that theology residing within the Eucharist will be a listening for the Father in Christ and by the Holy Spirit as well as a listening to each member of the Body in order to discern what is indeed being said to us. Theology involves a personal and a corporate listening.

Interceding

While listening to Scripture is determinative for the formation of theologians inhabiting the Eucharistic economy, it is not the only listening that takes place, that has a role in the realization of God's communion for us and for the life of the world. While we do listen for God in Scripture, we are called to then listen to the world. In the course of the Eucharistic enactment after the 'Liturgy of the Word', there is intercessory prayer or 'Prayers of the People'. This is when the gathered members of the Body of Christ, the priestly people, intercede to God on behalf of others, bringing the needs of those who are not there into the presence of God. The movement of the absent to the present is the movement from listening to offering. The concerns of the church and of the world are brought into the Eucharist between Scripture and Sacrament, between God's address and God's gift of life. For theological *askesis*, the appropriate perspective on the world, on that which is outside the Eucharist, is characterized by the movement from listening to offering. In this way, the world becomes present to God as theology speaks of the world to God always through the idiom of intercession. Thus, what can happen in the world from this theological perspective will always be attributed to God's agency, to the God who has listened to us. For the Eucharistic nature of theology, theology is not motivation to change the world. Rather, theology is the abiding intercessory movement from those who are absent from us into God's presence where we are now with them. When we do go out into the world from the Eucharist, we do so from this intercessory perspective, with our eyes open to the possibilities of God's Eucharistic agency. As faithful inhabitants of this agency, we are to look for ways to exercise it in the world. We enter God's Eucharistic agency from listening to the world to offering our prayers to God for this world, while suspended between God's Word and God's life. Listening to the concerns of the world with Eucharistic ears is not the same as taking the world on its own terms. The world does not change theology, nor does theology change the world.

Confessing Sin

We enter the Eucharist, we are gathered here and now, as both members of the Body of Christ and as sinners. In the course of the development of the Eucharistic liturgy, there emerged the act of confessing sins and receiving absolution for them. There is a consciousness of a gap between membership in this Body and actual human living, between our essence and our existence. Furthermore, the accountable horizon of this Body as the enactment of the Eucharist allows for a discernment of sin, of what does not reflect the life performed and received within the Eucharist. The possibility of the reconciliation that occurs as communion is entertained from the standpoint of separation or alienation from where and with whom we are called to be. The theological *askesis* arising from the Eucharistic nature of theology includes the confession of sin. As Eucharistic theologians we do not approach the object of our thinking from an objective place or perspective. We do take into account our own subjectivity. However, this subjectivity is not ours to express or construct. It is not ultimately regarded as an expression of the place from which we have come, but as a subjectivity that is now possible in the Eucharistic presence of God.

Facing the proper object of theology, theologians enter into a questioning of their own perspective, entertaining the possibility, perhaps inevitability, that their understanding will be marked by some distortion because it is *their* understanding. Theology will then always have a purgative dimension within its nature and a wariness of saying too much about God and about oneself. Such sensitivity to theological pride, the greatest of all sins, allows for the recognition that as theologians we are not deciding or determining anything regarding God. God is not waiting on us to see what we can think and write now. Rather, God is waiting on us to enter the realm of God's presence as the place to know oneself in this presence first before going on to know God as the one who is present to these confessing knowers. Thus, once again, the autonomous subject and pure reason do not reside here where sin is confessed, absolution sought and Christ's peace is exchanged. This *askesis* happens within the Eucharist and not in the seminar room.

Receiving Forgiveness

Receiving forgiveness of sins is receiving God's act on us; we receive from God what we cannot do for ourselves. This forgiveness places us in a relationship of reconciliation, of being brought into a relationship with God on God's own terms. Once forgiven by God, one is oriented towards God in a way that leads to communion, to the understanding of faith that is sought through forgiveness and reconciliation. To go in another direction now is indeed to sin again and to repent once again, to go in a different direction towards the place of communion. Theology, true to its Eucharistic nature, will be directed towards reconciliation with God received and enacted as God's unmerited gift. True theology changes the theologian and not God. Proper theological questions would include the self-examination of the theologian, the preparation required for making an authentic confession of sins. And this questioning brings the theologian into the disposition of receptivity towards what God can do in and with the theologian, to what God might reveal from the other side of forgiveness, the knowledge of God hidden behind reconciliation. Where does theology go from here? It goes to the altar of God. How does theology get there? It offers itself fully, without reserve or remainder.

Offering

The movement where communion is realized and given, the where and when of the arrival of Jesus, the movement begun in gathering, imagined in listening, and directed through confession and absolution, now reaches its *telos* by offering. In the Eucharistic movement, offering precedes the realization of the Bodily presence of Jesus' arrival and the consequential receiving of his life of communion. We offer ourselves towards receiving the offering of God to us, the exchange of life in the place where what poses for dying, for loss of self, becomes the posture of risen life, the communion of the resurrection, the resurrection of communion. What becomes the Body and Blood of Christ is first offered to God for this purpose. Along with the bread and wine, the gathered people offer themselves, including the offering of money with everything that this offering signifies. That is, what is offered to become the Body and Blood of Christ includes the lives of those who make this offering. Offering to God is not a movement that protects the oblationers from any divine interference in their lives; it is not giving something to God so that God will leave us to do and think what we see fit. Offering bread and wine to the Father is performed by those who already belong to the Son in baptism, having received the gift of the Holy Spirit, which is God's profound and incomprehensible movement within us (Rom. 8). Offering is then both response to God's initiative within us and our initiative towards becoming what we are here and in the age to come.

The theological *askesis* of offering excludes the theological disposition of only thinking about something. We do not think about God in order to articulate an understanding of God. We do not think about Jesus so that we can articulate a faith that is about Jesus. For the Eucharistic nature of theology, seeking understanding is offering of self towards the place, presence and agency of proper theological understanding. We understand faith when we begin to understand how, when, where, what and why God has acted on us for the purpose and reality of participating in God's life of communion bestowed in the Son and enacted by the Holy Spirit. This understanding is a reflection on God's Eucharistic place, presence and agency. And this reflection is possible for us because we have offered ourselves for the sake of this communion. That is, what is primary here, what is the ultimate *telos*, is communion in and with God and not our understanding of faith. This reflective understanding presumes both an *a priori* and an *a posteriori* consecrated reality and reality of consecration, substance and potency that precedes and follows any of our theological efforts. The Eucharistic faith is realized on the altar of God and is lived, believed and understood from that place.

Remembering

In the Eucharistic economy, offering takes us to the Eucharistic prayer, to the time of Christ's sacramental arrival. Whatever else that can be and is said about the various structures and developments of the Eucharistic prayer, we are permitted to identify two basic concepts or dynamics of such prayers: remembrance and invocation, or anamnesis and epiclesis. Thus, the Eucharistic faith is realized and understood through the modes of anamnesis and epiclesis. The substance of this faith is understood through remembrance, and the potency of this faith is understood as invocation. What is remembered, what is invoked, and why? The anamnetic movement of the Eucharistic prayer is the giving of thanks for what God has done in the creation of the world and for its redemption, locating the fulfilment of both in Jesus Christ sent, risen and returning. Salvation history is recalled, its presence made known through thanksgiving to the Father for his historical agency on our behalf. The *a priori* condition for such a Eucharistic act is recalled as such an act. The presence of this salvation history includes its potency as the possibilities that issue from divine agency. This is not a benign story, an impotent memory, because it occurs in the presence of God, and thereby is our offering of our history with God for the sake of God's own gift to us. The Eucharistic recounting of our history with God places us within the potency of this history; this history is God's gift to us. Hence the substance of faith is available to us as this remembrance of what God has done. Faith is not then a series of statements representing discrete meanings or an arranged set of things we believe. Faith is what proceeds from a relationship with God that is substantiated by anamnesis. However, this Eucharistic faith is not limited to faith about God, ordered towards saying something that is appropriate to God's essence or existence, or satisfied with remembering salvation history as its *telos*. Rather, this faith as a substantiated relationship seeks to move further into the presence and potency of God as it now exists here, in the moment when we once again call upon God's historical agency to create for us what we cannot give ourselves. We ask the Father for the sending of the Holy Spirit to fashion for us the singular gift of life that is the Body and Blood of Jesus Christ whereby the covenant made with God in baptism is renewed. We invoke the Holy Spirit to draw us more deeply and comprehensively into the life we entered at baptism when we became members of the Body of Christ. This life is always given to us as the Body and Blood of Christ through the distinctive agency of the Holy Spirit, 'the Lord and giver of life'.

The theological *askesis* appropriate for, adequate to, the Eucharistic nature of theology will include remembrance and invocation, anamnesis and epiclesis. Within Eucharistic praying, the object of our remembrance is what God has done. Remembering what God has done is to remember who God is; God is the God who has acted in this way. God's identity is available as God's history. While God is identified by this history, including creation, God is not this history. This history is possible because of who God is. As history for us by the agency of God, it is then appropriate to receive this history by thankful remembrance, by Eucharistic anamnesis. Thus, for the Eucharistic nature of theology, history is approached in a historical-anamnetic way; we do not stand over against history looking for signs of our agency. Rather, we regard this history as something remembered for the sake of giving thanks for God's agency; we place ourselves before this action, this acting God. As a theological reality, history is never neutral or objectified by our own requirements for producing knowledge. We always adopt a hermeneutic of anamnesis. However, this hermeneutic is not a general theory about any or all history; it is a distinctive interpretative disposition for a distinctive history. It is *this* history that identifies *this* God, and we approach this history in *this* way. Theology is not confined to the history remembered Eucharistically, but its study of history for theological purposes is to proceed from this Eucharistic place and posture. That is, there is the possibility that history can be placed within the sphere of anamnesis, that we can conclude our historical study in thanksgiving to God.

For theology, the *askesis* of anamnesis is abiding with the history that God has made in remembrance, present before the actuality and potency of God's agency. As such, theology is not the practice of open-ended speculation. We do not look for a God away from this remembered history. The question directing our seeking is not how do we think, or what is there to think about? Instead, the accountable question is what do we think about this God remembered in this way with this history? As abiding with this history, locating our minds within anamnesis, our thinking does not only have an objective relationship with this history, but a subjectivity that serves as horizon and not centre of our thinking. We think in the presence of God, whom we are directed towards in thanksgiving and remembrance, with whom we have a history of thought. We do not engage in speculative forgetfulness as if we are not standing before God, as if we do not have the witness of this remembered history.

Invoking

Along with this remembering, Eucharistic praying is the movement of invocation. We enter into a relationship with God's presence and potency through anamnesis and by epiclesis. We invoke the Holy Spirit over the bread and wine for God's own realization of the presence of the Body and Blood of Christ, and we ask for the Holy Spirit to descend upon us who are gathered as this Body and to receive it. Jesus arrives from the Father once again, and the Holy Spirit descends once again on the assembly of believers there to meet him. Remembering what God has done leads to the invocation of God's agency. God's history is fulfilled in Jesus Christ, and God's agency realizes Jesus Christ as an arriving presence, a gift to receive. God's history remembered in this way is handed over, is tradition, for those who reach out to receive what the Holy Spirit will place into their hands and mouth. God's subjectivity makes possible the objectivity of God's gift to us, which we receive objectively by the subjectivity of the Body of Christ in whom we are members. The Eucharistic nature of theology will reflect this subjective and objective interplay, the mutuality of divine and human agencies.

Theological *askesis* will then include the invocation of the Holy Spirit to render the possibility of not only understanding faith as a subjective seeking but will realize what there is to understand as an objective presence: 'When the Spirit of truth comes, he will guide you into all the truth; for he will not speak on his own, but will speak whatever he hears, and he will declare to you the things that are to come' (John 16.13). Thus, there is a pneumatological mediation of theology between the faithful seeker and the understood faith, between God and us as determined by God's active agency and our receptive agency. We ask for what we wish to understand, and this understanding is possible because there is the prior gift of presence, of a reality seeking those to understand insofar as they are willing to receive a life, a gift of truth. Once again, theology ventures forth not by speculative manoeuvres among the fragments of postmodern epistemologies, but through the willingness to approach the Father with an epicletic desire to know whom this Father will send to us, a seeking after more than a seeking for. This desire, this theological posture of invocation, emerges from the remembrance of God's history; we are led to ask, formed to seek. Theological knowledge is God's gift to us. Theological objectivity is constituted by our receptivity of the objective presence of God the Father in the object of the Son, rendered objectively by the subjectivity of the Holy Spirit. This pneumatological subjectivity is where we enter into the possibilities of speaking of the objectivity of theological knowledge, which is objective because it is always already God's bestowal of a real presence, the presence of God's reality as revealed for us to know. We remember though that this objective knowing is for Spirit-led living. We do not seek this knowledge elsewhere or through the epistemological modes of our capacities to seek. We do not construct a knowledge that belongs to us either objectively or subjectively. When we enter the Eucharist, we leave behind any pursuits of a natural objectivity or of an experiential subjectivity. Rather, we abide in that place where anamnesis is fulfilled by epiclesis, and where epiclesis refers to anamnesis.

Place, Presence and Agency

Throughout this initial exploration of the Eucharistic nature of theology, three fundamental concepts have emerged: place, presence and agency. Perhaps it is a misnomer to refer to them as concepts. They are not ideas or ideals that are employed in the various ways theology might address certain appropriate topics; they are not categories we keep 'at hand'. Place, presence and agency are dimensions of the Eucharistic nature of theology. They allow us to appreciate the scope and depth, the vivifying dynamics, of this nature. That is, place, presence and agency are not symbols for theology; they do not serve as significations of this nature. It is the direct effort to explore the theological nature of the Eucharist that has led to the identification of place, presence and agency as faithful ways to speak of what has been revealed. Thus, a further investigation of these contingent concepts, these integral dynamics, will allow for a keener appreciation of the Eucharistic nature of theology.

Place

Theology originates where a particular event takes place. This phrase 'takes place' conjures up both a beginning, a temporal occurrence, and a locatable event, a spatial reality. It has been asserted that the origin of theology is when Jesus arrives from the Father along with the sending of the Spirit. The promised, covenantal and normative place for this arrival is the Eucharist. The Eucharistic nature of theology involves the theological nature of this place. The faith that would lead us to enter this place, the faith that is nurtured here, that belongs here, is the faith that we seek to understand. Furthermore, we seek an understanding that also belongs here; this place is where we learn how to seek. The point of departure for theology is inhabiting this place, and then being formed there as seekers of what presents itself for understanding. We are located seekers, who attend to the particularity of this place. We are not disembodied thinkers striving for a general idea or basis upon which to build a system. This Eucharistic place is not any place, neither a modern universal nor a postmodern fragmentary place. It is a place we enter. As such, here are appropriate and inappropriate theological fundamental questions. The questions or directives that we find elsewhere, and that do not belong in this Eucharistic place, are as follows: Why are we here? (existential questions); What has happened here? (historical questions); What is here? (metaphysical questions); and How can here be changed? (ethical questions). Instead, these are the appropriate questions residing within the Eucharistic place: Why did we come here? What can happen here? What change takes place here? Who will meet us here? and Is there an agency here other than our own?

Presence

The definitive difference between what constitutes appropriate and inappropriate questions that may be posed in the theological place of the Eucharist is rooted in presence. This place exists for presence; it is the place of the presence for which we seek when we enter this place. Theology takes place in the presence of its object. Theological work is both the discernment of, and the transformation by, the presence that is known and encountered in the Eucharistic place. We are not alone with our theology; our presence is not the point of reference for our thinking and doing. This means that the 'turn to the subject' in modern theology cannot be the determinative trajectory of our theology. For the Eucharistic nature of theology, the turn to the subject is always already the turn towards the God who is present in this place in this way for a particular objective: communion with us as God's communion is given to us. Once again, we can employ the definition of theology as faith seeking understanding to illuminate what is being claimed regarding the nature of theology as formed by its Eucharistic place. Faith here is not only believing a content or upholding a substance. Faith is knowing the one in whom 'we live and move and have our being' (Acts 17.28). Faith is the how and why of being a member of the Body of Christ. What knowledge of God and of ourselves belongs to the Body of Christ? What can those who share the life of this Body know because they do share this life? Thus, we are incorporated into a presence not our own, and yet for us to be present here is to know ourselves in this other presence. Faith then is not understanding myself as a seeker of God, or a seeker after some 'spiritual' or 'religious' dimension to a human life. Faith is coming to terms with God's presence in the place where and whereby this presence is offered. The Eucharistic faith is always open to God's presence. Our availability to God, our awareness of God's presence as a radical difference waiting to happen, is our fidelity. When we seek to understand this faith, we do so in the presence of the one we seek, the one whom we faithfully seek. This is why theological understanding includes an offered presence, an arriving reality. Understanding is not confined to the exposition of doctrines or the exegesis of texts. Ultimately, we are not seeking to have a better or fuller grasp of a set of teachings, or to fashion teachings presumably more adequate to our own places and times.

Rather, we are seeking an understanding that is only available to us in this arriving presence of Jesus, enveloped by the presence of the Triune God. We understand that we are here in this presence, and that we are here to receive this presence as a communion of persons. Here is a mutuality of minds, a thinking characterized not so much as being 'about' something but a being 'with, in and towards' someone. This is a presence of movement; this is presence as movement. We seek as those whom God seeks. We are present as those to whom God is present. We understand as those who seek to share God's understanding of us as members of the Body of Christ. In this Eucharistic place, God the Father knows us in the knowledge of the Son that belongs here, the knowledge realized by the gift of the Holy Spirit. Therefore, we cannot really understand this Eucharistic faith that takes place here in the presence of God without taking account of divine agency.

Agency

The Eucharistic nature of theology has three dimensions: place, presence and agency. There is this place where this God is present who acts in this way. Each of these dimensions is identified with each other and as each other, and this identifiable dynamic resides with *this*. Attending to the particular is the initial movement of discernment, and theological understanding will not leave behind this particularity while striving for any general or universal ideals, values, experiences, religiosity, spirituality and most of all for any divinity. For the distinctiveness of the Eucharist for the nature of theology, the distinctiveness of place and presence, is what happens in its enactment, the celebration of the Eucharist. What happens in this place is an event of the presence that is known by its action. While there are two agencies operative in the one celebration of the Eucharist – God's and ours – these agencies are asymmetrical. We can easily yield to the temptation to think that the Eucharist is something we do just as we can think that theology is something we produce. The primacy of our own agency becomes almost inescapable. This is why theology often becomes almost inevitably reduced to ethics. For the Eucharistic nature of theology, God's agency is not only primary; it is also not singular, while still being unique. Indeed, any adequate consideration of God's agency will take up the mutuality and appropriateness of agency attributed to each of the Triune persons, the enactment of the Eucharist presents this trifold agency through the multiplicity of actions that constitute the Eucharistic economy. In the Eucharist and as the Eucharist, God addresses us, gathers, forgives, listens, shares, gives and sends us. The consequence for theology of this multiple Eucharistic activity of the Triune agency is that theology will neither reflect nor be guided by only one of these actions. Theology is not then confined to attending to God's Word addressed to us; theology is not defined by the thinking or understanding required for faithful proclamation of the gospel. Theology is not confined to that which assists our understanding of what we need to be doing. Theology is not the singular pursuit of what entails our salvation. The Eucharistic nature of theology requires a comprehensive account, a catholic discernment, of the wholeness of God's agency as enacted and known through the economy of the one celebration of the Eucharist. It would be theologically natural to assert that we invite God to celebrate the Eucharist with us so that we might have once again this Eucharistic faith and be renewed in this faith as we seek to understand it. With this introductory appreciation of the dimensions of place, presence and agency of the Eucharistic nature of theology we can now put before us a series of theses that will direct the more detailed and expansive rendering of the Eucharistic faith that follows in subsequent chapters. The Eucharistic nature of theology is movement rather than methodology; epiphany rather than existence; discovery rather than deconstruction; presence rather than absence; oblation rather than ethics; language rather than experience; and agency rather than speculation.

Our appreciation of the Eucharistic nature of theology from within its inherent dimensions of place, presence and agency yields three identifying characteristics of the Eucharistic faith.

Since the Eucharistic nature of theology has the defining dimensions of place, presence and agency, the Eucharistic faith that we are seeking to understand has three respective characteristics: it is located (place); sufficient (presence); and creative (agency). As Eucharistically located, faith will be shaped and animated by the dynamics or the economy of the Eucharist. Any entertaining of the existence of faith outside the Eucharist will be accountable to its Eucharistic location. That is, any reflection on faith, any theological effort to understand the Christian faith, will be guided by the question whether what we are saying or claiming belongs within the Eucharist. Put another way, we do not go seeking greener theological pastures outside the Eucharist. As the place of the arrival of Jesus from the Father, the presence of Jesus as this arrival, the Eucharistic nature of theology will be characterized by a regard for sufficiency. That is, the presence of the arriving Jesus in the way that he is arriving, and why he is here, is the sufficient reality and 'object' for theology. The arriving presence of Jesus to give us his life of communion, to share with us his presence from the dead and from the Father, is enough for us. We never take this presence for granted, and our minds never itch to hear something more interesting, useful, prophetic or provocative. However, the Eucharistic location of theology and faith, the presence of the sufficiency of faith, does not lead to a static or rigidly objective faith. The fidelity that is the location and sufficiency of the Eucharistic faith is creative, because it is the participation in God's own creativity. As the place and presence of God's agency, the creativity of God is at work among us. For any and all true theological creativity is what brings about the new creation, the resurrection of our minds, wills and bodies, the realization of the Body of Christ by the descending Holy Spirit. For what we are truly seeking through the Eucharistic nature of theology is not understanding of this or that, but life in Christ, the astounding and inexhaustible creativity that is the *perichoresis* of God.

PART 2

Seeking

3

Tradition

In the sixteenth century, tradition became a problem for those who regarded the current theological state of the church as at variance with their reading of the New Testament. Tradition, or that which had transpired between the closing of the New Testament canon and the contemporary church, was now primarily rendered by the nascent Reformers as a story of betrayal or infidelity. Somewhere and somehow along the way the church instituted beliefs and practices that were either distortions of original faith or direct contradictions of this faith. Thus, there was the effort to reform the church and its doctrines and liturgies along the lines of a renewal of biblical theology, a univocal *sola scriptura*. This Reformation proved to be a pervasive and comprehensive transformation of all aspects of church and theology. Tradition was cast aside so that faithful Christians can have a direct engagement with Scripture, without the mediation of ecclesial authorities or doctrinal interpretations.

The subsequent Counter-Reformation was thus a counter-argument for the nature and role of tradition, for the proper scope and content of the Christian faith as it existed authoritatively. Tradition was deemed appropriate, even necessary, for living into, and living from, the Christian faith. Tradition was not something added to Scripture. Instead, fidelity to Scripture generated tradition; they formed an organic theological whole. Theology, or sacred teaching, was the exercise of commenting upon the scriptural text. There was a tradition of engaging Scripture, and tradition was a consequence of this engagement. That is, tradition could itself constitute fidelity to the original faith and not a result of doctrinal, theological and ecclesial infidelity.

The problematic of tradition in its Reformation and Counter-Reformation version – whether tradition was primarily a problem or a possibility – was further developed by the rising tides of autonomous reason and historical consciousness that washed over the theological landscape in the eighteenth and nineteenth centuries. Learning to think for oneself and to take into account the historical process by which things came to be believed turned theology towards the authority of human agency and thinking. Both Scripture and tradition were taken before the judgement seat of reason and history. Scripture and tradition were subjects one could, and arguably should, approach from elsewhere, from the places where pure or objective reason and a historical-critical consciousness reigned. Even when regarded from a more positive viewpoint, Scripture and tradition became 'sources' of revelation and theology. They were studied for what could be taken from them and *now* believed (doctrine) or put to use (ethics). Again, Scripture and tradition are approached from elsewhere, while deeming both as sources of revelation or as necessary references for any authentic contemporary fidelity. Scripture and tradition were no longer *given*; they were *constructed* (modern) and then *deconstructed* (postmodern).

One of the principal products of this rational and historical engagement with Scripture and tradition was the appreciation for diversity and plurality. There is no longer 'the Scripture' or 'the Tradition'. Instead, there is a variety of scriptural texts, of redacted pericopes, texts within texts, and a variety of traditions strewn all over the history or histories and the geography or cultures of Christianity. The student of the Christian faith, and we might even speak of students who are not disciples, are confronted not only with change or development, but also with difference and multiplicity, both embedded in Scripture and tradition.

The historical study of theology rendered theology a subject for a discipline that was not necessarily and inherently theological. That is, theology can be considered historical theology or the history of theology. As such, theology is a sphere in which various contexts, cultures, politics, philosophies and ecclesial polemics have been at play. Theology is a subject understood as a product of these various influences or forces. Directly put, theology can be assessed as the consequence of human agency and thought. Theology is located within a temporal span, a historical epoch. We can speak of patristic theology, medieval theology, modern and postmodern theology. Theology is located within the currents of intellectual or philosophical movements; it is a narrative of argument and counter-argument. Theological exposition can be undertaken as a genealogy of thinkers, an account of misdirections and corrections. We convey this history or genealogy of theology by employing the rhetorical tools of pre-, post- and neo- this or that subject. The theological past has brought us to this theological present, and we can approach this present as a moment of continuity or discontinuity with this past.

This historical consciousness regarding theology, this location of theology within history, inevitably shapes what we consider tradition, and how we can consider tradition. As that which exists as past to this present, tradition is a subject of historical study and of theological discernment. Our theological present becomes a place from which to question our theological past; tradition is interrogated 'in light of' the present. Or, tradition is a past from which to question the present. Either way or direction, tradition is not an organic theological whole comprising both the past and the present. Employing the basic working definition of tradition as the dynamic of handing on and receiving the Christian faith, we can detect how primacy can be granted to either the handing on or the receiving. A critical *epoche* is inserted between the handing on and the receiving. The continuous movement of handing on and receiving can no longer be taken for granted as an abiding cycle of fidelity. Likewise, the receiving becomes a critical stance towards the handing on. The presumed linear movement of the past to the present can now be rendered the hermeneutical assessment of the present towards the past. Tradition no longer is who we are; tradition is something we choose or not. As we purvey the landscape of our theological past, we question what we see there that might be useful to us now, or what might be a decorative touch to the theological home we are constructing for ourselves, and what we wish to leave behind. That is, our decision about the past, our discernment of tradition, is the way we ask the question about our theological future. Our theological decisions about our past become decisions directed towards our theological future. However, what if our theological future has been decided already, and furthermore, we did not make this decision?

Eucharistic Liturgical Tradition

The establishment of a critical contemporary perspective towards the tradition, the bracketing of the past over against the present, does not lead inevitably to a rejection of parts of the past in favour of a more enlightened present. Engagement with tradition, the historical study of the theological past, can lead to an effort to make the present more 'traditional', to transform the present to resemble more of its traditional past. This is the case with the liturgies of the Eucharist as well as an important dynamic in contemporary expositions and evaluations of theologies of the Eucharist, for example ecumenical statements on the Eucharist. What customarily has been called the liturgical movement began in the nineteenth century as an investigation of the liturgical tradition for the purpose of a deeper understanding of contemporary liturgies: how things became the way they are. That is, studying the tradition can lead to a better or clearer explanation of why the liturgy, especially the Eucharistic liturgy (in this case the singular dominance of the Roman Rite in the West), is the way it is. However, this initial critical engagement with the tradition, the historical study of the newly discovered and accumulating sources of tradition, led to awareness of discontinuity as well as continuity between liturgical past and present. This study also led to an awareness that there are many liturgical traditions and not just the dominant one or one's own. The liturgical movement in the twentieth century comprised both a looking back and a looking around, an investigation of the liturgical past, privilege being bestowed on the patristic period, and the corresponding ecumenical movement of approaching other churches and their respective liturgies and theologies without the polemical posturing of the past. For several churches, this intentional exploration and exposition of the tradition resulted in the development of Eucharistic liturgies that were deemed more 'traditional' than their pre-existing liturgies as well as more like the Eucharistic liturgies of other churches. Likewise, a diversity was created within the liturgical life of churches that did not exist before, for example having available four Eucharistic prayers instead of one, or six forms of intercessory prayer instead of one. On the other hand, the Eucharistic liturgies of the different churches came to resemble each other in 'traditional' ways. The polarity between the Reformation and Counter-Reformation Eucharistic liturgies, which had enshrined doctrinal 'here we stand' Eucharistic prayers, was transcended and transformed by and through a determined accountability to an identified common Eucharistic tradition.[1]

Eucharistic Theological Tradition

A critical appraisal of the tradition, and the consequence of becoming aware of various traditions with crucial differences among them, was brought not only to the Eucharistic or liturgical tradition but to Eucharistic theology as well. At the very least, ecumenical dialogues forced the issue of different theologies of the Eucharist, and in many cases, the confessions of these theologies were meant to contradict the Eucharistic theology of other ecclesial traditions. The Reformation and Counter-Reformation had Eucharistic theology as an animating theological concern. What to do about these conflicting Eucharistic theologies, especially around the abiding neuralgic questions of the presence of Christ in the Eucharist and the relationship between the sacrifice of Christ on the cross and the Eucharist?[2] One approach, as was carried out by the Anglican and Roman Catholic dialogues, was to study together the common tradition of both churches prior to the polemics of the sixteenth century. That is, what tradition of Eucharistic theology do both churches appeal to for their respective understandings of the Eucharist, especially again regarding presence and sacrifice? Like the study of the Eucharistic liturgical tradition identifying a variety of traditions, sometimes referred to as liturgical families, the tradition of Eucharistic theology presents itself not as a monolithic set of firm statements about controversial questions that come later. Instead, there are different kinds of arguments, perspectives and emphases. Even the patristic era, or especially the patristic era, is a rich and complex field of theological expositions, affirmations, arguments and commentary on the Eucharist. It is not just a question of what is said about the Eucharist, but how it is said. Different theologians can be explicating Eucharistic theologies by commentary on different Eucharistic liturgies or traditions. And as theology becomes more of an enterprise involving contemporary philosophical concerns, Eucharistic theology, just as much as theology, will be expressed by employing some of the concepts and language of philosophy. That is, how one thinks about reality is employed in how one speaks of the real presence of Christ in the Eucharist.[3]

The towering example of this is the initial theological exposition that becomes the doctrine of real presence in the Roman Catholic Church, that is, transubstantiation. Of course, the doctrine of transubstantiation is not found in the fourth century, or in the patristic era as such. Or is it? When faced with the question of what to do about transubstantiation in the statement on the Eucharist by the Anglican–Roman Catholic International Commission, the compromise was struck among the Roman Catholic theologians to place the direct reference to transubstantiation in a footnote with the editorial commentary that some theologians regard this doctrine as an affirmation of Christ's presence in the Eucharist rather than as an explanation of this presence. The statement itself offers an affirmation of the multidimensional presence of Christ in the Eucharist but forgoes any explanation of how this presence comes to be there. Within the Anglican theological tradition, there is an emphasis on affirming Christ's presence, believing that Christ is present, but being 'agnostic' regarding how this presence comes to be, which in the literature is meant to be a rejection of transubstantiation as an effort of explanation.[4] Also, it must be admitted that there is another Anglican tradition of Eucharistic theology more aligned with some Reformation traditions that do not affirm Christ's real presence in the Eucharist. There is the distinction within the Anglican Eucharistic theology of presence, a distinction found in all Western Eucharistic theologies, of faith in the presence of Christ or the presence of faith in Christ. This snapshot of how transubstantiation is treated within one ecumenical dialogue is offered not as a painfully inadequate rehearsal of this enduring question of the real presence, but rather to gain a glimpse of how critical engagement with the Eucharistic theological tradition results in an appreciation of traditions, theologies and complexities in our answers over time to the same questions. However, could it be that this awareness of the variety of answers existing as Eucharistic theological traditions can lead us not only to the transformation of our answers but to our questions as well? Theologically speaking, can we allow the Eucharist to ask its own questions?

Tradition as Questions and Answers

The diversity within the tradition of Eucharistic theology, the variety of Eucharistic theologies and ecclesial doctrines, can be accounted for in part by how different questions are being asked, yielding an array of answers. Focusing on the abiding theme of presence within Eucharistic theology, we can begin to see the role different questions play in accounting for how the presence of Christ is perceived. We have noted already the fundamental distinction between speaking of faith in the presence of Christ and the presence of faith in Christ. Surrounding these two emphases on the subjective and objective natures of presence and faith (and it needs to be stressed that these emphases are not necessarily exclusive of each other) are other questions. We can ask, how is Christ present? What is the nature of this presence? Where is Christ present? And, why is Christ present? And the answer to this question can reshape our answers to all the other questions of presence. Framing these questions of presence as questions of tradition, we can ask what is the presence of handing on, and what is the presence of receiving? Or, what is being handed on, and is being received? How does this handing on take place, and how does this receiving take place? Are these different places or events, or are they 'substantially' one event in one place? Furthermore, why does this handing on take place, and why does this receiving take place? Can the answers to these questions fundamentally reshape our answers to all the other questions posed by and as tradition?

Why speak of tradition when reflecting on the Christian faith? One answer to this question will be rooted in the presumed necessity of continuity. The faith is something that can be identified as such throughout history and within a variety of cultural and geographical settings. The faith continues as it is without being absorbed into these historical, intellectual, even ecclesial, places. That is, there is a recognizable faith being handed on regardless of the vagaries surrounding the receiving of this faith. 'To contend for the faith that was once for all entrusted to the saints' (Jude 3b) requires a theological vigilance so that the 'once' remains so within the inevitable handing on and receiving that follows until the *parousia*. Tradition is our historical and temporal receptive act of fidelity to what was originally handed on.

Another answer to the question of why tradition is the direct acknowledgement that there has indeed been a history, a temporal span, between the original handing on and receiving from the beginning of faith until the present here and now. The question then becomes what to do with this tradition. We can study tradition looking to identify patterns of continuity and discontinuity, periods of development and distortion. Of course, such a study is pursued through the lens of whatever is taken already as faith or as appropriate fidelity. A primary critical directive can emerge that is the polar opposite of the one adopted by the Reformers. That is, instead of critiquing the present in terms of an original past, the past itself, including its original existence, can be assessed in terms of the present. Or, in terms of tradition, there are certain prior aspects of the Christian faith that can no longer be handed on in this context of possible reception. What can here and now be received becomes a critical filter to any handing on issuing from then and there. In fact, the theological moment might require not a receiving of the Christian faith but its abiding contemporary construction: What can and should be believed now becomes the hegemonic question.

Tradition as God's Fidelity

However, the question of why tradition, or what to do about tradition, is not theologically enveloped by the concerns, critical or otherwise, that reside within historical consciousness or temporal awareness. The story of tradition, again theologically construed, is not confined to the questions asked by human agents. The direct theological question put to tradition is: How is the essence of the Christian faith available throughout and as its own history? The answer to this question locates tradition initially within soteriology because we are asking about the endurance of salvation, about the God-difference the Christian faith proclaims and enacts. The answer to why tradition becomes the Christian faith. Tradition becomes ensuring that God's Word continues to be effectively heard and that God's saving act remains so. That is, continuity does not rest primarily on the patterns of speech and behaviour of Christians or churches. Tradition is the continuity of God's relationship towards the world; continuity is rooted in God's agency as the one who hands on what is being handed on ordered towards the faithful reception of this event. Thus, tradition is the faithful handing on and receiving that takes place as God's own fidelity to God's saving offer and relationship to the world, to humanity. We can say then that the tradition that is the Christian faith has its origin in the covenant tradition of Israel. God's establishment of a covenant with Abraham, and with the people of Israel, was God's initiative to constitute an abiding, mutual, and faithful relationship with the 'chosen' people:

> I will establish my covenant between me and you, and your offspring after you throughout their generations, for an everlasting covenant, to be God to you and to your offspring after you. And I will give to you, and to your offspring after you, the land where you are now an alien, all the land of Canaan, for a perpetual holding; and I will be their God. (Gen. 17.7-8)

> I will take you as my people, and I will be your God. (Exod. 6.7)

> And you shall be my people, and I will be your God. (Jer. 30.22)

God's 'steadfast love' for these people is to continue through particular places, practices and promises. God is a covenant-making God always willing to call these people to account for not keeping the covenant, and always willing to renew the covenant by offering a 'new' covenant. The arrival of Jesus in the midst of the people of Israel is God's definitive act of offering salvation, the fulfilment of God's covenant-making will. From now on Jesus is the centre of gravity for the covenantal sphere of fidelity to God, who is revealed as the Father of the Risen Jesus. As such, Jesus institutes the new, definitive and fulfilling covenant that is sealed by his sacrificial death. What follows this sacrificial death is the covenant that involves remembering this sacrifice as well as remembering the whole tradition of God's covenant-making relationship with the people of Israel. Therefore, and thereby, the arrival of Jesus through this remembrance of him and his 'new covenant in my blood' becomes the centre of gravity of the sphere that is fidelity to this covenant. The sphere itself surrounding this arrival, the continuity of this sphere, is the tradition of the Christian faith. That is, the tradition of the Christian faith is the Eucharist.

Tradition is the place where God's saving fidelity happens, where the arrival of Jesus takes place. As such, this place is appreciated as the sphere that takes shape around and as this arrival. This place where and whereby the centre of gravity that is the arrival of Jesus remains so. This is tradition because this is the normative place of the expectation (fidelity) and the realization of the arriving presence of Jesus with the offer of his life of communion (salvation). The content of tradition is therefore twofold: first, there is the content of expectation; and second, there is the content of realization. The content of expectation is what is customarily referred to as tradition. It is the faithful past that renders the existence of the faithful present, or at least the possibility of this existence. When we keep the tradition, we are keeping alive among us the content that has developed around the expectation of the saving presence of Jesus. Thus, a critical perspective towards tradition would be how this content is related to the presence of Jesus: how does content reflect the saving presence of Jesus? Put another way, is the tradition transparent and accountable to the presence of Jesus? If this content in question, content that presumes the questions of why, where, when and how of the arrival of Jesus, does not provide the answer sought, should this content be handed on? Should it be received?

Tradition as Expectation and Realization

The question of the content of tradition, now transposed into the twofold question of the process of tradition, calls into question the very nature and purpose of tradition, that is, the theological vocation of tradition. Keeping the tradition that is the content of expectation of the arriving Jesus is our fidelity; it is faithful human agency. However, this faithful human agency, this keeping the content of expectation, is not the accomplishment, much less the production or construction, of the arrival of Jesus with his gift of saving life. Jesus arrives as himself and not as one circumscribed by our expectations, traditional or otherwise. Even the tradition that we keep as expectation still belongs to his arrival. The tradition of expectation, that which is handed on from the past, stands as a sacrifice offered to God. This tradition is to undergo a transformation by passing through the expectation to the realization, by undergoing the paschal mystery of Christ, the passage from crucifixion to resurrection, the passover from death to life. The tradition from the past is not essentially and ultimately the story about ourselves; it is not the place to put down roots of our identity. Rather, this tradition from the past, and as expectation, is our vocation directing us towards the arriving presence of Jesus, towards belonging in the company of heaven. This is to say that the tradition as past and as expectation does not stand alone; it exists for the realization of the arriving presence of Jesus. The tradition surrounding the expectation of Jesus' arrival is accompanied by the tradition surrounding the realization of his arrival. Our sacrifice of tradition is met by God's gift of tradition.

There is a tradition of our handing on our expectations of God to God, and there is a tradition of receiving from God the realization of these expectations as the Body and Blood of Christ. There is a tradition of our way to God, and there is a tradition of God's way to us. There is a tradition marked by human agency, however it may be construed as Spirit-led or enabled, and there is a tradition of God's agency, the direct act of the Holy Spirit. However we speak of two traditions, or make this distinction between what is performed by human agency and by divine agency, we do so as the necessary faithful rendition of what tradition really is and why it is. We hand on to God so that we might receive from God. Tradition is a dynamic that exists in the presence of God. Faithfulness to tradition is then ultimately the willingness to sacrifice this tradition in order to be faithful to God. Abraham's willingness to sacrifice Isaac is an exemplar of the Christian tradition theologically conceived. We say 'theologically conceived' because we can speak of tradition, practise tradition, as if God is a bystander who cheers us on for 'keeping' or 'defending' the tradition, or who chides us for straying from this tradition. We can and do locate tradition as an immovable entity protected by the institutional or doctrinal walls of the church. We can 'cherish' the tradition, or 'loathe' the tradition. Either way, it is a performance of human agency, an act and an attitude that looks to us to do something about tradition. God becomes either someone 'enshrined' in the tradition, or God becomes the one who can only be truly alive outside the tradition. Both approaches to God and to tradition remove us from the dynamic exchange of the tradition of expectations for God, not to be confused with the expectations we have for ourselves as faithful agents, and the realization of these expectations that belong solely to God. The arrival of Jesus within the covenant tradition of Israel was both the fulfilment of prior faithful expectations of God and the unique realization of these expectations that is God's presence among us. Jesus remains who he is in his arrival despite the circumstances or context of this arrival. Where Jesus arrives does not obstruct or enable Jesus to be who he is, but there is a tradition of this arrival. Tradition does not determine who Jesus is; tradition is the place we inhabit in order to receive who Jesus is. It is possible that Jesus could behave in a disruptive way in this place; the Jesus who 'cleansed' the temple so that it could be renewed as a house of prayer to God, a place where God exchanges life with those who dwell there and not a place where we perform exchanges with each other. However, the arrival of Jesus in the Eucharist is not a replication of his historical arrival; the presence of Jesus is heard as the Word of God and is received as the Body and Blood of Christ. Thus, within the exchange of traditions that takes place as our sacrifice of tradition and God's gift of tradition, we receive the Body and Blood of Christ; there is a tradition of receiving this gift, and as a gift, it is both really there and always realized anew. We speak and know this Body and Blood of Christ by residing within the tradition of its expectation and its prior reception; and yet, we always receive the Body and Blood of Christ as a gift realized now among us gathered to receive it. This gift cannot be recognized as such without our prior expectation, and this gift always is given now for the sake of God's future for us. When we receive the Body and Blood of Christ, we are fed by and into God's future for us as the Body of Christ; we are not scouring around in our past trying to find something to eat that we might 'like' or 'need'.

Tradition as Eucharist

How then are we to conceive of tradition as a Eucharistic exchange of handing on to God and receiving from God? Are the conceptual categories of handing on and receiving adequate to this theological appreciation of tradition? That is, how do we escape the closed system of exchange among us, the enduring assignment of those who hand on and of those who receive, or the total rebellion against such assignments? Or, more likely, we strive for some ecclesial hybrid of traditional and contemporary, a regard for the past that comes under pressure from a different past, a hybrid of our own making between the they back then and we who are now. This hybrid of traditional and contemporary usually falls into the theological trap of approaching the future as something we achieve rather than the future God gives. There is an abiding distinction between what 'God wants us to do now' and what God gives us from God's future for us. Tradition as the Eucharist does not abandon the exchange of handing on and receiving. Rather, the Eucharist is the tradition of holding together, and within this holding together the exchange between our handing on to God and receiving from God, our sacrifice of tradition and God's gift of tradition, takes place. The image or dynamic of holding together returns us to tradition as the sphere that surrounds the arrival of Jesus; this arrival as the centre of gravity created by the power of the Holy Spirit operative both within the gathered Body of Christ and in the arrival of Jesus who is pneumatologically realized and given as the Body and Blood of Christ. Holding together for the sake of an exchange of offering and giving between God and the baptized allows us not to reduce the tradition of Christian faith to either a linear maintenance or a linear progression (or some hybrid of both). What are we holding together?

Our consideration of the nature and dynamic of tradition as theologically conceived, as characterized by God's fidelity towards God's will to save, to give us the life of communion that is the Body and Blood of Christ, has brought us to the Eucharist. We have acknowledged that there are various Eucharistic traditions and that this variety is not necessarily equated with pluralism but with a keener sense of what might be the essence of the Eucharistic tradition derived from the essence of the Eucharist itself. However, this reflective movement from tradition to Eucharist does not allow us to leave behind the existence and purpose of tradition. For we cannot explore the theological essence of the Eucharist, the Eucharist as the sphere existing around and as the theological centre of gravity that is the arrival of Jesus. Tradition and Eucharist are now being identified with and as each other. We are claiming the tradition as Eucharist. That is, the Eucharist is our holding together what surrounds the exchange between God and the baptized, our sacrifice of tradition and God's gift of tradition. In order to better appreciate the tradition as Eucharist, we now need to explore this question of tradition from within the Eucharist itself by attending to our fidelity to God and God's fidelity to us through time and as history that takes place within and as the Eucharist. That is, we will reflect directly on the Eucharist, its nature and dynamic with its normative theological categories. Certainly, given the diversity of the theology and liturgy of the Eucharist throughout Christian history as noted above, this effort to explore and exposit a normative Eucharist, a tradition that is the Eucharist, will be confronted with many challenges. These challenges come from all kinds of places, from cultures, contexts, churches, traditions, methods, philosophies and experiences. And yet, if we can abide within the theological perspective that the singular purpose of the Eucharist is for the exchange of the gift of life from the baptized to God and from God to the baptized, then our reflection on the possibility of a normative Eucharist can always be guided by this singular purpose. For it has to be acknowledged at the outset that the exchange of the gift of life between God and ourselves has, despite our infidelities, to either hand on our life to God or to receive life from God, an abiding existence, a tradition.

Our initial account of the 'institution' of the Eucharist states, 'For I received from the Lord what I also handed on to you' (1 Cor. 11.23a). Paul's admonition to the Corinthians regarding their practice of the Lord's Supper was an appeal to tradition. However, this was not an abstract tradition, a set of rules or doctrines out there to be upheld or defended. Rather, Paul speaks of what he has handed on to the church in Corinth, and he has handed on to them what he himself received from the Lord. The appeal to a normative tradition here is an appeal to be reoriented within the exchange between Paul and the church in Corinth that exists because of an exchange between Paul and the Lord. Tradition is a personal and relational fidelity that takes place because of what has been received from the Lord. Furthermore, as was discussed above, Jesus does not stand outside tradition, outside the tradition of covenant making, when he 'institutes' the Eucharist.[5] In the hands of Jesus, the Eucharist is both the fulfilment and the transformation of the normative faithful relationship between God and the people of Israel, and now becomes the normative relationship between God and those baptized into the Body of Christ. Thus, our effort to contemplate directly the theological essence of the Eucharist, and thereby the theological essence of tradition, is not done from outside the Eucharist. We are engaging in reflection from within the Eucharist and not in a scientific observation from outside the Eucharist. Our purpose for doing so is not the performance of a method or an effort to achieve a desirable or reasonable account. Rather, we wish to live and think within the Eucharist, to know the truth that is there, and this truth will set us free from all other theological speculations and constructions.

The Normative Eucharist

We will embark on this recognition of the normative Eucharist, on this appreciation of what is the essential dynamic and nature of the Eucharist, by asking some basic questions, the kind of questions that lend themselves to the possible existence of normativity. We will not begin by trying to describe the Eucharist while relying on the Eucharistic liturgy, because we know already that there is no such thing as 'the Eucharistic liturgy'. Posing the questions of normativity does not ignore or escape the tides of diversity and plurality that continually wash over any claim to a normative Eucharist. However, we will let the questions guide our reflection because we are not trying to describe or explain something; we are entering the place of conversion and formation.

Who

The first question is who gathers for the Eucharist, who enters into the Eucharist? The answer is the baptized, those who have been baptized into the death and resurrection of Jesus Christ, who have become members of the Body of Christ, and who have received the gift of the Holy Spirit. In the ancient church, one did not enter or participate fully in the Eucharist until one was baptized. Rather, the newly baptized are led into the Eucharist to take their place now, and not before, as the priesthood of all believers offering intercessory prayer and hearing for the first time the Great Thanksgiving prayer, exchanging the peace of Christ, and then receiving the Body and Blood of Christ. In short, we can say that the newly baptized are baptized into the Eucharist, into the Eucharistic life. The normative Eucharist is the place where the baptized gather; it is where the baptized go to live and know the life and truth into which they have been baptized. The normative Eucharist exists following entrance into the death of Christ; it exists as entering the resurrection of Christ. It is the place where one knows oneself as a member of the Body of Christ, and this identity belongs not to oneself, but is an identity always bestowed, the gift of a life that is rooted in knowledge of Christ and not in a pre-baptized self-knowledge. While the normative Eucharist has the boundary set between the baptized and the unbaptized, we can be tempted to draw other boundaries, to allow another gathering with its own terms of membership to overshadow, even deform, this Eucharist. Baptism is the boundary of the place that is the normative Eucharist, and we are to resist any other boundary drawing if we are to reside fully and faithfully within this normative Eucharist. Entering the normative Eucharist, entering the Eucharist, means leaving behind any competing identities, any theological concerns, any ecclesial allegiances, located elsewhere. Such concerns are washed away in baptism, and when they are revived from the dead, repentance is the path back to the Eucharist.

Where

Where is the Eucharist located? It is located where and when the baptized gather to celebrate the Eucharist. The normative Eucharist is where the baptized as the ecclesial Body of Christ enacts the Eucharist by intending to do so. Thus, the location of the Eucharist, the answer to the question of where the normative Eucharist is, is not defined or determined by any other concern. The location of the normative Eucharist is where the Eucharist is enacted. The location is where the Eucharist takes place, when it takes place. This means that we cannot allow the defining boundaries of other locations to circumscribe what is the normative Eucharist. We cannot say that the Eucharist can only be celebrated here or there. The normative Eucharist does not have a normative aesthetic. No group or entity beyond the gathered Body of Christ can claim an exclusive location or style for the Eucharist. The place where the Eucharist is cannot be determined by geography, culture, institutions, language, politics, nations or even ecclesial denominations. What is normative about the Eucharist, about its location, is solely determined and defined by the Eucharist itself. Why is this so? Again, because the theological reality of the Eucharist is the event of the arriving Jesus offering his life of communion to and within the gathered Body of Christ. This arrival is the theological centre of gravity which has its spherical place, its tradition of the taking place of this arrival. We can then say that the normative Eucharist is located where the normative Eucharistic arrival of Jesus takes place. This answer to the question where the Eucharist is will have us refuse to erect boundaries of our own making around this location. The risen Jesus can and does arrive behind all our locked doors; no wall can contain him. The tomb of Joseph of Arimathea was the last place where we located Jesus. After the resurrection, Jesus can arrive when and wherever we are. After the ascension, we can be located wherever Jesus is: 'And if I go and prepare a place for you, I will come again and will take you to myself, so that where I am, there you may be also' (John

14.3). The tradition as Eucharist is the tradition of abiding in that place prepared for the gathered Body of Christ, the abiding place where the Eucharistic arrival of Jesus expectantly and faithfully takes place.

The Eucharistic transformation of tradition, tradition as Eucharist, requires both a critical and a faithful regard for tradition as that which abidingly surrounds the arrival of Jesus. Tradition exists for the sake of the Eucharistic arrival of Jesus, but it does exist. We cannot do without this tradition as the Body of Christ. While the Eucharist defines tradition, there is no such thing as a Eucharist without tradition. Attending to, inhabiting, the normative Eucharist can bring us to a critical awareness of the diversity of our traditions, and whether we have erected 'traditional' walls that locate ourselves in places other than the place where and whereby Jesus Eucharistically arrives. A critical question addressed to any of our traditions is, does this belong in the place where Jesus arrives Eucharistically? Does this practice, doctrine or ecclesial apparatus belong in this place, and is it being pulled towards, shaped by, the Eucharistic arrival of Jesus? Does the traditional this or that take us to the place where the Body of Christ is gathered expectantly and faithfully to receive the offer of Jesus' life of communion? The location of the normative Eucharist, the tradition of this location, is a place of arrival and not a timeline to be continually drawn or disruptively redrawn.

When

When is the normative Eucharist celebrated? The Eucharist is celebrated whenever the gathered Body of Christ intentionally does so. Given this temporal freedom, is there a normative time for the Eucharist to take place? The initial answer to this question located within the tradition is that the normative time for the Eucharist is the first day of the week, because this day is when Jesus rose from the dead. The Eucharist is what the church does on the day that now belongs to the temporality of the resurrection. The time for the Eucharist is the time to meet the risen Jesus who arrives to share his risen life with the members of his Body. Furthermore, because Jesus has been raised from the dead, from the place and time in which he was placed by human agency, any subsequent time, as well as any subsequent place, always exists as the time given over to him for him to inhabit and give his time to those gathered. That is, there is an exchange of the present between the present of the gathered and the present of the arriving one. The present of the gathered exists from their past, while the present of the arriving one exists from their future, which he is. The baptized gather for the Eucharist because it is the time to meet the arriving Jesus and to share the time that is his to give. The Eucharist is the *koinonia* of past, present and the future. Thus, the normative Eucharist is not timeless, nor does it belong within the occasion of our time. The Eucharist is when we offer our *chronos* to be transformed by the *kairos* of the risen and arriving Jesus. Every celebration of the Eucharist becomes the fullness of time because this is when God's future for us is 'tasted and seen': 'O taste and see that the LORD is good; happy are those who take refuge in him' (Ps. 34.8). While the normative Eucharist is celebrated on the first day of the week, the day of resurrection, the day of the new creation (including the new creation of time), every Eucharist, whenever it is celebrated, is the enactment of the exchange of our present with the present of Jesus. Every Eucharist is both traditional and contemporary because it is the time to receive anew God's future for us, and because this future already has and is a history.

Every celebration of the Eucharist, whenever it is celebrated, is defined and determined by God's future bestowed in the arriving Jesus; every time that the baptized gather for the Eucharist is the temporal occasion for participation in this given future. We offer our now to be transformed into God's then; God gives us God's now to receive regardless of when this actually happens. Put in a more direct and practical way, the celebration of the Eucharist in the fourth century has the same relationship to God's future for us as a Eucharist celebrated in the twenty-first century, or the sixteenth century, and so on. Likewise, every Eucharist celebrated on a particular 'Sunday' has the same relationship to the temporality of the arriving Jesus. That is to say, that anytime the Eucharist is celebrated it shares the temporal reality of the risen and ascended Jesus, which is realized among us by the pouring out of the Holy Spirit. Tradition as the Eucharist is the abiding exchange of our time and history with the time of Jesus and his history for and with us, the historical place prepared for us to live.

Why

Why is the normative Eucharist celebrated? This question can be posed this way: Why a normative Eucharist? This question can be distinguished even further: Why the Eucharist, and why a *normative* Eucharist? We will take up the initial question of why there is the Eucharist before then addressing the qualification of 'normative'. The relationship between these two questions, between the theological reality that is the Eucharist and the possible and desirable existence of a normative Eucharist, speaks directly to the tradition of the Christian faith as Eucharist. Probing the question of why the Eucharist is the primary question that roots all other questions regarding the Eucharist. Why is there a Eucharist rather than nothing? This question leads us to identify the primary systematic theological category that serves as the abiding companion for a theology of the Eucharist. This category is soteriology rather than ecclesiology, anthropology or even a sacramental theology. These other categories are necessary areas of theological work, but it is soteriology that is primary. Why the Eucharist is another way of asking why Jesus, even though we are asking this indirectly. Eucharist is at the centre of God's saving will for humanity, for the world, for the renewing of all creation. Thus, soteriology itself is the primary theological category because it is derivative from, accountable to, theology itself; that is, what we essentially understand and proclaim of God. While we can then speak of the Eucharist in a variety of ways as liturgy, ritual or community event, we cannot allow the Eucharist to be subsumed by, circumscribed within, any other concern than God's saving will and definitive saving act, God's arrival in Jesus by the Holy Spirit, God's Eucharistic covenant with the Body of Christ. The centrality and primacy of the Eucharist for the Christian faith animates the question of why a *normative* Eucharist. The mutuality here claimed among God, Jesus, salvation and Eucharist renders the question of normativity inevitable and critical. Somewhere in the landscape existing between an immutable God and a mutable world is a normativity that allows for the recognition of this God who is unchanging yet faithful to that which is undergoing change. Indeed, the unchanging God by nature wills change for us and the world. God wills that creation become transformed into the new creation. Thus, theological normativity is the recognition of where and how this change from creation to the new creation takes place. Normativity is the abiding event of salvation; it is the recognition that, despite the diversities of contexts, churches, historical periods and intellectual currents, there is an abiding event of salvation. Tradition is this normativity; tradition is the normative Eucharist. This leads to a further distinguishing and defining question: What is *normative* about the Eucharist?

What

Such a question posed within our keener awareness of the differences among all the Eucharistic liturgies celebrated diachronically and synchronically as well as our ignorance regarding all the ways that the Eucharist has been celebrated cannot be answered by appealing to one Eucharistic liturgy, whether this liturgy had a long tradition of singular use, for example the Roman or Western Rite, or whether this liturgy can be traced from the fourth century to the present as is the case of the Liturgy of St John Chrysostom. We certainly can look for characteristics common to all or to the

great preponderance of known Eucharistic liturgies. We can appeal
to a basic structure or *ordo* of the Eucharistic liturgy that appears
in the second century in Justin Martyr's account of a Eucharist, a
structure that seems to have continued, and thus could serve as an
identifier of normativity. This approach to normativity would rely
on identifying certain actions in a prescribed order of enactment
as that which is the Eucharist regardless of other differences
among the collection of liturgies. That is, we would not be relying
on common texts for what is normative but common actions in
a common continuity of performance. While this approach to
normativity may prove reliable when addressing the variety of
Eucharistic liturgies located within the Eucharistic tradition, does it
serve as an adequate portrayal of the *theological* normativity of the
Eucharist? Does our comparative study of the Eucharistic liturgies
guided by an enduring structure so identified suffice to explore
the way in which the Eucharist is the event of the exchange of our
sacrifice of tradition to God and our receiving the gift of tradition
from God? For it is this exchange rooted in God's covenant-making
fidelity that is the tradition as Eucharist. Theological normativity
is not confined to our performance of a series of actions but is the
realm of the Father's faithful act in the Son and by the Holy Spirit.
The normative Eucharist is the event that relies sacrificially on the
normative God. This means that, while we begin with the common
structure of the Eucharist, we take this structure as an invitation
to explore what is the theological dynamic that both founds and
furthers this structure. Why is the structure a performance of the
handing on and the receiving of tradition that is the tradition as
Eucharist? How is this dynamic expressive of, and constituted by,
the exchange of handing on ourselves to God and then receiving
from God the gift of the Body and Blood of Christ? What does this
dynamic tell us theologically about the making and the renewal of
covenant that takes place between and among the Body of Christ?

The answer to these questions is the exploration of the
normative and mutual movements of the baptized towards
God and God towards the baptized: the gathering for and as

the Eucharist that is the Body of Christ, and the arrival of Jesus offering the gift of his life of communion to this Body. We, the baptized, the gathered Body of Christ, are offering ourselves to God; we are engaged in a movement into the life of God through the realization of this life among us, and by the reception of this life as gift. This is the movement from gathering to communion. In the Eucharist, the Triune God is arriving in our midst in order to renew and realize the life that God shares with us in the Son and realizes among us by the Holy Spirit. What we are doing in the Eucharist is ordered towards God, and what God is doing in the Eucharist is ordered towards the baptized gathered for this Eucharist, what is taking place here and now. What happens between these two movements is the purpose, the *telos*, of the Eucharist – the exchange of life – and hence, the handing on and receiving of life – the tradition. The normative Eucharist is constituted by these two movements towards each other, by human and divine agency, and by the giving and receiving of the life of communion. As such, these two movements have their proper and respective theological dynamics and categories of understanding: Anamnesis and Epiclesis.

Anamnesis

Tradition is not the place to escape to the familiar; it is, at its essence, an encounter with God, an invitation to leave one's previous life and to follow Jesus into God's future for the Body of Christ. Tradition is the occasion for *metanoia*. We regularly have to be displaced from the repose of the familiar, the comforts of the customary as well as from the enticements of a self-generated novelty, striving to make a difference on our own terms. The movement from our life as we would have it into the life God would provide for us is the movement of anamnesis. In baptism, we die to our past and are raised into the memory of the Body of Christ. We move from the past as our recollection into the anamnesis of the past that we receive. The anamnetic past is a

99

place of exploration, discovery and renewal because this past is not what we have created for ourselves; it is a past God has re-created for us. The tradition of the Christian faith is what follows the command, 'Do this in remembrance of me.' Tradition is the event of remembering Jesus and the act of inhabiting the memory that is Jesus. By doing this, celebrating the Eucharist, we remember Jesus, which is to say that we remember the Triune God. This memory is not static; it is not an object to bring to mind. This is the memory of God's saving will, the memory of God's history with and for us. The remembrance of Jesus, the remembrance of God, the God who is remembered this way, is the cross where the 'turn to the subject' goes to be sacrificed. 'Do this in remembrance of me' ought to haunt all our efforts to root our theologies in ourselves, and all our efforts to turn tradition into a comprehensive story about ourselves, for good or ill. The Eucharistic performance of anamnesis loosens our grip on the past, on history, and thereby on our own constructed identities. Anamnesis is the sacrifice of the mind and will so that our minds and wills can enter into the fecundity of the memory of the Body of Christ. Keeping the memory of Jesus propels us to hand ourselves over to him so that we might we receive the abundant life that he came to give, that he is in his Body. Anamnesis of God's mighty acts in history renews the tradition of the Christian faith by placing us where we hand on to God so that we might receive from God. Anamnesis is the act of handing on.

Epiclesis

While Eucharistic anamnesis is our sacrifice of tradition, the handing on to God, Eucharistic epiclesis is the reception of the gift of tradition, receiving now the gift of God's future for us. Tradition as Eucharist is the movement from anamnesis to epiclesis and the movement from epiclesis to anamnesis; the movement of the baptized to God and the movement of God to the gathered Body of Christ. The invocation of the Holy Spirit to realize the Body and

Blood of Christ as the gift of the life of communion, and to renew this life among those gathered, takes place when the anamnesis of the Triune God in remembering Jesus has brought us there. While anamnesis is loosening our grip on our identities and histories, our past, the epiclesis is placing ourselves into the hands of God, the hands that make something out of nothing, that take dust and make a world, the hands that raise the dead, and the hands that gather us into the praise filled future where the weight of God's glory is truly our incredible lightness of being. But this is not a foreign land, one more exile to endure. Rather, the Holy Spirit realizes a familiarity that has been nurtured and wrought by anamnesis: 'Surely the LORD is in this place – and I did not know it! … How awesome is this place! This is none other than the house of God, and this is the gate of heaven' (Gen. 28.16-17). Tradition is a twofold reality; it is handing on and receiving, anamnesis and epiclesis. Being received into God's future for the Body of Christ is not to leave behind the anamnetic past of this Body. When we invoke the Holy Spirit to realize the communion of the Body and Blood of Christ, we are receiving the communion of God that is the past, present and future of this Body. We do not enter into God's future for us in the present without also receiving once again as gift God's past for us as well. The Holy Spirit does not lead us down a path that has not already been prepared by anamnesis. Tradition as Eucharist is the necessary mutuality between anamnesis and epiclesis, between handing on what we have received from the Lord, whether this receiving is what was, what is or what will be.

The Marian Tradition of the Body of Christ

Tradition lives on the brink between past and future, from the old for the sake of the new. When we remember Jesus, we remember his birth, life, death, resurrection, ascension and his coming again: 'Therefore every scribe who has been trained for the kingdom of heaven is like the master of a household who brings out of his treasure what is new and what is old' (Matt. 13.52). The mutuality between God's past and future for the baptized, the mutuality that exists in the Eucharistic present, the mutuality between anamnesis and epiclesis that is the tradition of handing on to God and receiving from God, is the mystery of how the Body of Christ is created and re-created. It is the Marian nature of the tradition of the Christian faith, tradition as Eucharist. The conception of the Body and Blood of Christ, the birth of Jesus, took place according to Mary's yes to the Holy Spirit *and* Mary's yes to Joseph. Mary's yes to the Holy Spirit is her yes to God: 'Here am I, the servant of the Lord; let it be with me according to your word' (Luke 1.38). She said yes to God's future for her, a future she previously could not ask for or imagine. Mary said yes to God giving her a life that would now be hers. She said yes to the gift the Holy Spirit would conceive within her. While Mary said yes to this future that only God could give, the unexpected and unfamiliar life, she did not abandon her yes to Joseph. She remained steadfast in the place where tradition had brought her, betrothed to a descendant of David, the awaited nuptial event between the past and the future of God's will for the people of Israel. Mary's yes to the Holy Spirit took place where Mary's yes to Joseph had brought her, and while she did indeed receive the gift of God's future for her, she did remain where her yes to Joseph had brought her as well. Her yes to the Holy Spirit and her yes to Joseph were mutual. Tradition had placed her where God's re-creative act 'deigned to dwell'. Tradition as Eucharist has this Marian vocation to say yes to anamnesis and yes to epiclesis, yes to handing on and yes to receiving, yes to the sacrifice of our tradition, and yes to the receiving the gift of tradition from the Father, in the Son and by the Holy Spirit. Each past, present and future of the Body of Christ, when speaking Eucharistically, cannot say to one another, 'I have no need of you' (1 Cor. 12.21). Therefore, tradition as Eucharist, the tradition that is the Eucharistic faith, is the mutual continuum of past, present and future, the communion of time that exists as the Body of Christ. That is, our temporal reality as created is transformed into the temporal dimensions of the Body of Christ. The Body of Christ knows itself by knowing the members who entered it from the past, in the present and from the future. These members are known to each other in Christ, who welcomes them into the place he has prepared for them. This welcoming constitutes its continuous existence, its procession into the place where the future defines its common life. Tradition as Eucharist is the *koinonia* of our common future in and as the Body of Christ.

Notes

1 For a comprehensive treatment of the liturgical movement of the twentieth century and its shaping of what we consider the liturgical tradition, see the chapter 'Tradition' in my *Eucharist: A Guide for the Perplexed* (London: T&T Clark, 2010).

2 Again, for a fuller treatment of the subjects of presence and sacrifice in the Eucharist, see the chapters 'Presence' and 'Sacrifice' in my *Eucharist*.

3 This is why any evaluation of the developments of Eucharistic theology, especially regarding the question of Christ's presence, would do well to examine the philosophical currents at play in each period of its tradition and drawn upon by each theologian. The classic example of this is Thomas Aquinas relying upon Aristotle's use of the categories of substance and accidents to speak of Christ's transubstantiated presence in the bread and wine. Of course, Aquinas adapted these categories for his own theological purpose. Furthermore, while there was a rich and diverse exposition of the assertion of Christ's presence in the Eucharist, this belief as such did not become a controversy until the ninth century, and the fact that it did can be accounted for due to philosophical developments. A concise review of this controversy is available in Paul F. Bradshaw and Maxwell E. Johnson, *The Eucharistic Liturgies: Their Evolution and Interpretation* (Collegeville, MN: Liturgical Press, 2012), p. 222f.

4 A good and balanced presentation of Anglican Eucharistic theology regarding the questions of presence and sacrifice is H. R. McAdoo and Kenneth Stevenson, *The Mystery of the Eucharist in the Anglican Tradition* (Eugene, OR: Wipf and Stock, 2008).

5 The broader context for this statement, for the role of the so-called institution narrative in the primitive and developing Eucharist, is the subject of Chapter 1.

4

Scripture

Where is Scripture located? Or, where do we locate Scripture? Posing the question of Scripture's theological existence in terms of place, making location our theological point of departure, provides a more accountable direction for our reflections on the proper appreciation and realization of Scripture's role in the theological imagination and performance. The reader can be alerted already to some fundamental postulates for what follows. First, I will be considering 'Scripture' rather than the 'Bible'. That is, as will be argued below, I am dealing with the canon of Scripture or the church's Scripture rather than a collection of texts commonly known as the Bible. Second, I will not be constructing a theology of Scripture, and certainly not a theology of the Bible. Rather, my concern and focus is the location of Scripture *within* theology. This is why the question of location is the initial theological venture when addressing any other questions about Scripture. The second question of where we locate Scripture recognizes the hegemony of personal agency in any contemporary regard for the interpretation of Scripture. Of course, this type of autonomous personal agency has no place within the Eucharistic economy of theology where we are called to enter into this economy through the sacrifice of such agency. The question will become not where we locate Scripture but where are we located when we hear the proclamation of Scripture. Where would the faithful encounter with Scripture take us? In order to appreciate and clarify that the proper theological location of Scripture is within the Eucharist, we will survey briefly other candidates for Scripture's or the Bible's location and some of the theological consequences of these locations.

Several locations, or versions of one location, share the same basic trajectory: the past. If we want to interpret Scripture, discover its meaning for today or to ask whether this event really happened or these words were really said, we go back to the past armed with our present tools of investigation and the latest state of mind. We ask, what did this text originally mean? What was the author's intent? How would the first hearers and readers of this text have received it? And can we find historical and textual parallels for the text under investigation that could provide some reference for what this was about back then? Furthermore, we can ask, what kind of texts are these? Are they historical, mythological, literary or religious? How might these texts have been constructed and conveyed? We assume that any answers we might have for these questions put to the past are going to be different from any answer we might give to these questions addressed to the present. For we are weighted down with an acute awareness of our difference from the past, a past from which we have historically, theologically, epistemologically, culturally and philosophically *escaped*. Thus, in order to arrive at the meaning of this text for us, in order to regard it as appropriate to this place and time, we will have to deliver it from its past, removing its religious, cultural and mythological shackles so that it can join us in our freedom from this past. Within this trajectory, hermeneutics provides the key for this unlocking. Our desire is that once we have identified (constructed?) a fixed meaning we can apply it to ourselves. The past is to be mined for artefacts of meaning that we then can bring to life through our use of them. We search the texts we find in the tombs of the past, and whether they have life or not depends upon their possible accommodation to our life now and here. The text stands over against us as an object to our subject, and we presume this is possible because our subjectivity can operate objectively when disciplined by a method whose purpose is rendering objective conclusions.

As the masters of interpretation, the judges of applicable meaning, we come to realize that not only is the text other than ourselves as something written back then and there, but that when we turn our heuristic light on ourselves we discover the otherness that exists among us. Meaning for us becomes meaning for me but not perhaps for you, meaning for them but not for us. Furthermore, this assigning and possession of meaning(s) might conceal the exercise of the powerful over the powerless. Who gets to say what this text means?[1] There might not be one transcendental subjectivity inherent in human knowing but a diverse cultural, natural and experiential plurality always and everywhere at play, never to be brought together under one totalizing tent. Now the present is the horizon of meaning, and this horizon looks different from the perspective of different viewpoints and vantage points. Indeed, there are different horizons.[2] Also, this regard for the present and its inherent plurality and difference can lead to an approach to textual meaning that is not for its own sake, not to get the text right. Rather, the text can either be rendered an obstacle to, or a directive towards, the purpose for which the interpreter comes to the text. Does this text serve the desired agenda that exists outside it or not? The agent here is the reader or interpreter who assigns the text a place in an economy for which she or he is a worker. In order to construct a new world for myself I deconstruct other worlds, worlds from which I need to escape so that I can inhabit this newly constructed one. The objective no longer reigns over the subjective. The subjective has slain this ruler and creates for itself textual objects that can adorn the palaces located at the centre of its self-referential kingdoms.

Our hermeneutical strategies have allowed us to escape our common past, and now we have developed strategies to escape the hold of the presence of others. Is there a haven from all this interplay between the subjective and the objective, a place where we do not have to be concerned with either the difference of the past or the differences of the present? Doctrinal ideology, and its absolute and universal ecclesial guarantor, can provide such a haven. Here there is one meaning to one text as conveyed by one purveying authority. The text is taken from our temporal, historical, cultural and experiential reality and placed within the vault of timeless truth and abiding meanings where modern tools and postmodern cudgels cannot break the door down. Only those few who are authorized to have the key to this vault can enter it and come back out and tell us what is in there. The tombs of the past and the enclaves of the present now yield to the vaults of the future, from which textual meaning cannot escape. However, is it not a valid concern that the location of Scripture be a place that is safe from modern grave-robbers and postmodern invaders? As the Word of God with a presumed authority of its own, should not Scripture be regarded as above the fray of our intellectual reinventions and epistemological jousting?

The relationship between Scripture and theology is itself a varied and shifting one. We can say that theology was once considered essentially as commentary on Scripture, even if this commentary had different registers, different senses of meaning.[3] We also have the Reformed appeal to *sola scriptura* whereby theology was no longer commentary on Scripture, often with the accusation that this commentary served the ecclesiastical status quo, but now theology was derived directly from Scripture. Theology had to prove itself before Scripture without appeal to tradition or reason, or for that matter without authorization of the church. Scripture was granted an autonomy of its own, which theology was to maintain. Theology became exposition of the content of Scripture. However, Catholic theology sought a continued role for tradition in the development and articulation of the Christian faith as well as the pairing of Word and Sacrament. Scripture was not the sole authority or source for the Christian faith. Rather, Scripture was engaged by Christians living within an ecclesial life and guided by an ecclesial tradition. Further down the historical and intellectual road, reason supplanted tradition for theology, a reason unfettered by tradition, doctrine and church. That is, reason was to operate without any *a priori* canons of understanding except the ones developed by reason itself. Once Scripture was considered autonomous, and when the reader or interpreter was rendered autonomous as well, not needing any mediation of church or authorities, having these texts in one's own language with the text at one's own home, we can move from Scripture alone to alone with Scripture. Everyone can become their own theologian, and then they construct the theology that they need, like or find useful for whatever use they wish to put it. What can we find in Scripture that we can use for our lives? Theology needs to be practical, relevant and applicable. Now, Scripture is located in our own personal lives.

Where is Scripture located? Answers can be provided from appeals and renderings of the past, from our present contexts ('for us'), from an ideal church and from our existential concerns ('for me'). Each of these locations, or regard for the inherent hermeneutical dynamics of each and every location, has the capacity both to reveal and conceal, both to proclaim and distort, the 'true meaning' of Scripture. For indeed Scripture is located somewhere, and we as possible interpreters of Scripture are located as well. That is, Scripture is not an inert text sitting there waiting for us to take some interest in it, picking it up and reading a few lines until we come across something useful or inspiring, or until we get bored with it. The argument about the relationship between Scripture and theology, whether we are talking about basing theology on Scripture or the role of Scripture within theology, is really and essentially first about the location of Scripture and about our own theological location. Might Scripture and theology share the same location, both inhabit the common theological place so that the relationship between Scripture and theology is constituted by a mutually involving accountability to the dynamics of this one place? Here, I hesitate to speak of this place as a theological one lest we disregard the distinction between theology as our talk about God and as God's address to us, and how this distinction is played out in various other places. And what about those trajectories of the archaeological past, the existential present and the protected future? Will we encounter, should we look for them, these trajectories within the one mutually involving place of Scripture and theology? Do they have a place here too? Scripture is located within the Eucharist. The Eucharist is the theologically normative place of Scripture. Ultimately, what Scripture means will make Eucharistic sense because these texts are ordered towards the communion shared with and as the Body of Christ. Scripture belongs to and within the Body of Christ: The Word of God is embodied now and forever as this Body. It is here that the proclaimed Word ushers us into the presence of this Word; hearing and receiving are taken into the Trinitarian economy of place, presence and agency enacted through speaking and spiration. The trajectories of past, present and future are not absent here but reoriented towards the presence and consummation of God's life for us, from Genesis to the Book of Revelation.

Remembered Past

Our Eucharistic relationship to the past is constituted by anamnesis, by the remembering of God's acts through thanksgiving. We are thankful for this remembered past within the event of worship of this God. The distance that we have from this past does not alienate us from it. Rather, through Eucharistic remembrance, the past allows us to have this present. We do not adjudicate a relation to the past that may or may not correspond to our present outside the Eucharist. This anamnetic and theological past presses upon us to shape us into the embodied Word. Given this memory, our identity and vocation as the Body of Christ is realized and renewed.

Scripture provides the substance of remembering the past as God's active presence. We primarily remember this past as the sphere of God's agency. While human agency constitutes this past as well, this agency is remembered within the history of God's action upon, and speaking to, God's chosen people. God chooses to whom and on whom God will act and speak. Even though God's agency might be hidden within human agency, this human agency is contingent upon God's agency. God has given us the substance of this remembering even though we are the ones who remember. That is, we do not choose our Eucharistic remembrance. We do not get to choose our history as God's people. Thus, the whole scope of human history is not available for Eucharistic remembrance, and we only have this Eucharistic relationship to what is remembered as Scripture within the Eucharist. There is human history and there is Eucharistically remembered history. Furthermore, this remembrance is textually realized.

Our remembrance of God's history with us does not exist without these texts recounted within the Eucharist. We are not attempting to get behind these texts, the purpose of this recounting is not to give us something to analyse or to discuss. Since the presence of these texts is the presence of the Word, we hear them attuned to this presence and are inquisitive about it. This is not a benign presence, something interesting to think about. Rather, these texts present an array of possibilities now and here. Thus, the historical question primarily presented by these texts is not did it happen, but can it happen now? And if it does happen, what will it look like, and how are we to talk about it? However, the questions of action and speech are not open-ended, questions awaiting our answers. These questions are not answered from nothing. We are confronted by the questions of possible action and speech, questions arising from our proclamation and hearing of these texts, within the Eucharist. What can happen now is the Eucharist, and how can we talk it about is through Eucharistic praying. For theology then, any potential pursuits of historical investigation do not possess an objectivity established outside the Eucharistic economy. Any attempts to craft supposedly more adequate, appropriate or desired language for God will not stray from the Eucharistic idiom of language displaced from ourselves and placed before the presence of God as Eucharistically present. In the Eucharist, we do not have our own history or language, history and language no longer belong to us. They exist here within the economy of gift and reception; history and language are given, offered and received.

Offered Present

When we enter the Eucharist, we enter into the Eucharistic present, the present as known here. This entering of this present that is only here and not elsewhere is the movement of offering. The present within the Eucharist is an offered present. We offer ourselves as we are present to ourselves, but this is an offering towards the presence of God. We offer who we are now to who is God now, who we are here to who God is here. Thus, a distance opens up from the present before offered to this offered present. This distance is not an alien one to be overcome by the terms of the past-present but a space for discovering what can be known and imagined within this offered present, the present-presence of the Eucharist. The meaning of Scripture exists as meaning for us, and not what we might think it means. While these texts precede their Eucharistic proclamation and hearing, they now belong here, and as such, they are not available for our attempts, however sophisticated, to render them objects over against our subjectivity. We do not get to name our own subjectivity; we have offered who we are having died to our own hermeneutics.

Whoever we are, our presence to ourselves, our presence to others, this present world, is offered in the Eucharist. Offered does not mean abandoned or forgotten. The reality of who we are, and where we are in the world, is the *from which* we enter the Eucharist and the *to which* we will return. The offering of this present, its presence, is the movement to view it from the Eucharistic place, the Eucharistic perspective or hermeneutic. Thus, we encounter Scripture through our offered present; we do not locate Scripture in some hermeneutical enclave of the non-Eucharistic present. The removal of Scripture from the Eucharist is to bury it in our lives rather than to allow it to narrate the life we have come to the Eucharist to renew and to receive as gift. The meaning of Scripture cannot be allowed to be something we discover by peeling away the layers of cloth wrapped around a dead body. The meaning of Scripture lives within the Body of Christ. What Scripture meant and what it means is a false dichotomy within the life of the Body of Christ, within the Eucharistic temporal spectrum. The animating question is not what does Scripture mean or not mean where I live, but what might my temporal, historical and cultural location look like after it has been offered towards the proclamation of Scripture, the hearing of Scripture within the Body of Christ? This is a question that cannot be answered by holding my present in one hand and a Bible in the other.[4] Scripture is not an analytical device, a guidebook or a manual for living. The proper Eucharistic hermeneutical question is not, what does Scripture say about an identified question or issue in our life or world? Members of the Body of Christ are not to carry our Bibles around looking for problems to solve, conflicts to settle or arguments to win. We offer our present towards an invoked future.

Invoked Future

Scripture located within the Eucharist is the narrative proclamation of a possible future that has a remembered past and an offered present. This future is why Scripture exists. Thus, Scripture is heard and interpreted in view of this Eucharistic future. Scripture is approached within this Eucharistic horizon of fulfilment. However, this possible future does not supersede Scripture or render it obsolete. It is still future and not the offered present or the remembered past. While this Eucharistic future is the *telos* for our reading and hearing of Scripture, we cannot relate to this future, indeed, we cannot imagine it, without Scripture. For the Eucharistic future is not available for analysis or interpretation; it does not exist as an object of thought. We do not study the Eucharistic future. We invoke it. We ask for it. Furthermore, we do so having remembered this scriptural history and having offered the present. Scripture brings us to the place of invoking the future we can now begin to imagine, that is now possible. Therefore, the future is not a guarded place; it is not a time that protects us from variation and change. We do not look to the future to stabilize the present or to ensure the continuity of the past. There is one fundamental reason for not allowing the future to protect the status quo or to maintain the hegemony of the past. The Eucharistic future is enacted by the unfettered agency of God. The invocation of this future is asking God to act on us, to transform us more deeply and comprehensively as the Body of Christ. This future is the horizon of God's definitive presence and agency. We cannot project ourselves into this future; we can only receive it as gift.

The location of Scripture within the Eucharist provides us with the hermeneutical question: How do the various texts of Scripture relate to the future of God's agency? In what ways does Scripture present us with the contours of an invoked future where and whereby God fulfils this remembered past and offered present? The task of asking what a scriptural text meant back then in order to establish a meaning for the text now, the effort to translate meaning from past to present, stands under the judgement of what meaning God will give the text in the future. Actually, a more adequate way to speak of this judgement is to entertain how a scriptural text will signify the meaning of God's fulfilling act. Narrative will be subsumed into event. Text will be a way to talk about what is happening now. However, for this Eucharistic now, Scripture is how we learn to speak of this possible future, this imaginative invocation. We do not inhabit this fulfilled future. Scripture is our way to this future. Scripture forms us as those who are called to remember this past and to invoke this future. Scripture is formative for the Body of Christ; it is not a collection of texts that inform lives existing outside this Body. Located within the Eucharist, Scripture is located within the temporal spectrum of the Eucharistic past as remembered, the Eucharistic present as offered and the Eucharistic future as invoked.

Scripture Within the Eucharist

The Eucharistic location of Scripture has two vectors of direction, two active movements ordered towards an encounter with each other through the proclamation and hearing of Scripture: God and us. Our location within the Eucharist for this encounter with Scripture requires the primacy of this location above all other possible and real locations. Not only do we not approach Scripture without primary regard for its Eucharistic location, we do not perceive ourselves as hearers and readers of Scripture without the authority of its Eucharistic location. That is, when we hear, read and interpret Scripture, we do so primarily as members of the Body of Christ. We are accountable to this Body for any meaning we might derive from the scriptural text. Thus, any and all approaches to Scripture contingent upon our various contexts as readers must be subservient to the authority and primacy of the Eucharistic location in which we hear Scripture with the expectation of the Trinitarian arrival of Jesus, the Word of God. While we may indeed take into account our various contexts in which we engage Scripture, we are not to locate Scripture within them. Scripture is not to be uprooted from the Eucharist and planted anew in our cultural, ethical, political or intellectual contexts. Outside the Eucharist, contexts are not hermeneutical grids but patterns of existence that are meant for Eucharistic transformation. So we do attend to these contexts as possible places of Eucharistic illumination and transformation. We cannot carry our Bibles around with us wherever we go and forget the Eucharist. The Word of God exists as always the reality of the Eucharistic fulfilment of this Word. Scripture cannot be disembodied from the Word of God as the

Body of Christ: We cannot forget Scripture's Eucharistic narrative. The hermeneutical question becomes not where are we now, but where are we called to be and become? The question is not primarily where do I live, but where must I go to find life and find it abundantly? Not what is my context, but what is my commitment? What is our commitment as the Body of Christ? There is a fundamental theological distinction between those places we either have inherited or have made for ourselves and the place God has prepared for us. There is always the temptation to find a place for Scripture or Jesus or God in our contexts or homes, rather than sacrificially inhabiting the place where we are at home with God. Scripture is ordered towards our remembrance of God's arriving presence and action towards and on us in the Son by the Holy Spirit. Scripture loses its plot when it becomes a tool for better living here. The ultimate theological movement is not God to us but we to God, and the Eucharist is where and whereby we enter this movement. When we do, we are prepared to hear Scripture the way it was meant to be proclaimed and heard.

Nonetheless, we have to enquire initially whether this focus on the Eucharistic location of Scripture in contrast to the diversity and plurality of contexts yields a singular meaning to any given scriptural text. Is there always a Eucharistic meaning assigned to a text, and if there is, how would this even be obtained? The abiding question of the possible relationship between the one and the many, in this case adjudicated among one text and many meanings, is placed within the Eucharistic economy of presence and agency. Thus, any given scriptural text exists within the Eucharist among a multiplicity of agencies that constitute the mutuality of presence that is the gathered Body of Christ receiving the arriving Body of Christ as the indivisible work of the Trinity. Any effort to establish a one-to-one correspondence between a text and a meaning will either deny or distort this communion of texts and agencies, this manifold presence. Rather than any singularity of meaning, or the superseding of meaning due to shifts in conceptual accessibility, the Eucharistic economy offers a *perichoresis* of meaning. This is meaning as referral to other texts and to other persons all present within the one moment of hearing and proclamation. We do not just listen to these texts within the Eucharist, we proclaim them. We are called to say something about them that serves what God wishes to say to us. Our Eucharistic hearing of Scripture cannot be unhinged from the presence of God who is never separated from the Word of God. As Jacob wrestled with the angel in the desert and discovered the gate of heaven, the place of worship, we are to wrestle with Scripture at this same gate, limping our way to Jerusalem and not running back to our contexts with something useful. The meaning of Scripture is not determined by us, nor is it confined to our own times and places. The communion of Eucharistic meaning belongs within the remembered past, the offered present and the invoked future. That is, scriptural meaning is something recognized within the communion of saints, within the ongoing tradition of Word to Sacrament. The text of Scripture then does not become an object that sits still for our exegetical analysis. While there is an objectivity to the text, it is enveloped by the subjectivity of the Body of Christ. So instead of assigning the meaning of a text either behind, within or before, the meaning surrounds the text. The effort to assign meaning to the authorial intent, to the literal text or to the meaning the text generates over time can only be an entry into the meaning that is going on around and through the text. However we approach the Word of God, whether this approach is historical, ecclesial or contextual, we are to remember that the Word of God is surrounded by the Body of Christ. And, the Body of Christ is never speechless, never without the Word of God. How does the Body of Christ hear, proclaim and interpret its own identifying narrative?

Eucharistic Formation of the New Testament

Prior to turning directly to the consideration of the proclamation and realization of the Word of God within and as the Body of Christ, we will reflect on the original formation of the canon of the New Testament within the primitive Eucharistic church. That is, we will reflect on the reality that the celebration of the Eucharist, the Eucharistic assembly of Christians, existed prior to the development of both the writings and the designated canon of the New Testament. Before there was a New Testament, there was the Eucharist. However, what truly garners our attentiveness to the origins of the Eucharist and the subsequent canonization of the writings of the New Testament as such is not simply, or only, this chronological priority of the Eucharist to the New Testament. Rather, what concerns us is the possible compatibility between the origin of the Eucharist and the origin of the writings of the New Testament, especially of the Gospels.[5] This compatible origin, what originates both the Eucharist and the New Testament, is the primary and abiding effort to keep the memory of Jesus. This keeping of memory involved seeking his presence and following his teaching. What he did and said prior to the ascension was available to the early Christians because Jesus himself was still available to them. Likewise, the early Christians sought to remain in the company of those who were in the company of the pre-ascension Jesus; this is the authoritative regard for apostolicity. In his *From Jesus to the New Testament*, Jens Schroter addresses this mutuality between the development of the New Testament canon and the Eucharist as follows:

> Christianity developed two institutions that serve its obligation to its own roots and their representation in the respective present, namely the canon and the Lord's Supper/Eucharist. With the canon early Christianity created a corpus of writings that gave expression to its faith confession and from which writings that contradicted it – such as those that advanced a docetic

Christology – were excluded. From the beginning the Lord's Supper served to make present the salvation that came in Jesus in which the community symbolically shared in the celebration of this meal. With this it simultaneously becomes clear that the worship service is the central place of recollection for the Christian community. Here there were readings from the accepted writings; here the shared meal was also celebrated. Therefore, in Christianity the reference to its own history must not be separated from its ritual-making present in the celebration of the worship service.[6]

The early Christians kept the memory of Jesus alive by enacting the event and attending to the writings by and through which Jesus still lived among them. Thus, the Eucharistic celebration itself became a perspective on the emerging acceptability of whether writings belonged within the canon of the New Testament or not. What belonged in the Eucharist came to belong in the New Testament. Therefore, one cannot take up the origin of the New Testament writings and their authoritative status without the Eucharistic context for this origin and development. Here we are speaking of the Eucharistic formation of the New Testament.

The earliest Christian writings, Paul's letters, were written to churches that would have heard them read in the midst of their assemblies, within the Eucharist. This presumption of the Eucharistic context of the addressees of Paul's letters is not just one of ritual or liturgy but of theology as well. Paul indicates as much in his reference to handing on what he has received of the Lord's Supper narrative, the so-called institution narrative in 1 Corinthians 11.23f. Clearly, the church in Corinth already celebrated the Eucharist with its attending theological significance. Paul was exhorting them to return to an existing Eucharistic practice and meaning. By stating 'what he received from the Lord', Paul is stressing the 'keeping the memory of Jesus' of the Eucharist. Paul's rendition of the words of Jesus at the Last Supper is the only one of the four that includes the double inclusion of the command 'Do this in remembrance of me', which would eventually be found in the great majority of Eucharistic prayers beginning in the fourth century. When we turn to the Gospels, we recognize that there are some texts with strong Eucharistic overtones. The three accounts of the Last Supper in the synoptic Gospels provide a theological perspective on the upcoming passion of Jesus, which is anchored in the words associating the Blood of Jesus with a new covenant/testament. The crucifixion of Jesus will come to have a salutary relationship with the Eucharist. Again, the Eucharist is at the heart of fidelity to the memory of Jesus, to his saving work and to his promised presence. The risen Jesus in Luke and John renews his relationship to his disciples through meals that are enacted by the Eucharistic acts of taking, giving thanks, breaking and giving. These same actions are found within the feeding stories in the Gospels.[7]

While the Eucharist is the event where and whereby the early Christians faithfully keep the memory of Jesus and 'proclaim the Lord's death until he comes' (1 Cor. 11.26b), it is thus the way they inhabit the new covenant God has established in and through Jesus. The Eucharist, with its initiating narratives of a 'new covenant', is located at the centre of the gospel of Jesus Christ, the way Christians inhabit the place and life God has provided with this new covenant. The new Israel is identified as those people who celebrate the Eucharist. Anything else that can and will be said about the Christian faith and life as the early Christians begin to speak for and as themselves will resonate with Eucharistic overtones. The Eucharistic assembly is where Christian speech is first heard and learned; it is where Christians are most themselves as the gathered Body of Christ. They are the people of the new covenant who imbibe the Blood of Christ and feed on his Body. This is why we are not permitted to separate, or even alienate, from each other the questions of the origin of the New Testament writings, the origin of the Eucharist and the origin of Christian theology. There is an intrinsic and abiding mutuality between the proclamation of the Word of God and its Eucharistic realization. Before turning directly to this Eucharistic realization of the Word of God, let us further consider the question of formation beyond the emerging New Testament as a Eucharistic phenomenon to the Eucharistic formation of New Testament studies.

The theology or 'meaning' of the New Testament, whether as a whole or fragmented into its various and diverse pericopes, is not derived ultimately in isolation from the Eucharist. Again, the primary and principal theological context of the New Testament, and the Old Testament as well for Christians, is the celebration of the Eucharist. The Word of God is not to be de-fleshed from the Body of Christ. The texts of the New Testament are not to become dead tissue placed under the historical-critical microscope having been surgically removed from the living Body of Christ. We do not take Scripture from the Eucharist and forget where we found it; we do not take up the study of Scripture unless we do so as keeping the memory of Jesus. This means attending to how the Eucharist forms our study of the New Testament, how the celebration of the Eucharist is the horizon of theological accountability for what the New Testament provides for the Christian faith and life. We are formed by Scripture within the Eucharistic dynamic of the formation of the Body of Christ. There is no Scripture alone and neither is there alone with Scripture. Of course, there will be ways to study the New Testament and Scripture as a whole that do not proceed directly from this Eucharistic dynamic. All of the typical scholarly concerns are still viable. However, the life that is being nurtured and formed is the Body of Christ risen from the dead of history and arriving as Lord of history in every celebration of the Eucharist where this Body has gathered for another resurrection appearance, another ascension, provoking worship and hope. A more comprehensive scope for the study of New Testament writings in light of the Eucharistic faith and life of the early church would include how keeping the memory of Jesus guided how the church or Christians dealt with a variety of questions and contexts that were not directly about Jesus. That is, how did the Christian faith and life continue when faced with questions and issues not directly addressed by Jesus.[8]

Eucharistic Realization of the Word of God

Scripture is the textual Word of God that conveys the narrative of the arrival of the Word of God. As Word of God, Scripture is the way we enter into the place of God's address to us with and as God's Word. That is, the proclamation of Scripture, the hearing of Scripture (and directly not the reading of Scripture for oneself) ushers us into the movement of where the Word of God will take us, which is to the addressing God as this God who is the Word as well as the speaker of this Word. The horizon for the faithful hearing of Scripture is God and not the world, not ourselves as such. In the Eucharist, we do not hear Scripture proclaimed and then go back out into the world. The Eucharist does not stop with the Word of God heard and proclaimed. We are in the Eucharist for the arrival of the Word of God in the person of Jesus Christ who arrives from the Father in the power of the Holy Spirit to give us his life, his life of communion. The proclaimed Word of God becomes the arrival of the gift of life created anew as and in this Word. The Holy Spirit hovers over every gathering for the Eucharist. Thus, instead of speaking of Word and Sacrament, the Eucharist is the movement of Word to Sacrament. The *Word* of God becomes the Word of *God*. Thus, the primary teleological movement of Scripture as the Word of God is towards God and not towards us. We pass through Scripture on our way to the promised land, but Scripture itself is not this promised land. We are called, if you will, not to inhabit the biblical world but the Eucharistic world, but we do so as those who have been formed to imagine this Eucharistic world by the proclamation and hearing of Scripture.[9] The Eucharistic future enacted for the sake of the arrival of Jesus, who is the consummated Word of God, is always preceded by the scriptural past, the always expectant Word of God. Jesus always arrives to his Body within the Eucharist having been narrated by Scripture. We are formed to recognize him in the breaking of bread. The presence of Jesus in the Eucharist is perceived by the scripturally narrated Body of Christ. Likewise, when we return to Scripture in other places and in other ways, we are to keep this memory of Jesus, to remember that Scripture exists for and as the consummation of the Body of Christ, the announcement that there is a place prepared for us to belong to God. We have heard the Word of God when we offer ourselves to enter into this place where God shares God's Word with us. This is the Eucharistic movement of the *Word* of God becoming the Word of *God*. The *telos* of Scripture is not our edification, or even enlightenment, but our embodiment within God: The Word of God takes flesh as the substance of the new creation.

These reflections on how the Eucharist preceded and served to form the New Testament as well as on the realization of the Word of God as the teleological movement from Scripture into God's own mutual address lead us to one comprehensive claim: the gospel as Eucharist. What essentially is the gospel, and how then are we permitted to speak of this gospel as the Eucharist? Furthermore, how does this claim frame all the questions regarding the proper theological interpretation of Scripture, if this concept of 'interpretation' is still viable? The gospel, the good news of Jesus Christ, is that God has and is acting definitively on our behalf. God is present in the arrival of Jesus to both announce the coming reign of God over the whole world and to enact this reign. Jesus both proclaims and enacts the kingdom of God. This reign of God is nothing less than the re-creation of the world: the resurrection of Jesus begins the new creation. As such, the world itself is not here as an object of analysis, a reality to be understood in some putative theological way. The *telos* of theology is not understanding the world but its re-creation by God. This is why we theologically cannot separate acting from thinking. The Word was made flesh, and the Father has raised

Jesus from the dead, are not God's ways to have a meeting of the minds with us. Theological speculation is ordered towards participation in God's redemptive and re-creative arriving presence, towards witnessing to the catholicity of salvation. Everything and anything that might garner our theological attention is to be located within the event of re-creation, this enacting of the kingdom of God by the proclamation of the coming of the Christ in expectant proximity to the reality of his arrival. Thus, the Word of God is an announcement of an event and the event so announced. The gospel is both the invitation and the event itself to which we have been invited. The gospel is the summons rendered through the sending of the Son by the power of the Holy Spirit, the summons to what God has done and is doing in the place where this summons is both heard and answered.

Eucharistic Economy of the Word of God

The initial employment of Scripture for Christians, what came to be rendered the Old Testament, was both to proclaim and to understand what has happened in Jesus and its implications, its consequences, for how we speak of God and of ourselves in relationship to this God. Hence, Christian theology involves the creation of the New Testament through the interpretative availability of the Old Testament to speak of, to think through, what God has done. God has acted, God is acting in and as Jesus by this outpouring of the Holy Spirit, and our Scriptures are both fulfilled and transformed by this act, by this arriving and re-creative presence. This movement from Scripture to its fulfilment and transformation, the movement from narrative to the event, which then transforms the narrative itself, is the movement of the economy of the Eucharist. The is the movement from summons to answer, from Old Testament to New Testament, from the narration of God's history with and for God's people to the present enactment of the eternal will of God for creation, all of which remains the summons to God's future for the Body of Christ, so gathered as a hearing Body, so offered as a living Body and so consummated as a risen Body. Scripture is read and studied, proclaimed and heard, for the sake of the Eucharistic present and Eucharistic future, which is temporally mediated in each celebration and teleologically anticipated as the end of time, the fulfilment of the creation of time itself.

The proper theological hermeneutic of Scripture is attentiveness, awareness, of the movement of God towards the world and of the world towards God that is both announced and enacted in the celebration of every Eucharist. Scripture is not an object for us to find something useful or relevant to do with it, nor is Scripture a text for the sole purpose of pronouncing judgements on this or that theological issue. Scripture is the narrative of going to the place God has prepared for us before the foundation of the world. Scripture, both Old and New Testaments, is the summons into the theological imagination where Jesus is Lord of all and to what it might really be when God is all in all (1 Cor. 15.28b). We interpret Scripture for the sake of God's Eucharistic 'interpretation' of us who have arrived in this place where God the Father will once again send the Son to share his life, this life realized by the Holy Spirit from hovering over creation to being outpoured on the new creation. Essentially, Scripture exists as the gift of the new creation and not as a relic of the old creation. Scripture is not lodged in the past so much as it is breathed from the future of God (and this is how we can speak once again of the inspiration of Scripture). The bones of Scripture do not lie before us collecting dust strewn about the historical-critical desert. Rather, these bones are meant to live again as the Body of Christ, and the Eucharist is how they come to this new life.

The location of Scripture within the Eucharist is the location of Scripture within the theological economy of the Eucharist. Thus, the relationship that Scripture has to history and time is constituted Eucharistically. When we do consider the broader questions of the relationship of Scripture to history and time, we are guided by this Eucharistic constitution. The centre of gravity for any theological approach to Scripture is the Eucharist, and this means that we view all other perspectives within the gravitational pull of the Eucharist. Our focus then will be in the Eucharistic present, the present time of the celebration of the Eucharist. The Eucharist is always enacted in the present, and it is from this present that we consider past and future, the history that has been accomplished as well as the history that is possible now. In this way, Scripture is reintroduced to its history and invited to inhabit its future.

Scripture is located within the temporal spectrum of the Eucharist. Scripture is read, heard and expounded in the Eucharistic present. Yet, this present is not bereft of memory or hope; it is not a timeless or ahistorical present. Actually, to understand this present, to know its inherent meaning, the past and the future are required to be brought to our awareness. When we are aware of the past and the future, we do not forget that we are located within the Eucharistic present. We do not step outside the Eucharist to get another perspective, to gain a knowledge somehow unhinged from the Eucharistic economy of history and time. We remember the past that has brought us these scriptural texts, while these texts no longer belong to this past. They belong in the Eucharistic here and now, but this present is what it is in the company of this remembered past. Likewise, these scriptural texts are read, heard and engaged because we are moving into a Eucharistic future to which they witness. This future has a scriptural textuality; we inhabit this future with a scriptural imagination. We remember the scriptural past within this present for the sake of a gifted-realized future. The scriptural text does not stand alone as a product of its own past. We are not translating past to present; what did it mean translated to what it might mean now, always giving priority to the non-Eucharistic now. Rather, we are entering into the transition from the Eucharistic present towards the Eucharistic future, and we are taking our Eucharistic past with us.

Eucharistic Exegesis of Scripture

The exegesis of Scripture can then be shaped and directed by this Eucharistic location ordered towards its proper realization as the Word of God. This shape and direction can have two mutual forms: anamnetic and epicletic exegesis. Anamnetic exegesis is when the concern for the historical setting of the text will be accountable to the keeping of the memory of Jesus, to the comprehensive scope of the memorial of God's words and actions on our behalf. Historical background to a text will be viewed in light of the horizon that God has spoken and acted historically, and the text is a witness to this horizon of God. Anamnesis is remembering the past as belonging already to God. The anamnetic past is not theologically neutral or 'objective'. The scholarly study of the text, the effort to interpret a text in view of a historical context, while not diminished, is qualified by the enveloping scope of remembering that God would meet us here. Memory, as a liturgical and theological idiom, is claimed by God for God's presence to and with us. In this way, we can speak of the Word becoming flesh, Word becoming history, as a movement that reaches its definitive fulfilment in Jesus, and as such, opens the possibility of fulfilling all other memories, all other pasts and all other histories. The tomb of Jesus did not contain him, and remembering this movement of Jesus from his tomb, opens all other tombs to the possibility that turning over the stones of the historical past might indeed release a resurrection to new life and not reveal the bones of the dead past. The exegesis of a text of Scripture is not dusting off a headstone of a grave; it is standing at the gate of heaven. However, this heaven does not exist in the past; it is present as future. The movement to this future, as the study of Scripture, now involves epicletic exegesis.

The texts of Scripture arrive in our presence through the anamnesis of the Eucharist, and as such, these texts are a narrative gift to those who are called to imagine the coming kingdom of God. In a Eucharistic sense, we are remembering where we have been in order to imagine where we are going now. The remembrance of Scripture in the Eucharist invites the homiletical question: Where do we go now? Any meaning the text might have is uncovered on the journey of the future-directed now. Therefore, our ultimate question to a scriptural text is not really what happened historically, or what is the timeless truth we might discover in order to apply it to our lives? We engage these texts to imagine what is now possible because the arrival of Jesus has happened in time and history, and this arrival is now expected among us. Jesus arrives in our time and history with the gift of his history and his relationship to our time. We remember the history of Jesus as both the Logos of all creation and firstborn of the new creation.[10] We enter into this temporal spectrum, we inhabit this teleologically charged history, when we enter the place defined by the two horizons of the Eucharistic anamnesis and epiclesis. Remembering Scripture within the Eucharist as the pneumatologically gathered Body of Christ means that we do not enter the biblical world. Rather, we pass through it from past to future, from death to life.

Epicletic exegesis transcends anamnetic exegesis. After the text has been recognized as a memorial to God's acts and words, while keeping in mind that we cannot separate God from this memorial, from this text and history, and vice versa, we are called into the expectation of the coming kingdom of God that is announced now by the invocation of the Holy Spirit. Again, within the Eucharistic economy, the scriptural text is remembered and is not a product of a historical-critical method. We do not stand at the door of the church waiting to celebrate the Eucharist until someone brings us the latest historical-critical consensus on any particular text, pericope or postmodern fragment. The Eucharistic act of remembering these texts presents a narrative for the future that now stands before us. This is not any future, not any kind of effort to speak of what we want or need, or of a world, society, culture or nation that is on the brink of being fixed or solved of its problems. Standing at the Eucharistic gate of heaven is not imagining any open-ended future; it is actually a place to repent of such idealized, idolatrous, projections. The epicletic horizon, just as the anamnetic horizon, is determined ultimately and absolutely by the vision of God.

The Eucharist is a movement from creation into the new creation. Within the celebration of the Eucharist, Scripture is located within this movement; Scripture provides the narrative of this movement without being its realization. Scripture is the proclamation that we are on our way to the new creation, but the way to this new creation is through Scripture. Scripture is a passage from death to life; it conveys the paschal mystery as witness and as itself undergoing this mystery. Scripture does so within the economy of the Eucharist. How is this so? The Holy Spirit gathers creation and leads it into the new creation that is the Son. The Son shows forth the Father; the Son shares his vision of the Father with those who belong in the Son. The Father sends the Holy Spirit so that we might hear and respond to the Father's address to us in and as the Son. Thus, there is a Trinitarian movement from the Father as the Spirit for the Son, and consequently by the Spirit to the Son before the Father (before the Father in the sense that we come to the Father in this way, and before the Father in the sense of countenance). The location of Scripture within these reciprocal movements means that lying behind the Eucharistic existence and proclamation of Scripture is the depth of the Holy Spirit. Out of this depth ('too deep for words', Rom. 8.26), the Holy Spirit introduces us to Scripture. This introduction prepares us to hear and to know the address of the Word of God. We are invited into that place where only the Word of God is heard; where this Word creates anew. This is why our arrival in this place is an offering of ourselves, the sacrifice of the life created outside the Eucharistic economy. As the narrative of the transition, the transformation, of the old into the new creation, Scripture is bounded by anamnetic and epicletic horizons. However, this is not a status position; it is a movement because the Word of

God is an address that embodies its own response. God speaks so that God can be seen. The Word of God is the embodiment of the vision of God. Entering into this Word leads to sharing the Son's life and vision.

Scripture exists within the movement from the depth of the Spirit to the vision of the Father, and the Son is this movement. The Word of God introduces us to his vision of the Father. The embodiment of this introduction is the Body of Christ. Our regard for Scripture is to know these texts as suspended between anamnesis and epiclesis, between depth and vision, as the address that leads to an announced and envisioned future not known anywhere else. The text of Scripture is suspended between earth and heaven. Our understanding of Scripture, our theological perspective on Scripture, is never to seek an abolition or absolution of this suspension. To resolve this suspension in either direction by abandoning the past as anamnesis or by seeking another future besides the epicletic one is to leave the embodied address of the Word of God; it is to approach Scripture as if the Eucharist was not celebrated. There is no proper theological meaning of Scripture outside the Body of Christ. While there can be legitimate study of Scripture outside the bounds of its Eucharistic location, any results of this study are to be offered at the altar.

Consummation of the Word of God

As located within the Eucharist, Scripture is taken within the movement that is the economy of the Eucharist. We as the Body of Christ are gathered into this economy, this Eucharistic place, and it is here that we discover Scripture anew. What are we to do with this discovery? Scripture is a gift from God, and as such, it exists to become our gift to God. The economy of the Eucharist is the exchange of gifts. Scripture is to be offered back to God for God's own purpose. When we offer God a gift for the singular purpose of God's agency, we offer this gift at the place where only God is active, where we ourselves enter only in thanksgiving, praise and petition. We place Scripture on the altar, and we pray over it passing through the thankful anamnesis of God's history and moving into the place where the Holy Spirit descends realizing the presence of the Word of God for the life of the world. What happens to Scripture when it is placed on the Eucharistic altar?

Scripture becomes the narrative of the consummation of our life with and within God's life with and for us. The *suspended* text between anamnesis and epiclesis moves towards becoming the *transparent* text before the vision of the Father. What has happened as anamnesis, what is happening now as epiclesis, becomes transparent to what will happen as the present future: the arrival of the Word of God in glory. At the Eucharistic altar, we theologically move from speaking of the *inspiration* of Scripture to the *illumination* of Scripture. Scripture becomes God's address to us from the consummation that resides solely in God's present and presence but stands before us in the present as the presence of God's future for us. Through Scripture we behold the vision of the Father, we see what the Son sees, because we participate in the clarity of the Holy Spirit. The canon of Scripture itself entices us into this narrative of the Eucharistic vision, the text that exists not so much for reading as it does for seeing.

> The revelation of Jesus Christ, which God gave him to show his servants what must soon take place; he made it known by sending his angel to his servant John, who testified to the word of God and to the testimony of Jesus Christ, even to all that he saw.
>
> Blessed is the one who reads aloud the words of the prophecy, and blessed are those who hear and who keep what is written in it; for the time is near. (Rev. 1.1-3)

These beginning verses of the last book of the canon of the New Testament can now be for us an exhortation to enter into the Eucharistic place and Eucharistic economy of Scripture. The place where Scripture yields the vision of the Father, and of the Son and of the Holy Spirit: the doxology of the Eucharistic consummation of Scripture. The revelation that is Jesus Christ, the Son of God, existing in Scripture as the revelation of the Word of God, now shows us 'what must soon take place'. The embodied Word of God arrives to take what we have offered to the Father as moved by the Holy Spirit and realizes it as the presence of the Body and Blood of Christ. Blessed are those who read aloud Scripture, hearing it and leading lives according to what they have heard, for in this Eucharistic place, within this Eucharistic now, it can always be said, 'These words are trustworthy and true, for the Lord, the God of the spirits of the prophets, has sent his angel to show his servants what must soon take place' (Rev. 22.6).

The celebration of the Eucharist is the manifestation of what it looks like for God's creation to enter into the age of the new creation. Here and now is that sacrificial movement from death to life, from the life *of* the world into the life *for* the world, from what we are looking *at* to what we are looking *for*. Scripture is the narrative fulcrum of this movement, the libretto of this manifestation.

> Then I saw a new heaven and a new earth; for the first heaven and the first earth had passed away, and the sea was no more. And I saw the holy city, the new Jerusalem, coming down out of heaven from God, prepared as a bride adorned for her husband. And I heard a loud voice from the throne saying,
> 'See, the home of God is among mortals.
> He will dwell with them;
> they will be his peoples,
> and God himself will be with them.' (Rev. 21.1-3)

The proper theological engagement with Scripture belongs within the economy of the Eucharist because Scripture itself belongs within this economy. Belonging within the Eucharist, which is not the same as existing exclusively there, Scripture is both a distinctive narrative from the Eucharist as well as a narrative that is located, formed, realized and consummated within the Eucharist. As located within the Eucharist, Scripture is enveloped within all that happens there, Scripture is not left alone, objectified by the intellectual, cultural and existential whims of our own non-theological subjectivity. This location places Scripture within the Body of Christ as it is being formed, realized and consummated. As such, Scripture has had a prior liturgical formation as canon constituted by the Old and New Testaments. Likewise, the Body of Christ is to be Eucharistically formed by Scripture. Scripture exists to form the Body of Christ. This relationship between Scripture and the Body of Christ is mutual; it is an 'admirable exchange'. Thus, the realization of the Body of Christ as and within the Eucharist is the realization of the Word of God that re-creates all that is placed before the Father who speaks this Word along with the outpouring of the Holy Spirit. Scripture is the Word of God within the Eucharist; Scripture is the narration that introduces us to the realization of this Word among us as the Body of Christ, which is the narration of our consummation in Christ before the Father. The Body of Christ enacts the Eucharist; the Body of Christ is realized anew within the Eucharist. The economy of the Eucharist is the Trinitarian movement of the mutuality of past, present and future. These dimensions of temporal existence are, in the offered presence of God, gifts to each other. Scripture is taken up into this temporal and historical communion; it is not an inert collection of texts to be taken from the shelf when we need to consult it for our own purposes. Scripture belongs to the consummation of the Body of Christ that proceeds from God's future for us. Scripture becomes an epiphany of the Eucharistic future. Scripture is the witness to the new creation.

Notes

1 A good guide for this discussion of meaning and text is Kevin J. Vanhoozer, *Is There a Meaning in This Text? The Bible, the Reader, and the Morality of Literary Knowledge* (Grand Rapids, MI: Zondervan, 2009).

2 The approach taken here will not be an argument for a 'fusion of horizons' as advocated by Hans-Georg Gadamer, *Truth and Method* (London: Bloomsbury Academic, 2004). Rather, as located within the Eucharist, Scripture always stands before the horizon of God.

3 The classic work on the four senses of Scripture in the tradition of biblical interpretation is Henri de Lubac, *Medieval Exegesis: The Four Senses of Scripture*, Vols. 1–3 (Grand Rapids, MI: Eerdmans Publishing, 1998, 2000 and 2009).

4 The assertion that we ought to preach with the Bible in one hand and the newspaper in the other has been attributed to Karl Barth. He did say this on various occasions through interviews and informal talks, but it has been taken up as a mantra by many preachers and writers on preaching. While certainly the task of preaching is relevant to any consideration of the relationship between Scripture and theology, especially as Scripture is located within the Eucharist, I will address directly the nature and task of preaching in the third volume of this systematics, *The Eucharistic Church*.

5 An argument for, and analysis of, how the celebration of the Eucharist by the early Christians shaped the writings of the New Testament is provided by Denis Farkasfalvy, 'The Eucharistic Provenance of New Testament Writings', in *Rediscovering the Eucharist: Ecumenical Conversations*, edited by Roch A. Kereszty (New York: Paulist Press, 2003), pp. 27–51.

6 Jens Schroter, *From Jesus to the New Testament: Early Christian Theology and the Origin of the New Testament Canon* (Waco, TX: Baylor University Press, 2013), p. 68.

7 Luke's account of the risen Jesus encountering the two disciples on the road to Emmaus and its implications for speaking of the Eucharistic context for the appearance of Jesus will be taken up at the conclusion of the next chapter, 'Knowledge'.

8 I owe this consideration of a further comprehensiveness of New Testament study in view of the centrality of the Eucharist for the primitive church to Stephen Fowl. For a good overview of the relationship of Scripture to theology and the life of the church, see his *Engaging Scripture: A Model for Theological Interpretation* (Malden, MA: Blackwell Publishers, 1998).

9 Thus, I disagree with the notion that the task of theology is to inhabit the world of the Bible as this view is proposed by George A. Lindbeck in his monumental work *The Nature of Doctrine: Religion and Theology in a Postliberal Age* (Philadelphia: The Westminster Press, 1984). An example of Lindbeck's argument is: 'These same considerations apply even more forcefully to the preeminently authoritative texts that are the canonical

writings of religious communities. For those steeped in them, no world is more real than the ones they create. A scriptural world is thus able to absorb the universe. It supplies the interpretative framework within which believers seek to live their lives and understand reality' (p. 117). My argument is that the Eucharist is 'the interpretative framework' for faithful understanding. Also, I am not only arguing against this 'postliberal' approach to Scripture but against the 'liberal' approach that seeks to 'translate' Scripture to our world(s), and this is where I do agree with Lindbeck.

10 I will explicate 'The Eucharistic Logos' that is Jesus as Son of God at the conclusion of Chapter 7 on 'Truth'.

PART 3

Understanding

5

Knowledge

Do you want to know God? This is the initial question that will begin to guide us towards developing a Eucharistic epistemology. However, in order to appreciate the direction this question sets forth, and thus why this question will lead us into the Eucharistic place of knowing God, we need to review other questions that may be, or indeed are, asked when the subject of epistemology in general is raised, or especially when the direct concern for the knowledge of God is expressed. After a brief review of these other misguided theological questions, we will proceed with an overture to what constitutes a Eucharistic epistemology. Then, we will have to address what the Eucharist is prior to encountering it as the place to know God. The Eucharist *qua* Eucharist is how we know the God we wish to know. Finally, the bulk of this chapter will be a reflection on the economy of the Eucharist as the knowledge of God, an articulation of a Eucharistic epistemology.

Non-Eucharistic Epistemology

Our initial question is not how we can know that there is a God. We do not proceed from within the realm of absence and its teleology of possibility. This question leaves the question of God as ambiguous and open to the temptations of projection from our prior comfort and utility as knowers of our worlds. That is, the question becomes how we can know that there is a God *beyond* ourselves, one who exists outside where we are, whether this outside is formulated in cultural, experiential, historical or cognitive terms. If we do come to the affirmation of God's existence, then we can venture further into the possible knowledge of the God that now exists. The arrival of God into this existence established within our question of the possibility of this existence means that God is already present on our terms, again whether they are historical, cultural, experiential or cognitive. We have the agenda for God's existence to us. When we ask the next question, how can God be known, we have already begun to answer this question for ourselves. For surely, we will know God the way we know that God exists. We will have moved from our presence and the presumptive absence of God to the presence of God known alongside of knowing our own presence. One could say that the arrival of God from the shadows of non-existence into the self-generated light of our presence is something we now have achieved. Thus, we will want our speculative success to continue and to come to its 'natural' fulfilment. The achievement of knowing that God exists will be pursued along the historical, experiential, cultural and cognitive continuum towards knowing this now existing God.

Asking how we can know that there is a God, or asking how we can know God, includes at the outset a prior understanding of knowledge, an already operative exercise of knowing this or that. We presume our own existence as knowers, and then we establish a hierarchy of what can be known. As the knowers we are, what is the most important object of knowledge for us? The answers to this question have varied over the whole course of asking such questions. We might ask, and we have asked, how we can know the world, the real, Being itself, the Absolute, the Ideals, etc., and then we discovered the most powerful and intriguing question of all: How can we know ourselves? Or, how do we know ourselves? We turn the question of knowing from its outward perspective to the vector of introspection. We can become a question to ourselves. The knowing subject turns away its gaze from the outer and possible objects of knowledge and looks within: How do *I* know myself? And this question then becomes how I know other things, all that is outside of myself in the terms set forth by knowing myself as this knower and not otherwise.

Once we have reached some form of certainty, stability or security of our knowledge of God's existence through knowledge of ourselves, we can begin to ask what good this knowledge of God does for us. Having achieved a knowledge of God as the performance of our own agency, we can look for ways to extend this agency by co-opting our knowledge of God into our will for ourselves. Knowing becomes doing; knowing for the sake of doing. While we may have attained knowledge of God on the basis of a prior knowledge of ourselves, or the world, we can venture forth into the realm of how this putative knowing of God will allow us to know and do other things we wish now to know or do. God moves from an object of our knowing to a subject at the disposal of our will. Of course, this will can be 'religious' and 'well-meaning'. We can want God to help us do what surely God wants us to do. However, again, having approached the question of the will and of act by way of our agency, God's actions can be a projection of our own idealized behaviour. We have re-entered the realm of possibility from another gate, from whether God can be known to whether we can do this with God's assistance. As such, we destroy the idols of speculation to erect the new gods of practicality. We vacate our enclaves of modern subjectivity in order to relocate ourselves within postmodern contexts.

Are there any problems with this account of the questions posed thus far, with what we have entertained in contrast to the identified initial question of a proper theological epistemology? Where is the agency of God in this account? How is God not just available to our knowing efforts, but a participant in our knowing? Where is God's Word and deed, God's speaking and doing, God's epistemological agency? Put another way, are we not to move away from the possibility of knowing God towards the potential this knowledge has for us as knowers? How might knowing God change us as knowers? Where is the epistemological sacrifice for knowing God?

From Possible to Potential Knowledge of God

Do you want to know God? Posing this question transgresses the open-ended realm of possibility. This question is addressed to a potential knower of God. Instead of asking our own questions, maintaining the primacy of ourselves as questioners of God, self and world, a question is addressed to us. The questioning 'I' becomes the questioned 'you'. Our existence, our subjectivity, is placed in question by this question of knowing God. This question presumes an unknowing of God, a knowledge of God that does not yet exist even though we already exist as ourselves within a known existence. It could be entertained at this juncture that what is being questioned is our absence from God, rather than the presumed absence of God at all, or the absence of God from us. That is, knowledge of God will not be a movement from our presence to God's absence, but the movement from our absence to God's presence. For the question is an invitation and a proclamation. The 'you' addressed is invited into a knowledge of someone who is now unknown, but who could be known. There is an invitation to enter into a knowing that may not be 'natural' to the pre-existing knower. What knowing God will involve, what it will take to know this God, is as yet unspoken. Likewise, this question is a proclamation that God can be known, and furthermore, this God can be known as this God. The question resonates with particularity and specificity, with the potential sacrifices of love that only exist intersubjectively.

Do you want to know God? Between this you and knowing God is the question of 'want'. Is it your desire to know God? Do you desire to know God? Do you have the will to come to the knowledge of God? The fulcrum point between our subjectivity and knowledge of God is our desire for this knowledge, our desire to become knowers of God. Desire transcends and transforms the epistemological avenues of 'thinking about' or 'feeling dependent upon'. Desire will not allow us to stay put and try to figure out the how, what or that of a possible knowledge of God. However, our desire to know God is a precondition for knowing God; it does not constitute this knowing. The realization of our potential knowledge of God is God's desire to be known by us. This is why the primary theological trajectory is not our movement to God, but God's movement to us. Our desire to know God is a trust that we will discover an answering desire to be known. That God desires to be known by us ushers us into the realm lying on the other side of the next question: how does God desire to be known by us? We are introduced to the how question by the mutuality of desire to be known and to know.

When the theological epistemological priority has been granted to God's willingness to be known rather than our capacity to know God, the argument becomes God's revelation in contrast to, or in conflict with, with any natural knowledge of God. We have here the opposition between revealed theology and natural theology, the opposition between dialectic and analogy, or perhaps a contest between faith and pure reason. It is not my intent at this stage to enter into this debate but rather to consider the existence of revelation as God's desire to be known. After this consideration, and as I proceed with the exposition of a Eucharistic epistemology, the subject of a possible natural knowledge of God will be taken up; however, not on its usual terms but as related to the Eucharistic place within which God desires to be known. God's movement outside God, yet proceeding from God, to those created in God's image, is God's desire to be known as God. The desire to be known as oneself will involve the giving of self to be known. That is, God does not desire to be known other than as God: 'you are not to have any idols before me'. God's revelation, in whatever mode we assign to it, is, at least, God's demonstrative will to say and act in such a way that there is no mistaking who this God really and truly is. For an abiding condition on our side of the revelatory relationship is to get this God wrong, either to seek other gods or to distort what a faithful relationship to this God really is. God entered into covenants with the people of Israel so that they would remain steadfast to the God who created and called them, the God of Abraham, Isaac and Jacob. Jesus is the revelation of his Father, and we are now to know God as the Father of Jesus. As God's desire to be known, God's revelation is both the offer of self to be known and that seeks an answering offer of self by the potential knower. Thus, knowledge of God by us is an encounter of mutual desire. We as potential knowers are called to move from our places in the world, our epistemological environs, towards the place God has prepared for us to know God. Just as God does stand outside this place and say come and know me, we are not called to stand in our places, our worlds, and say either how can we know God or how can God be where I am already? Knowing as the desire to be known involves a kenotic movement towards the 'object' to be known, the 'object' of our desire. God's subjectivity objectifies us as knowers within this epistemological place. We are called to know God in the way that God has called us to become knowers of God.

Revelation

This reflection on revelation as God's desire to be known as God, with its kenotic movement of known to knower and knower to known, means that revelation is more than an address to us, a speaking to the world. The question of the nature of revelation is raised not just as an epistemological one; it is the question of theology itself. Theology at its essence is not only a speaking about God, an exercise in understanding who this God is so that we might say something about God, whatever our motives and purposes are for such speaking. Rather, at its essence theology is a faithful and truthful relationship with and within God. Of course, this is itself a theological claim. One does not stand outside theology in order to talk about its nature and method objectively. Theology is not one more academic discipline among the reigning pantheon of intellectual pursuits and trends. The question that concerns us here is not whether theology belongs in a university. Rather, does theology belong in the presence of God? Thus, the question of revelation is again not the question of what is possible for us to know and say regarding God. The question of revelation becomes how we know and speak of God within the presence of God. This emphasis on presence transforms how we are to understand the difference between God and ourselves, the difference through which revelation is navigated, or in some theological efforts, negotiated. In order to appreciate this transformation of what we take revelation to be, where we locate it, let us briefly rehearse some of the customary approaches to revelation in the history and development of theology.

While revelation has always been a dynamic of theology, it has not always been a distinctive subject in the study of theology. It is really at the Reformation and Counter-Reformation in the sixteenth century that revelation becomes a direct subject of consideration precisely within the context of polemic and debate. That is, the Reformers' appeal to Scripture alone constituted their perspective on revelation, while the Counter-Reformation theologians argued for tradition as a companion of Scripture in the economy of the revelation of God, or what God wishes to reveal to the church as authoritative teaching. This debate over the nature and purpose of revelation is found in their arguments over the church, salvation, sacraments and all principal theological subjects. As such, at least in Western Christianity, revelation is incorporated within different ecclesial contexts and theological frameworks. Speaking of revelation became a self-conscious theological exercise. Once revelation has in a sense been removed from its home within a coherent and assumed theological and ecclesial environment, and once such environments themselves become divergent and contested, revelation can be taken up as a subject itself according to whatever intellectual, historical, ecclesial or cultural interests and strategies are currently at hand. Thus, with the rise of the Enlightenment in the eighteenth century, revelation is treated from the perspective of reason held to be universal and objective. The more epistemological territory is conquered by reason as an inherent exercise of the human mind, the more revelation is pushed into a land one enters only by 'faith'. If revelation is allowed to transgress the border between reason and faith, between the visible and invisible, empirical and transcendent, then revelation will become circumscribed by what is *a priori* deemed reasonable, what is 'possible' here where the modern mind belongs. When, in the nineteenth century, the development of rationality took into account not only conceptual minds but historical agents, revelation had to prove itself beyond the question of how we can know this by reason with the further question of could this have happened within our history. How can the revelation of God fit into how we understand ourselves and within the course of history as we know it? Or, how does God belong in this world, in this life, as we know and experience it? In this way, revelation was regarded as existing within our subjectivity; God is revealed within our own sense of dependency or as an interior movement towards transcendence. This location of revelation within human subjectivity was countered by placing the realm of revelation within the course of history. God is revealed not so much by consciousness within us but by actions on ourselves. God is known not through our knowing, but God is known as an agent within our history, whether God's agency is viewed as more disruptive or compliant with this historical agency.

In the twentieth century, there were theologians who claimed that these homes for God's revelation in our minds, experience and history were actually prisons where we held God captive. True and faithful knowledge of God knows the freedom of God to break into our cognitive, historical, experiential and cultural captivities, setting us free for faith in this God. The ultimate act of this freedom is the resurrection of Jesus. Jesus cannot now be known as an extension of what we already know; we are called to know Jesus in the way that he now knows himself as arriving from the Father through the rationality of the Holy Spirit. What is possible for us is transformed into God's potential for us before the risen Christ. All our epistemological endeavours will now be confronted by the abiding newness of God. All our analogical strategies for knowing God will belong within the new creation and not conceptually bound by the pre-resurrection creation. And yet, the revelation of God is for us, so who we are and how we live is indeed of critical importance to what revelation truly and really is, to why there is this revelation and not some other. Revelation exists between God and those to whom God is revealed. Revelation is both a revealing of God and a revealing to us. Revelation is a movement from God to those who seek to encounter this movement. How then are we to contemplate rather than to conceive of a place for this encounter? I say contemplate rather than conceive because this place is given and not constructed. That is, our theological efforts here are directed towards coming to terms with what already exists through the potential God gives and not because of a conceptuality that we deem possible for us *qua* us. For this place to remain one of encounter, the overriding and ultimate reality of this place will be the presence of God. God is present here to be encountered by those who have come here to be so encountered. This is a place where the Revealer is never separated from revelation, and where revelation participates in God's presence. It is a place where not only is revelation never severed from the Revealer, and thereby becomes a subject for our study (for we cannot really know what this revelation is unless it is part of the living God); it is a place where and whereby revelation fulfils its purpose for existence: communion with the Trinity and communion within the Body of Christ. This revelatory, and thus epistemological, place is the Eucharist, and we enter this place through the waters of baptism having been anointed into the mind of Christ. How then are we to speak of this Eucharistic place of the revelation and knowledge of God that we enter through baptism? What kind of knowing takes place here and not elsewhere?

The Eucharistic Location for Knowledge of God

The Eucharist as the primary and paradigmatic place of God's revelation, and hence of knowledge of this revealing God, means that some of our customary perspectives on both revelation and knowledge need to undergo a transformation. One such transformation is to cease talking of the sources of revelation as distinguishable modes of revelation from each other. Whether we are speaking of revelation in terms of Scripture, tradition, reason, doctrine or experience, each of these is no longer an individual source to be exposited from the others. Within the Eucharist, all such sources yield to a multidimensional presence. Presence does not have sources; presence has attributes or features of the one who is present. Presence has modes whereby the one who is present here presents oneself to others. Again, the primary movement within the Eucharist is the arrival of God as Jesus realized by the Holy Spirit. This arrival has modes of arriving presence. Thus, we do not identify sources of revelation that we once so identified and then explore them with our prior conceived hermeneutic or theological method. Rather, we are called here within this Eucharistic place to become adapted to how God is revealed as present to and for us.

The revelatory movement of God within the Eucharist means as well that we cease from regarding revelation as *to* us in any exclusive way. That is, revelation is not to us either as outer address or as an inner experience. Rather, the revelation of God surrounds us, we are enveloped by it when we enter the Eucharistic place. This is why we will emphasize the 'within' of revelation instead of the 'to' of revelation. This emphasis will involve abstaining from any consideration of the correspondence or correlation between God and ourselves, between the human and divine. Within the Eucharistic place our questions posed from elsewhere are not carried into this presence looking for answers that may or may not fit the accountability of this elsewhere. Rather, while we indeed may have questions once we inhabit this place, we also may find ourselves being questioned within this Eucharistic presence of God. When we arrive within the presence of God's arrival, theologically, we are not striving to arrive at a correspondence or correlation between our questions and God's possible answers. We do not move into the Eucharist to look around for things that will help us or fix us elsewhere. We move into the Eucharist for communion and not correspondence. Communion is a multidirectional reality characterized not by a being at but a being with and within. Communion exists as participation among others that then constitutes a shared life. The revelation of this life will at the same time and in the same way be the realization of this life among others. As a Eucharistic reality revelation will not be within the confines of God's address to us; revelation will always be a gift of self. Gift is a more comprehensive, sacrificial, reality than an address. Gift will not allow the giver to remain distant from the recipient of this gift. God does not speak to us from elsewhere either; God speaks as one who is present here with a gift, the gift of God's life for us. It is the gift of communion where 'we are to live, move, and have our being'. We do not come to the Eucharist looking for answers; we come seeking life in Christ.

Eucharistic Epistemology

The Eucharistic transformation of revelation from 'to' to 'within' is the transformation of knowledge of God from the standpoint of how we are present to ourselves to how we are present within the presence of God. Within this enveloping Eucharistic presence of God, knowledge of this God is not achieved or acquired. We are not striving to find an epistemological path we walk to other known places and then walk it into the Eucharist. Knowledge is an encounter with a presence not our own, with the arrival of the one seeking us. Jesus arrives within the Eucharist as the epistemological way to the Father, and the Holy Spirit animates our walking through this way to the knowledge and love of God. This epistemological way, this location for the knowledge of God, is for us to inhabit and be formed within it as knowers of God. Again, entering this epistemological habitat is a movement from the known to the unknown, not as an epistemological move but as an ascetic one. What was known recedes into the background of absence as we move into the presence of the one we seek to know. The epistemological move is from absence to presence. However, this absence is not absolute. Rather, our prior ways of knowing, our previous locations of knowledge, are to become present to us once again, but as that which has been offered to God and received as God's gift to us having been sanctified through the dynamics of communion. This is the epistemological transformation from the old to within the new creation. There can be an analogy between the old and new creation, but it is an analogy given to us from, and from within, communion with God. God is not known as this God outside communion within this God. Knowledge of God is a consequence of our giving ourselves over to the known. Contrary to customary theological epistemologies, knowledge of God does not exist within reason, within history, within our subjectivity nor even within the church apart from the Eucharist. Knowledge of God exists within the Eucharist where and whereby the essence of this knowledge arrives and abides. However, knowing God within the Eucharist does not entail the absolute absence of the rational, historical, subjective and ecclesial dimensions of this knowledge. Within the Eucharist we discover and contemplate, we articulate and proclaim, how the knowledge of God within the arriving presence of God is indeed rational, historical, subjective and ecclesial. Such is the task of a Eucharistic epistemology.

Baptized Knowers of God

Before exploring and explicating a Eucharistic epistemology as such, there is the question of entry into the Eucharistic place of the knowledge of God. Who goes to this place, and how do they get there? Asking these questions already moves us away from any generic epistemology, any effort to construct a universal account of what it means to know, and certainly any reliance on the modern conceit that reason will guide all of us to the promised land of pure objectivity. That is, we are not asking the question of knowing and knowledge from a putative perspective that somehow does, or is able to, belong to all of humanity under the right circumstances, or according to the appropriate method. We are not asking what is possible for human knowers and knowing. When we enter the Eucharistic place for the knowledge of God, we are leaving the modern world and the postmodern contexts behind. Moving from the world into the Eucharist is a sacrificial passage from any claims of secular reason, from any pretence of being scientific, to a new place, even a new world, where we are called to learn its ways by living its life. Who goes to this place? How do they get here? They are the baptized; the baptized enter the Eucharistic place in order to receive the gift of life, the life that will grant them knowledge of God.

Theology proper will not first develop an anthropology and then possibly 'baptize' it. There is for theology always the priority of a baptismal anthropology, a reflection on the baptismal passage from the old to the new creation in Christ.

> Do you not know that all of us who have baptized into Christ Jesus were baptized into his death? Therefore we have been buried with him by baptism into death, so that, just as Christ was raised from the dead by the glory of the Father, so we too might walk in newness of life ... We know that our old self was crucified with him ... We know that Christ, being raised from the dead, will never die again; death no longer has dominion over him. (Rom. 6.3-4, 6a, 9)

All proper theological epistemology begins with the 'knowing' that we are baptized into the death and resurrection of Christ; we have passed through the knowledge that leads to death into the knowledge that is life in Christ. Thus, our attentiveness to any object of theological knowledge will have the knowledge of dying and rising in Christ as its point of departure. This text from Romans does not stand alone in our consideration of a proper theological anthropology, and thus, a proper theological epistemology. When we take into account the practices of baptism in the first four centuries of the existence of the Christian faith, this passage from the old to the new creation, the entry of the baptized into the Eucharist, is enacted by the church. The baptismal passage from the old self to becoming a member of the Body of Christ is performed; it takes on a life of its own. This is why there was a lengthy preparation for baptism involving the examination of how you lived and thought, and how you are transformed into living the life of the Body of Christ and entering into the mind of Christ. That is, there were behaviours and beliefs, habits and thoughts that would have to be left behind if you were to enter the waters of baptism and receive anointing as a newly conceived Christian. This passage from the old self into the Body of Christ was taken as the defining reality of your life. So much so, that if you strayed from this new life into any of the behaviours and beliefs of your old self, you had to start over with another course of self-examination, purging of old ways, and relearning the life and faith of a Christian. Why? Not because you have gone from being a good person to a bad one, but because you had turned away from the life that you had been given. The transgression was not essentially ethical; it was infidelity.

The comprehensive reality of baptism is not centred in fixing inherent defects of the human person or rectifying the human condition. Rather, baptism is entry into the comprehensive life of the Body of Christ and receiving the gift of the Holy Spirit. Again, the primary question of the self is not introspective, but the exploration of who I am here in this place where I have been led. And we are not alone in this place to figure it out for ourselves, according to our own noetic light. One of the primitive appellations for newly formed Christians was the 'illuminated': those who are led now by the light of Christ. Speaking directly to the customary categories of epistemology, the baptized do not possess an individual subjectivity or an autonomous mind.

> From now on, therefore, we regard no one from a human point of view; even though we once knew Christ from a human point of view, we know him no longer in that way. So if anyone is in Christ, there is a new creation: everything old has passed away; see, everything has become new! (2 Cor. 5.16-17)

Having left behind the old ways and entered into the new creation, leaving behind individual subjectivity and autonomous reason, the baptized are not to practise the old epistemological ways that seek a knowledge that they can possess and use for their own benefit. This new creation and its ways of knowing with its inherent gift of knowledge are realized in three modes: the subjectivity of Christ within, the subjectivity of Christ without and the subjectivity that is living into Christ. While these are three distinct modes of subjectivity, they belong in communion with each other.

The Subjectivity of Christ

The Apostle Paul proclaimed that 'it is no longer I who live, but it is Christ who lives in me' (Gal. 2.20a). Baptism bestows two mutual movements of subjectivity: the movement of Christ within the person and the movement of this person into the Body of Christ. The movement of Christ within the baptized person is accompanied by the gift of the Holy Spirit. Therefore, the baptized subject is not left alone as a possible knower of her or his life or world. Prior to any act of knowing is the depth of the movement of the Holy Spirit rendering this person a potential knower of God (Rom. 8). That is, God is subjectively prior to this person's desire for the knowledge of God. Any judgement that God is indeed known is preceded by God's agency to be known by the baptized.

God is active in this person as knower of God. The baptized comes to know God by being placed within the movement of how God knows God. The baptized knows God by participating in God's agency of knowing. This agency co-exists with the human agency of the potential knower of God. Indeed, the agency of the Holy Spirit is what transforms the possibility of knowing God to the existence of a potential knowledge of God. God is here to be known; knowing is knowing that God is here. The agency of the Holy Spirit within the depths of the baptized subject is not an amorphous existence. The Holy Spirit realizes the presence of Christ. The Holy Spirit is given in baptism so that this person can become a knower of Christ as and when this person knows themselves as they truly and really are.

> So if you have been raised with Christ, seek the things that are above, where Christ is, seated at the right hand of God. Set your minds on things that are above, not on things that are on earth, for you have died, and your life is hidden with Christ in God. When Christ who is your life is revealed, then you also will be revealed with him in glory. (Col. 3.1-4)

The dwelling of Christ within the baptized never becomes an object to be known by the self as the self: 'Abide in me as I abide in you' (John 15.4a). Any objectivity that might have been gained by a critical distance between the autonomous subject and the object of knowledge has been washed away by the waters of baptism. Now, through the relentless agency of the Holy Spirit, the baptized come to know themselves in the very act of knowing Christ. The revelation of Christ to them is the revelation of who they are in Christ. Christ is the objectivity of knowledge given through the subjectivity of the Holy Spirit dwelling within us as potential knowers of God, potential knowers of ourselves. In this way, any epistemological effort to move within will simultaneously become a movement without. The baptismal knower will be led from an awareness of Christ within to the Christ without, from introspection to pilgrimage. Knowing Christ is knowing him in the resurrection, in the passage from who we are to where we are in Christ. This is the knowledge not constructed from the materials bequeathed to us from our past built with the current tools of our present. Rather, this is a knowledge to which we are invited from the future that belongs to the company of heaven. Thus, there is a baptismal transcendence that is the movement from Christ within to Christ without, from the creation originally wrought by the Holy Spirit to the new creation, the passage now from death to life. Any proper theological concept of transcendence or category of the transcendental will ultimately be this movement from the hidden in Christ to the revealed as Christ. The resurrection of Christ is the absolute, ultimate and transformative gift of transcendence. Knowledge of God is participation in the resurrection of Christ. Knowing God arrives by offering our empirical existence and our categorical minds. Once we leave the tombs of our own epistemological making, where do we go?

Knowing Within the Body of Christ

Knowing ourselves as members of the Body of Christ is realized within the Body of Christ among its other members. The movement of Christ within to Christ without, while it indeed has an eschatological trajectory, it first brings us face to face with our fellow members of the Body of Christ. The Christ who arrives to us, who awaits our arrival to and in him, is not encountered without his Body, without the other members of this Body. Thus, baptismal knowers will know themselves and will know Christ as they share in the knowledge of God that belongs within the Body of Christ. That is, we do not get to claim our own autonomous or individual knowledge of God. As knowers of God, we are accountable to the other knowers of God. While we each have a distinctive subjectivity as members of the Body, a distinctive sense of the Christ within, we all share a common reality of the Christ without. As knowers of God, we cannot say to our fellow knowers within the Body of Christ 'I have no need of you' (1 Cor. 12.21). Each member is accountable to each other for what this knowledge is, but they are all accountable to the Christ without who bids them to know him as he is and to know the Father that he knows. The subjectivity of our fellow members of the Body of Christ ought to mitigate any temptations to objectify the knowledge of God that alienates this knowledge from the presence of God. We are called to know God in the company of other knowers of God, and our knowledge of God will be shared among us as we all participate in the life of the Body of Christ. For baptismal knowing is not only in the mode of Christ within and of Christ without; it is a knowing by living.

The bringing of persons into the Body of Christ with the gift of the Holy Spirit in baptism is the beginning of a new life, a new way of living. As part of their formation the catechumens of the early church would undergo not only examination of their old life, they would be guided by those who were leading the new life of the Body of Christ. Before you became a Christian, you were required to learn how to live as a Christian. While it certainly became this in later centuries, both liturgically and theologically, baptism was not primarily something 'done' to someone, especially an infant. The principal reality of baptism was not located within an individual, much less confined to that individual, but was located within the Body of Christ and this Body lives in certain ways. For our purposes then in this chapter, the knowledge of God that is the Body of Christ inhabited by baptismal knowers is a knowledge into which one lives as a member of this Body. Knowing God is a way of life and not something confined or defined by the mind of the potential knower. Furthermore, our minds are being formed by the way we live, where we live and with whom we live. This is why catechesis was both learning to live as a Christian as well as learning what Christians believe: the formation of mind and body. Therefore, any proper theological questions regarding Christian epistemology will include probing the habits and disciplines of actual Christian lives as well as questions of mental states or capacities. The attention to living will exclude any basis for epistemology within a preconditioned mind or within a mind dedicated to navigating its natural or cultural context.

I have reflected briefly on what I have called three modes of baptismal subjectivity, three mutual dynamics of baptismal knowing: Christ within, Christ without and living into the life of the Body of Christ. These are not modes by which a pre-existing reality expresses itself. There is not a substance of knowledge behind these modes; they are not ways that a pre-existing object reaches three modes of subjectivity. Rather, these modes of a baptismal subjectivity are trajectories into a knowledge of God that arrives from before the knower. The knowledge of God arrives from the future and is not a reconstruction of the past, nor is it a way to make sense of a currently existing present. The entrance into the life of the Body of Christ, the exploration of the mind of Christ, is always a movement into this life and mind. Again, baptism is not essentially the bestowal of a status, but the introduction of the baptized to Christ who is always introducing his Father to them, while being animated by the Holy Spirit. This movement never ceases; it does not lose its capacity for joyful discovery. While this baptismal movement never ceases, and while it begins in baptism, where does it take us now? Where do the baptized go, where is this place and life of the knowledge of God that is always a joyful discovery, where the Body of Christ gathers to celebrate the life and knowledge that only belongs here and not elsewhere?

The Eucharistic Economy of Knowing

The Body of Christ goes where it belongs as this Body; it gathers to meet the arrival of Jesus who will give his knowledge of the Father to them. The baptized gather for the Eucharist; they are led by the indwelling Holy Spirit to inhabit that place where the true knowledge of God is received. Attending to the Eucharist is attending to how God is known by those who seek this knowledge. As such, we will consider the Eucharist as the sphere in which God is known, where and whereby Eucharistic knowledge takes place. Thus, the question of what the Eucharist is cannot be separated from the question of the knowledge of God. The first task towards a Eucharistic epistemology is to review what constitutes the Eucharist. The next task is to take up the dynamics and contours of the Eucharistic as realizing the knowledge of God. Eucharistic epistemology is first and foremost Eucharistic. We are seeking the knowledge of God that takes place within the Eucharist. We are not trying to fashion an epistemology by cobbling together some Eucharistic parts. We are accountable to the Eucharist and not to any reigning epistemological concerns or theories lying elsewhere. What then does the Eucharist *qua* Eucharist reveal about the knowledge of God? How does our baptismal immersion into this Eucharistic place bring us into the knowledge of God through the mind of Christ illuminated all the way by both the indwelling of the Holy Spirit and by its invocation to realize the 'object' of our knowledge as the arriving presence of the Body and Blood of Christ, the gift of communion?

The Eucharist is a continuum of actions related mutually to each other. That is, there is an order to these actions that constitute the event of the Eucharist. The Eucharist is what it is because of certain actions in a particular order. These actions constitute an event, which has its inherent purpose and reality. This event possesses its own objectivity and resists all efforts to objectify it from the concerns and concepts that exist outside its economy of the true and the real. Whatever one may or may not think about the Eucharist, it is still the Eucharist and remains so. We do not invent the Eucharist; we inhabit it. The Eucharist is not a performance of innovation; it is a faithful receptivity to transformation. We have identified the constitutive actions of the Eucharist in a previous chapter, considering them as essential concepts of the Eucharistic nature of theology. These actions are gathering, listening, proclaiming, confessing a common faith, intercession, confessing sin, receiving forgiveness, sharing peace, offering, praising, thanksgiving, remembering, invoking, receiving and dismissing. These actions not only constitute a singular event as such, but this event is repeated. As a repetitive event, the Eucharistic actions are performed and engaged anew. The givenness of the Eucharistic actions is the abiding 'context' in which a gift is received as always new. The givenness of the Eucharist is the place where the gift of the Eucharist is received. Those who enter the Eucharist do so in order to be gifted and not to employ what is Eucharistically at hand in order to express themselves or to do and say what is 'needed' in their self-referential now. With this brief review of what constitutes the Eucharist *qua* Eucharist in mind, we can now consider the Eucharist as where the knowledge of God takes place.

The entering of the Eucharist by the baptized, the movement of inhabiting the Eucharistic place, is not directly or ultimately for the sake of knowledge of God. The Eucharist exists in order to realize, share, participate in and receive the gift of the life of communion that is the Body of Christ. The Eucharist is not taken up as a method for knowledge of God; it is not directly an epistemology. Knowledge of God cannot be dissected from the life of the Body of Christ; flesh cannot be peeled away from the Word. The Eucharistic actions are performances of fidelity before they can be rendered dimensions of knowledge. Eucharistic epistemology is an epistemology because it is always Eucharistic and not vice versa. This means that knowledge of God, or a Eucharistic way of knowing anything or anyone, does not reside within any *a priori* concepts or concerns of the human mind, nor does this knowledge belong substantially to whatever context in which this hypothetical knower resides. Knowledge is not located within the knower, nor is it located in the natural, intellectual, cultural or historical provenance of the knower. For Eucharistic epistemology, the knower is located within the

Eucharist. What constitutes the Eucharist is what constitutes knowledge of God. Furthermore, the economy of the Eucharist, although it is the economy of knowing God, is always given to the knower. Within the Eucharist, there is no method or theory of knowledge. Rather, there is the presence of God as the arrival of Jesus realized by the leading and the outpouring of the Holy Spirit. Knowledge of God is a consequence of, a reflection upon, this presence. Thus, the dimensions of knowledge are the ways we enter into this presence as well as the ways this presence is encountered on its own terms and for its own sake. Thus, Eucharistic epistemology involves the *askesis* of asking the 'how' question: how can God be known? The 'how' of this knowledge is transformed by the 'that' of this knowledge. We ask 'why' is God known in this way because we ask why is God present here, and why are we present here? Eucharistic epistemology is a pilgrimage into the gifted presence of God who arrives to know us as those who receive the gift of communion. God knows us here Eucharistically. Eucharistic epistemology is knowing God as God knows us. Hence, any notion of objectivity is not that an object is now known, either by the terms of the knower or as the thing itself. Rather, Eucharistic objectivity is that the objective of the Eucharist is being fulfilled; we have become knowers of God because we participate within God's life for us. There is no knowledge of God without *koinonia*. As a repetitive pilgrimage, Eucharistic epistemology always exists within the dynamic tension between what is known and what will be known, between what has happened and what will happen, the present between past and future. This why again Eucharistic epistemology is not the methodical movement from the known to the possibility of knowing, that unknown that is only reached by the known.

Let us consider the basic movements of the Eucharistic prayer as the basic movement of Eucharistic epistemology. These movements are: praise, thanksgiving, anamnesis, epiclesis and communion. We begin in praise of God as God is now accompanied by 'angels, archangels, and all the company of heaven'. We begin with 'lifting our hearts' and joining in the heavenly liturgy of praise: 'Holy, Holy, Holy, Lord God of hosts'. We begin by abandoning the calculations of our minds for what is useful and possible, and we leave behind the securities and satisfactions as well as the perceived needs of our self-realized and self-referential contexts. We abandon ourselves to God's unknown and yet living reality which we approach by sharing in its idiom of praise and worship. Knowing God is belonging to the company of God's presence. However, this abandonment of praise is not bereft of referential content, of the recognizable consequences of God's agency on our behalf. There is something to be known as such; there is a commonly shared knowledge between God and us that, although it will always elude the temptations of foundationalism, will nonetheless abide as the place to traverse on this epistemological pilgrimage to communion. This content, or shared knowledge, is named by thanksgiving and known as anamnesis.

The shared knowledge between God and ourselves is first acknowledged as that which God has done on our behalf among us. Our relationship to this content is characterized by thanksgiving. We approach this narrative history with thanksgiving and not with suspicion. We do not encounter this narrative history as something that has to be first critiqued and analysed for what may or may not be useful or relevant. Furthermore, we do not choose what we are thankful for; it is not available to us within any personal proximity. We were not there when this happened, but we give thanks that it did. We have thankful knowledge of a history in which we are not agents. Our agency is introduced by this thanksgiving and exercised by keeping the memory of this content. What we know here is given to us to keep, to abide within, for whatever we will know of God will not dispense with what we have remembered. This knowledge is present to the mind without being constructed or constituted by it. This is an 'object' of thought that retains its own location within God's historical agency while also being available to our knowing of it. Yet, we know it as remembered; we are keeping this memory. It is not our memory as such. Rather, we are first stewards of a content of knowledge, custodians of its authentic objectivity. Memory here is a sacrificial event whereby we are renewed in the identity of those who keep this memory, the knowers of this God remembered in this way. However, knowledge of God is not a repose in the past; it is not limited by the content that has been given. Knowing God is knowing the God who acts and calls, the God who arrives and seeks, who steadfastly gives life to be shared, the participation in and realization of communion. We do not truly and really know God unless we know God's active presence, the expectant giving of life: 'We believe in the Holy Spirit, the Lord and giver of life.' Anamnetic knowing yields to epicletic knowing. The object of our knowledge of God is realized by God; it is for the knowers of God to invoke the Holy Spirit to provide the 'object'. This object, the arrival of Jesus, the arrival of the one whose memory we keep, is provided by and as the free agency of God. As object of our knowledge of God, this object cannot be known without the free, non-necessary and non-contingent subjectivity of God. God remains God's own objectivity, and God will be known by those who participate in God's *perichoresis* of subjectivity and objectivity. God then is known as here because God has arrived here. God is known as here 'on the altar' and 'at the communion rail' because God cannot be located here before this epicletic arrival. The knowledge of God is always God's own gift to these baptismal knowers. And knowledge of God is not the objective here. Communion with God is the objective of Eucharistic epistemology. We know God as those who receive God's life for us, and this life never belongs to us; we always belong to this life. Communion is an epistemological reality in the sense that knowledge of God is a dimension of life with God and is always shared with those whose life is this *koinonia*. Thus, there is no expertise or special status among the knowers of God as the

Body of Christ. Knowing God is not the product of education or intellectual ability but is our capacity for anamnesis, epiclesis and receptivity of the gift of communion. The primary attribute of knowledge of God is holiness, the transparency of our lives to the arriving of Jesus, the animation of our lives by the outpouring of the Holy Spirit, and by the language we employ to speak thus: 'Holy, Holy, Holy, Lord God of Hosts; heaven and earth are full of your glory.'

Epistemology on the Way to Emmaus

We have an account of Eucharistic epistemology as one of the accounts of the risen Jesus appearing to two of his disciples, and of how this appearance becomes an arrival. We are speaking of course of Luke's account of the appearance of Jesus to two of his disciples on the road to Emmaus (Luke 24.13-35). We will reflect on this account as it both reveals and summarizes how the knowledge of Jesus takes place within the economy of the Eucharist. While the two disciples are going towards the village of Emmaus, having left Jerusalem, they are having a conversation about what happened in Jerusalem with Jesus. While they are no longer located geographically in Jerusalem, the events of this place remain their topic of language. They are not talking about some other place and some other events. The Eucharist exists between the Jerusalem of history and the Jerusalem of heaven. The origin of what happens and why it happens in and as the Eucharist resides with this historical Jerusalem, and the *telos* and purpose of the Eucharist is the movement towards the heavenly Jerusalem.[1] They are not engaged in speculative meanderings; they are discussing what happened to Jesus in Jerusalem.

'While they were talking and discussing, Jesus himself came near and went with them, but their eyes were kept from recognizing him' (v. 15). While they were talking about Jesus, the presence of Jesus is introduced, and this is a presence that is still part of the disciples' own presence to themselves.

Jesus accompanies them on the way that they are going; his appearance is not yet an arrival. The disciples did not recognize him as Jesus, but they did know that someone was present. We could say that since he was not known as himself, Jesus appears but does not arrive yet to them from the dead or from the Father. The phrase that 'their eyes were kept from recognizing him' could be an indication that they are to recognize Jesus in another way than as just someone who shows up. That is, how Jesus is to be known as himself henceforth will be in another way than how anyone else might be known or not. The way to know Jesus now is unique to him. Jesus enacts his own epistemology. While Jesus is with the disciples, he does not remain mute; he asks them questions. He questions them about the topic of their conversation, and he questions them to give their account of this topic, to tell him what they know already. As such, they refer to Jesus as a stranger: 'Are you the only stranger in Jerusalem who does not know the things that have taken place there in these days?' (v. 18b). Jesus is the stranger in Jerusalem, while everyone else knows and recognizes each other. The Eucharistic economy of knowing is to move from the familiar to the strange so that what first appears as strange becomes the arrival of knowledge, the type of knowledge that will never have a place within our prior locations of the familiar. Jesus questions us in order to lead us into his strangeness from us, so that we might share his strangeness from us. Jesus invites us to become strangers to our previously known selves, the self that exists prior to baptism, the self that is not known within the Eucharist. We sacrifice our familiarity, our ways of locating each other and ourselves in other places for the sake of being in the company of this stranger, the one who is estranged from death, from all knowing that ceases at death.

'He asked them, "What things?"' (v. 19a). The two disciples not only answer Jesus' question with a robust account of all that had happened to this Jesus of Nazareth, but they speak of their own desire for its significance: 'But we had hoped that he was the one to redeem Israel' (v. 21). They know what had happened to Jesus, but this knowledge was accompanied by their own desire for its meaning, for the consequences that they had projected into the future. Instead of this consequential future, the disciples have faced a quite strange future, one that they could not understand. There had been reports from others in their company who had visited to the tomb where Jesus had been located, and he was no longer there. Some women were told by angels that Jesus was still alive, but the women had not seen him for themselves. Others went to the tomb and saw for themselves that it was empty. Many had seen the empty tomb but had not seen Jesus. When we look to know someone where our experience and history tells us that this is where they were, where they belong, we are not within the economy of Eucharistic epistemology. Our knowing of Jesus must first be displaced from all other locations of knowing. Jesus is not known within the categories of our subjectivity nor within the crevices of our history. Before the appearance of the risen Jesus all of these categories and crevices are empty awaiting their own transformation as rooms prepared for us in the presence of the ascended Jesus.

Jesus ceases asking questions; he begins to speak for himself; he begins to arrive as himself with these words: 'Oh, how foolish you are, and how slow of heart to believe all that the prophets have declared! Was it not necessary that the Messiah should suffer these things and then enter into his glory?' (vv. 25-26). When we are gathered into the Eucharist, into the economy of knowing Jesus, there is a recognition that we may have known the basics of the faith, we are able to tell the story of Jesus, but we still do not know what this faith is, what this story really and truly means. Furthermore, while we have known a great deal about Christianity, or possibly in our telling 'spiritual' things, we really have not known what God has sent us to know. Properly speaking, when we enter the Eucharist we can be admonished for our prior ignorance! We have ignored the presence of Jesus by cultivating our own presence with or without him. We can become so enamoured with our own ecclesial, religious or spiritual conversations that our 'eyes are kept' from recognizing the presence of Jesus. Jesus arrives to us when we are open to his questions, to his admonishment, to when and how he speaks for himself as himself.

Perhaps, ironically, the way to Emmaus is not the way to knowledge of Jesus. 'As they came near the village to which they were going, he walked ahead as if he were going on. But they urged him strongly, saying, "Stay with us ... So he went in to stay with them" (vv. 28–29). While Jesus had begun to arrive to the disciples, they had not begun to arrive to him. They had not offered their presence to his presence. Even though the disciples saw that Jesus was walking on ahead of them, they did not follow him to see what he was going to see, to go wherever he was going. Instead, they asked Jesus to remain with them, where they were going, and in this way, Jesus would see whatever they would see. Jesus does not refuse their request; he stays with them. Ironically, Jesus does not suggest that if the disciples really cared about getting to know him better, or to continue their conversation, they must go with him. At this point on the journey, Jesus does not tell them no; he does not insist on his own way. By not insisting that he gets his own way, Jesus remains who he is, and if we are to know Jesus, we are to know him as who he is. Jesus has never insisted that he gets his own way; he has sought to do the will of his Father, to be driven and led by the Holy Spirit, even to the point of shedding blood in Gethsemane and on Calvary. Jesus did not insist on the resurrection; he was raised from the dead by the will of the Father and by the power of the Holy Spirit. And 'once for all' that this has happened to him, he remains in the presence of the Father by the Holy Spirit, and this presence arrives when he does. Jesus is always who he is as he is in the presence of the Father, and as the Holy Spirit realizes this presence. To know Jesus is to know him in his presence, in this presence from which he arrives with the offer to share this presence, to share with him how he knows himself as the one who arrives both from the dead and from the Father.

'When he was at the table with them, he took bread, blessed and broke it, and gave it to them. Then their eyes were opened, and they recognized him; and he vanished from their sight' (vv. 30-31). Jesus would be recognized by the disciples at the table he shared with them. This table was to be the place where their eyes would no longer be kept from recognizing him as who he is; their eyes *were opened* and let us note here the passive voice. Recognition of who Jesus is, knowing him as himself, is an event that happens to us. We do not recognize or know Jesus by insisting on getting our own way, by our epistemological efforts. Knowing Jesus is God-given, but God gives this knowledge by not ignoring what is familiar between God and us. It is just that God gives the familiar circumstances for the gift of a strange knowledge of the stranger who arrives in the Eucharist to be known, and to know us there and then, in this way. The actions of Jesus at the table - took, blessed, broke and gave - are familiar to the disciples. Many of his disciples, even crowds of people who came to hear him teach, had witnessed Jesus perform these actions. However, the familiarity of these actions does not reside within themselves – others had performed these same actions – but with the one who performs them. That is, we cannot separate the recognition of Jesus from these actions while not allowing Jesus to be reduced to them. The recognition of Jesus is realized by these actions and by his own agency. He bestows his own familiarity with the Father, the familiarity he shares with the Holy Spirit, on the disciples through the actions he has shared with them when he has given them what sustains life. Thus, there are actions, agency and purpose that are located at what happens at the table where Jesus presides. This is the economy of Eucharistic epistemology.

As for the nature of Eucharistic epistemology: 'Then they told what had happened on the road, and how he had been made known to them in the breaking of the bread' (v. 35). The inviting strangeness of knowing Jesus, even when this strangeness exists within our familiarity with Jesus, is when 'he vanished from their sight' (v. 31b). Knowing Jesus in the breaking of bread, within his actions (not ours) at the table, does not lead to his ongoing epistemological availability to us. These actions at the table, what we have called the economy of Eucharistic epistemology, does not establish a state of knowing, an object that is placed among us to know when we exercise whatever epistemological strategies at hand. Knowing Jesus as his arriving presence belongs within the actions of this knowing. What we are not saying is that Jesus is not known except within the Eucharist. What we are saying is that Jesus is not known as his *arriving presence*, as his arrival to give us his Body and Blood, to receive us into his life of communion. Jesus is present in other ways for other purposes, other places with other actions. However, the knowledge of Jesus that is the knowledge of God, the *koinonia* of knowing each other as each other is known by God and as members of the Body of Christ, is the knowledge abiding within the Body of Christ. Eucharistic epistemology is knowing the Eucharistic Jesus, who is the arriving presence of the Eucharistic God.[2]

Notes

1 For a similar reflection of Jerusalem as both origin and destiny of the vocation of theology, see my chapter 'What does Canterbury have to do with Jerusalem? The Vocation of Anglican Theology', in *The Vocation of Anglican Theology*, edited by Ralph McMichael (London: SCM Press, 2014).

2 I realize that I am making fairly grand theological claims in this last sentence, claims that provoke a strangeness of what I am saying, departing the customary familiarity of our theological habits and predilections. I will say more about these claims in the Epilogue to this volume, but my real endeavour to explore these claims for a Eucharistic Jesus and a Eucharistic God will be presented in the next volume, The Eucharistic God.

6

Language

Theology is the nexus between God and language in that order. While practically speaking there is no theology without language, it is possible to do theology without God. That is, in our use of language we can ignore God until we are ready to say something about God based on what we are talking about already. Our initial and governing reference for language might be ourselves, our experience or thinking, even our customary use of language. We can venture to talk about God, to address the existence of God, after we have already begun a conversation; now that we are talking this way, how we do we say something about God? This exercise of language for theological purposes inverts the order of our premise; theology becomes the nexus between our language and God. Our task becomes, how can we talk about God? God here is an object of language, something that seemingly does not have a say in how it is rendered linguistically. There is a presumed distance, whether characterized at this point by alienation or by compatibility, that we will bridge with our language. We might turn to prior theological language as a resource for our contemporary effort to say something about God, for example Scripture, creeds or confessions. Almost by definition, these resources for a contemporary idiom for theology will require 'translation' so that our language about God can be understood by these current speakers, writers and readers. Not only is there a bridge to cross between God and us, but now there is a bridge between past language about God and any viable contemporary language about God. Of course, there is an argument to be made for putting language prior to God in the operation of theology. We are the ones doing this theology, and we are keenly aware that language changes and develops along with our understandings of ourselves and of the world. Furthermore, there are a plethora of human languages all of which originate from particular and distinct places and times. How then can this history and plurality of language be brought to bear on the question of an eternal and unchanging God, a God who is not defined by, or confined to, any place, time or language?

There have been two basic approaches to answering this question. One approach is that language cannot be placed in a direct relationship to God. No matter how traditional, or how experiential, or how rational, our language is, God will always be beyond it and will elude its grasp. Metaphor becomes the currency of theological language, or for its more ambitious practitioners, it will be analogy. The distance between our language and God will be maintained even when we claim some theological propriety for this language, though the truth of it is held in abeyance if not totally excluded. The other approach to the question of our language for God is the direct one. The presumption of theology is that God has either given us the language to use for God, or God has guided us in the creation and development of such language. Theology is to be accountable to this language even though theology is always more than its repetition. These two approaches whereby we are either fashioning language for God, or we are accountable to the language that God provides, can be further elucidated with regard to movement. Language does not exist solely as language: it is employed by persons who wish to do something with it. Language is spoken or written so that others may hear or read what is being conveyed. Language exists between persons, either immediately as spoken or anticipated as written. That is, the use of language presumes a relationship of some sort. We can even entertain the possibility that the kind of relationship presumed will shape the kind of language that is used within it.

There are different kinds of idioms belonging to different kinds of relationships among persons. The operation of language between or among persons characterizes how persons relate to each other. Thus, when we entertain the nature of theology as the nexus between God and language, we are exploring foundational presumptions as to how God and humans relate to each other or are called to relate to each other. As such, we are delving into the movement of God to humanity and the movement of humanity to God. The attempt to fashion our theological language for ourselves is the movement of ourselves to God, while the attempt to be accountable to the language that God has provided represents the primacy of the movement of God to us. Do we address God with language that makes sense to us; or do we address God in the way that God has already addressed us? This is the abiding question of the relationship between God's revelation and our faith, the question of the nature and existence of theology itself.

At this point it has to be admitted that what is often considered theological language does not exist between God and ourselves, but rather exists among ourselves. This is the language whereby we talk with each other *about* God; God is the topic for our conversation or discussion. It also has to be admitted that what is regularly deemed theological language does not actually have God as the principal topic of its use. Instead, we can have discussions about the church, about our spiritual or religious selves, and we consider this theology. God can either be ignored or taken for granted in our theological language. Language can become a way to move away from God. Are we indeed left to our own theological linguistic devices? If we do want to take God seriously in the nature and existence of our theological language, how would this happen? What would this look like? Answering these questions would require us to break out of the hermeneutical circle of language about God, or language about ourselves that takes place before the horizon of God. We are required to consider our language *to* and *with*

God; the language that takes place within our relationship to God, God's relationship to us, the movement between God and ourselves that exists as communion.

The Word Was Made Flesh

Theology is the nexus between God and language in that order, but what is the nature and existence of this nexus? This is not a decision we have to make, nor is it a theory at hand that needs to be employed for the sake of some outside interest such as a presumed rationality or semiotics. Rather, theology exists because 'the Word became flesh and lived among us' (John 1.14a). God addresses humanity with God's Word, and this address creates a Worded-humanity. The proper theological movement for appropriate theological language, for language as theology, will always be from God's address in and with this Word. Theology ought not to presume that we have to make our way to God according to our best linguistic devices. As the Word becoming flesh, any repose into theological language that remains within the idiom of 'about' God will by definition remain inadequate. God did not issue the Word 'about' humanity; in the fullness of time God did not offer the best description of humanity that was currently available to God. Also, 'flesh was not made the Word'. Our theology as language is not a *creatio ex nihilo*. Theological language is not essentially self-expressive. While we are speakers of this language, we are not the primary referent of this speaking. All of our proper theological language is a response to this primal address of God in and as God's Word. Our language for God is a response to God's 'language' for us. Furthermore, as Worded-flesh, we participate in God's address to us when we address God; this is the movement of the Holy Spirit within us and towards us. This mutuality of address between God and us, this nexus between God and theology, is the gift and realization of the communion of language, or the speaking of language within the communion between God and the baptized. Before going any further with this argument about the true nature of theological language, we need to acknowledge two conditions of its development. The first is that there was theological language before 'the Word became flesh'. The second condition is that God does not speak in a human language. Before there was the New Testament there was the 'Old' Testament. And, much of this New Testament, especially the Gospels, draws upon the existing 'Scriptures' to speak of who this person is, who is God and what does it mean for us as consequence of the Word being made flesh. Christian theology was developed by appealing to this prior 'Word of God'. The task of developing this theology, of speaking and writing that is faithful to who and what Jesus is and represents, was one that could not rely on a particular language or idiom that God directly and immediately used. Hebrew, much less *Koine* Greek, was not the sole language of theology. Theology as language was not going to be either a repetition of what had already been said or written, nor was theology going to become an imitation of what had already been said or written. Theological language is generated from its origin in the Word made flesh, and theological language would be how the Body of Christ addresses God.[1]

The nexus between God and language is the mystery of the Word made flesh, of flesh being transformed by this Word. While flesh was not made the Word, and theology is not the pursuit of words that are suitable to the flesh, we further have to acknowledge that flesh is flesh. Flesh is the reality that must be taken into account in all its particularity. Flesh is not and cannot be rendered one more abstract concept for us to engage with our current speculative strategies. The 'postmodern' recognition that we must take into account history, culture, society and context when we are doing theology is surely correct. We do not have a flesh that is not temporal, historical, cultural and social. Flesh is a physical reality and not a metaphysical one. Flesh is really not a good fit for a universal and modern ideal of humanity or of human nature. This recognition of the particular reality of flesh, its concreteness, can and does tempt theology to collapse the Word into flesh. We would then have different Words for different flesh, different gospels, different gods, different saviours, for every human *différance*. This is a theology that reverses the order of God and language; theology is the nexus between language and God in that order. Can we be faithful to the nexus of God and language in that order, speaking and writing from and towards the mystery that the Word became flesh and still lives among us?

While flesh exists always within the particularities of actual human life, a life that is social, cultural, historical and linguistic, this does not mean that the task of theology is to find a place for the Word within those particularities as they exist on their own terms. To do so would ignore the theological reality of baptism, of the church, the proper theological claim that the Body of Christ has its own culture, history, society and language. Theology is not the mediation between God and the world; theology does not make the Word into flesh or flesh into the Word. Theology is the exploration of that mystery whereby the Word was and is made flesh when the Word sent by the Father arrives in flesh by the pouring out of the Holy Spirit. This flesh is not an abstraction nor is it the reality determined by the particularities that exist outside the Word's arrival in its midst. When God addresses humanity in God's Word – the arrival of Jesus in the flesh – what happens to our language for God? How does the Word become flesh transform theological language? Furthermore, how does the arriving Jesus who continues to arrive in our midst transform theological language, which is another way of asking how does the arriving Jesus in our midst transform theology itself?

Word as the Arriving Jesus

The task of theological language at this stage is to be faithful to the movement of the Word become flesh, thus to the arriving Jesus, within that social, historical, cultural and linguistic reality of and as the Body of Christ. However, lest we begin to construct this ecclesial location of our theological language for ourselves, yielding to the same temptations that beset the search for appropriate language from non-ecclesial locations of particularity, we need to attend to this flesh that has become Word, for this flesh itself bears the marks of particularity. The incarnation is not the sole principle of theological language because Jesus himself has and is his own particularity; he has a social and cultural existence, a history and an identity that is conveyed with its own language. The arrival of Jesus begins with the incarnation, but the person of Jesus has a life; he has a history that is constituted by his ministry, the crucifixion, the resurrection, the ascension and the expectation of his second coming. Thus, attending to the particularity of the flesh of Jesus, while upholding the initiative and primacy of the Word, means that our theological language is accountable in some sense to these prior and inherent particularities. As a transformative movement of Word into flesh, theological language will be transformed as the movement of not just talking about Jesus but talking as Jesus. Our theological language will not be so much the effort of saying something about the incarnation, life and ministry, crucifixion, resurrection, ascension and expected second coming of Jesus, as it will be the effort to convey this history, this theological reality, as it speaks. The history of Jesus becomes the transformative 'grammar' of theological language, of theology itself. Theology is not just talk about Jesus; it is the how, when, where and why of Jesus becoming our talk about God, ourselves and the world. We inhabit this grammar of the arriving Jesus when we are baptized; when we are immersed into the language of the Body of Christ.

Eucharist: Location of Language as Theology

Now we are prepared to claim that the task of theological language, the exercise of speaking faithfully about God, self and world, is first and fundamentally faithfully abiding within the Body of Christ.

Only by way of this abiding, this inhabiting of the life of the Body of Christ, its 'form of life',[2] do we learn proper theological language, the way to speak from and as the Body whenever we speak about any and everything. The language that is spoken within the fullness of the life of the Body of Christ, the language that serves as both the epiphany of the arrival of Jesus and our response to it, will be the language that forms us as faithful speakers of God, self and world, regardless of where and when such speaking takes place. So, how do we abide within the life of the Body of Christ, learn to speak its language, formed as speakers of the Word made flesh? Where and how does the grammar of the arriving Jesus take place, transforming our particular language into the particularity of theological language? The Eucharist is the where, when, how and why of theological language. The Eucharist is where true and faithful theological language takes place. Of course, not all theological language is confined to the Eucharist. We do speak theologically outside the Eucharist, but we should do so Eucharistically. We will explore the Eucharistic transformation of theological language in two stages. First, we will attend directly to the language that exists within the Eucharist. Secondly, we will then consider how theological language can be transformed by bringing it into an accountable relationship with Eucharistic language.

Language Within the Eucharist

Before directly exploring the theological reality and resonance of the language that exists within the Eucharist, we will first pose the question of the origin(s) of Eucharistic language. Then, we will consider whether we can trace any development of Eucharistic language, that is, does it have a genealogy? Lastly, in this initial treatment of Eucharistic language, we will reflect on the different types of language found within the Eucharist.

The origin of Eucharistic language is hidden from us. That is, we do not have any sort of *Urtext* for the Eucharistic liturgy. We do not have this *Urtext* because it has not yet been discovered in some desert cave; we do not have it because it does not exist.[3] Furthermore, the origin of Eucharistic language is not located within any textual tradition just as the origin of the Christian faith is not located within any particular text. Just as the origin of the Christian faith is the arrival of Jesus, realized by the Holy Spirit, the origin of the Eucharistic language lies within the sphere surrounding and expecting the arrival of Jesus, the place so charged by the Holy Spirit, that language begins to erupt in praise and thanksgiving. Jesus did not write any text, and therefore any faithful text is a sign and sacrament of his presence. The text serves the arrival of Jesus and not vice versa. This is why the textual tradition of the Christian faith was essentially an effort to convey the presence and significance of Jesus; texts are to speak of Jesus without becoming surrogates for his presence. The celebration of the Eucharist with its actions and language precedes any later development of a clearly identifiable Eucharistic text. Simply put, there is Eucharistic language before there are Eucharistic texts. The origin of Eucharistic language is the life of the Body of Christ gathered for the arrival of Jesus in its midst. The origin of Eucharistic language is the linguistic effort to speak thanksgiving to God for Jesus and to pray for the gift of his life of communion. While this language was not textually located, this language did emerge from a linguistic tradition. The Jewish oral tradition of liturgical prayer was the background of the Christian oral liturgical tradition. Christians adapted the Jewish traditional way of praying extemporaneously. There was praying the tradition before there was ever praying traditional texts. Jewish liturgical prayer had a normative structure, with certain themes for the liturgical occasion in which the leader would pray without following preassigned words. The fidelity of this prayer is located within the faithful performance of that which was known and recognized as the faith so enacted. The origin of the Eucharistic prayers of the church is this enactment of the faith then being celebrated and proclaimed. Eucharistic language emerges from the faithful intention of this is what we want to say to God, this is what we believe, and this is what we desire from God.

Given then this origin of Eucharistic language from within the faithful celebration of the Eucharist, a celebration that did not yet have a textual tradition, any consideration of a genealogy or development of this language will be fraught with insuperable scholarly difficulties. In fact, current scholarly appraisal of a possible genealogy of Eucharistic texts is deemed terribly misguided.[4] Previously, the discovery and identification of Eucharistic documents containing liturgical texts led to the attempt to draw developmental vectors from document to document, for example from the *Didache* to the *Apostolic Tradition* then to the *Apostolic Constitutions*, thus moving from the second century to the third and then to the fourth. A great deal of scholarly work has sought to make the connections between the documents and texts that we do have, seeking to identify possible developments from one Eucharistic text to the next. However, along the way we had forgotten what little we knew as well as taken for granted the authority and influence these texts may or may not have had, especially regarding the so-called *Apostolic Tradition* of Hippolytus. The theological point for our purposes is that these Eucharistic texts are still emerging from the liturgical life of faith. They are primarily witnesses of the Eucharistic faith rather than liturgical formularies to be followed. It is not until the fourth century that we get the pronounced existence of the texts of Eucharistic prayers and a more expansive account of Eucharistic liturgies. That is, it is only in the fourth century that we have the beginnings of a textual Eucharistic tradition or traditions. Of course, the fourth century is a dynamic and productive period of Christian faith and theology including the debates that were taking place with its councils and creeds. There is a mutual ferment between the creation of these great Eucharistic texts, the Eucharistic prayers and the exercise of theological development and clarity of expression. However, while we can speak of a corresponding dynamic between these Eucharistic texts and theological developments, they do not share the same idiom, the same way of speaking and writing the faith. The great Eucharistic prayers emerging in the fourth and fifth centuries do not share the same idiom of creeds and definitions. They also do not contradict each other. Just as we cannot draw clear trajectories between Eucharistic texts from century to century, and between texts in the same century, we cannot draw clear trajectories of influence between Eucharistic liturgies and theological expositions proper. We are not able to construct a hybrid genealogy among our various Eucharistic and theological texts of the fourth and fifth centuries.

The theological reality that accounts for this lack of genealogical trajectories, for the lack of a clear mutuality among the various texts emerging from the church, is the abiding and primary horizon of God. Eucharistic texts are ways of speaking to God regarding all the ways that God has spoken to us in the Son. Theological texts proper are ways to speak truthfully about how God has spoken to us in the Son. In other words, we do not have at this stage of theological and Eucharistic textual development the fixation on how the texts speak for us, or how these texts are ways to speak to each other *about* God, self and world. The accountable theological reality is doxological. We are either speaking directly to God, or we are speaking in such a way that God is glorified. God is not explained but explored. At this point, that is all we can say about any putative development of Eucharistic or theological language, and we cannot speak of any genealogy of Eucharistic texts.

Another relevant observation about the emergence and development of Eucharistic prayers and liturgical texts is that once these texts are produced and employed in the fourth and fifth centuries, and in the case of the Roman Canon the sixth century, they are used for several subsequent centuries.

Thus, we could say that there was no further development of Eucharistic texts until the sixteenth century. This lack of intentional development, and the absence of any genealogical stages of 'growth', does not mean that Eucharistic language now possesses a satisfactory precision of theological formulation. The essential doxological character of this language is still its governing dynamic. God is the horizon of this language, and God is still the God who receives our thanksgiving and praise. We are not yet theologically self-conscious or reform-minded regarding this language. That will come in the sixteenth century with the creation of new Eucharistic liturgies that express new Eucharistic theologies and pieties. Of course, there are a myriad of developments between the fourth and sixteenth centuries of how the Eucharist is enacted. Attending to Eucharistic language and texts does not tell the whole story of the development of various ways that the Eucharist comes to be celebrated. In fact, this variety of celebration serves to foster a good bit of the pressure for reform and renewal of Eucharist liturgies, especially the above-noted creation of self-conscious theological texts as Eucharistic texts. From a contemporary perspective, the creation of new and various Eucharistic texts and liturgies can be attributed to not only a theological self-consciousness, but a traditional one as well. That is, knowing the tradition of what lies behind Eucharistic liturgies led to their reform and renewal. Knowledge of the tradition of Eucharistic language directly shaped the creation of contemporary Eucharistic language and texts. The proper theological question regarding this 'renewal' of Eucharistic language is what does this have to do with God, or our relationship to God?

There are two directions from which to address this theological question regarding Eucharistic language; one direction is the Word, and the other direction is the flesh. The Word, or the Word of God, does not change; this Word is always the Word regardless of historical developments and linguistic mutations. This Word is spoken from an unchanging God; the horizon of

God for our theological language abides. However, this Word is spoken to someone, and this speaking takes place in some way: The Word is made flesh. Flesh does undergo historical change and is ensnared in linguistic mutations. Flesh speaks in a variety of idioms. The immutable Word is made the mutable flesh. The question becomes how does Eucharistic language embody this abiding address of God's Word as flesh speaking this Word faithfully back to God? We can be assisted in our reflection on this question by first acknowledging what types of language we find within the Eucharist. Basically, there are two types of language within the Eucharist: proclamation and prayer. Scripture is proclaimed both in reading it aloud and in its homiletical exposition. Eventually when the Nicene Creed is recited in the Eucharist, this text is proclaimed as a confession of a common faith. However, the preponderance of language within the Eucharist exists as prayer.

Eucharistic Language as Prayer

The Eucharist is an act of prayer, and its language either is prayer or is directed to prayer. Language within the Eucharist is more than the language of prayer; it is language as prayer. The consummation of this Eucharistic enactment of prayer is the Eucharistic prayer. Thus, if we wish to grapple with the nature of Eucharistic language, and how this language ought to shape our understanding and employment of theological language, then we need to reflect on language as prayer. Furthermore, we are to remember that all Eucharistic theological language is either prayer or is meant to become prayer. We do not do Eucharistic theology outside the bounds of that place that is the movement of prayer welling up from our depths by the Holy Spirit, finding a dwelling place in the Son, who takes this prayer as his own to the Father.

Prayer is the seeking of a relationship between the one who prays and God; prayer itself is a type of relationship. Prayer to God is the existence of language as incomplete, even impoverished. Turning to God in prayer is a turning away from our self-referential language, for even if we do 'talk about ourselves', we do so seeking the presence of God. To pray is to decentre ourselves, to leave self-sufficiency behind. Of course, many if not most people do not turn to prayer, understood here in the most basic way as turning to God, until they are undergoing some crisis, a threat to their self-sufficiency or autonomy. This prayer can become a request for God to restore what was the case: 'God, give me my life back.' True prayer is never this request; it is always directed towards God's gift of life, God's re-creation of our lives. Prayer is the language of transformation. The language of prayer recognizes a horizon beyond us, especially a horizon beyond our needs and desires for ourselves. Thus, the language of prayer cannot capture or define the 'answer' to our prayer. God's possible response to our prayer will not be on our own terms. The language of prayer always involves this instability between language and reality, reality as what God would realize among us. Prayer is the language that refers to God; it is turning our language to God as our response to God turning God's language towards us: 'The Word was made flesh.' That is, we speak to God because God has first spoken to us. Here we begin to move more deeply into the nature of prayer or the language of prayer. For the language of prayer, the language within the Eucharist, is not any language attempting to say anything. The language within the Eucharist is not a generic spiritual idiom; it is not a general prayer language. This inherent particularity of language as prayer, the Eucharistic language, is rooted in the particularity of God's language to us. God gives us in God's address to us, within us, the way to address God. We could claim at this point that the way to salvation, to God's will for us, is through this language as prayer, the language within the Eucharist. We exercise the Christian faith by how we talk to God. Our language to God embodies the salvific life. The Body of Christ talks this way and not otherwise.

We enter into God's gift of the life of communion, into the saving presence of God, through the language that is given to us as prayer, as offer, as the sacrifice of praise and thanksgiving. In order to probe more deeply into the nature of this language that leads us into God's gift of life arriving as God's Word among us, we do reflect directly on this 'Word was made flesh.' Our response to God in language participates in God's living address to us. Thus, we desire to be faithful in our language to God, faithful to God's way of speaking to us. Our reflection on God's address to us begins by reminding ourselves of what is being said when stating that 'the Word became flesh and lived among us'.

> He was in the world, and the world came into being through him; yet the world did not know him. He came to what was his own, and his own people did not accept him. But to all who received him, who believed in his name, he gave power to become children of God, who were born, not of blood or of the will of the flesh or of the will of man, but of God.
>
> And the Word became flesh and lived among us, and we have seen his glory, the glory of a father's only son, full of grace and truth. (John 1.10-14)

The Word was in the world and was still unknown and unaccepted. The Word came to what was his already, and yet the Word remained unknown and unaccepted. The movement of the Word into flesh, the arrival of this Word in our midst, does not immediately lead to recognition and acceptance of this Word. The Word can be ignored; we can be ignorant of this Word even though we are 'his own'. Theological language is not a natural language. Left to our own language, even though we might claim that grace perfects nature and does not destroy it, or that grace perfects language and does not destroy it, this language does not lead to knowledge and acceptance of this arriving Word. Perhaps we might be able to say we have the capacity to be aware of this Word, but that is not the same thing as its knowledge and acceptance. However, in this passage from the prologue to John, we are indeed speaking of a 'passage' from ignorance into knowledge. That is, we are not speaking of a revelation that will be layered over nature; we are not adding revealed language to natural language. Instead, we are speaking here of the transformation of speakers, and thus the transformation of their language. For 'all who received', 'believed in his name', were given the 'power to become children of God'. They were not born through any human or natural will but were 'born of the will of God'. Baptism is the passage from natural and cultural language into proper theological language. We die to what we can do with our language and are raised into what God can do with our language; the language that now exists in the Word of God, the linguistic life of the Body of Christ. We are baptized into Eucharistic language, the language that belongs within the Eucharist, the language that emerges from the gathered Body of Christ. God creates a people by the power of God, who have received the gift of the Holy Spirit in baptism, who are given the capacity to speak to God in the way that God arrives to speak to them. We are baptized into the language, the Eucharistic language, that is capable of recognizing and accepting the arrival of the Word in our midst.

'And the Word became flesh and lived among us.' This Word did not arrive to be there or here as an inert and mute object. This Word lived; this Word was embodied and living as the person of Jesus. Jesus spoke and acted; the arriving Jesus speaks and acts. The Word of God continues 'to be living and active' among us. The Word has lived among us; the Word lives. This living Word, this Jesus, has a history, a tradition, of speaking, of addressing those in whom he lives. Our language is transformed into the form of the language of this Jesus; we inhabit his linguistic life. We inhabit his prayer before the Father; the Spirit-led opening of his mouth. The language within the Eucharist is the inhabiting of the Christological transformation and pneumatological dynamic of the life of Jesus as now the life of the Body of Christ.

The language within the Eucharist is the language that belongs to the form of life that is the Body of Christ. Thus, we do not speak an alien or foreign language; we speak our language that has been transformed into the language of the Word. Our flesh, our language, has become Word-ed within the Body of Christ. This is why it is proper that the language of the Eucharist be 'understood by the people',[5] while still having the character of transformation. It is a false signification to turn our language into another language, either as a foreign language or as their language back then. We undergo transformation; we do not manufacture it. Eucharistic language has the potential for understanding, and understanding that will be donated. Eucharistic language is not understood as an act of translation, or an act of inhabiting another cultural or temporal age. As a form of life, as a way of life, Eucharistic language requires the potential to become our living language. That is, there is the potential that how we speak to the Father in the Son, and by the Holy Spirit, will form how we speak to each other within the Body of Christ as well as form how we address the world with this Word. Eucharistic language does not leave behind the flesh that speaks it, nor does it speak as this flesh.

'We have seen his glory.' The language within the Eucharist, the language of Word-ed flesh, is the language that leads to vision. The purpose of this language is not description, definition or analysis. This language is not even doctrinal in the strictest sense, language ordered towards teaching the faith. This language is the faith. This Eucharistic language never reaches the satisfactions that belong to language itself. When we speak this language, we are to know that we will never say enough; and yet, our unsatisfied language is not dissatisfied. We speak truthfully without ever fully speaking the truth. So, Eucharistic language forms those who can see the glory of God, and it is worth noting the question whether we could see this glory without this language. Seeing the glory of the Word, the glory of the Son, the glory of Jesus, is to see the glory of God's address to us, of how God appears to those who inhabit the language where and whereby God wills to speak to us, to know us in the way that the Father knows the Son. Seeing the glory of God as speakers of Eucharistic language is the arrival of the 'weight' of this language. Our transformed language receives its substance as vision.

'We have seen his glory, the glory of a father's only son, full of grace and truth.' While our language undergoes transformation such that it will not achieve the satisfactions that would 'naturally' belong to it; the speakers of this Eucharistic language are granted the vision of the fullness of what or who is seen: the fullness of grace and truth. There is an exclusive quality to this language, this vision, and to this fullness. It is the Word that has become flesh. While we can speak of all flesh – 'and all people shall see it together' (Isa. 40.5) – we are not speaking all words. There is only one Word, and there is only one-begotten Son. Yet, this exclusive character of Eucharistic language is what allows fullness to be beheld. We speak this language to have this vision of his glory, of this grace and of this truth, which is the fullness granted to our exclusive fidelity. This exclusiveness is not our drawing of boundaries around us so that only we are included. The exclusiveness of the Word is for the sake of the catholicity of flesh. Thus, this exclusiveness is really a direction, a linguistic directive, a language transformed by being directed towards the Father in the Son; the Holy Spirit is directing us towards the vision of the fullness of grace and truth that only we can see, exclusively, where we have been taken through this language. This is the fullness granted beyond our limits; God includes us into the fullness that belongs only to God. We behold this fullness only in this Son.

We have now arrived at the *telos* of the original and faithful transformation from ignorance and non-acceptance of the arrival of the Word to the recognition and acceptance of the arriving Jesus within the company of those who are speaking the Eucharistic language. The language within the Eucharist has the character of recognition and acceptance; it is directed towards the fullness of this recognition and acceptance. This language does not represent what is already there to talk about; it is not a language ordered towards expressing what has already been fully recognized and fully accepted. Fullness always lies beyond the speaking, when the speaking becomes seeing, when the seeing becomes the revealing of the one to whom we have spoken. We undergo a transformation of language, a transformation of sight, of knowing, and this transformation is faith itself. Eucharistic language is the Eucharistic faith.

When the baptized, the members of the Body of Christ, enter the Eucharist, they are given what they are to say and do; they are given language. This language precedes them; this language becomes theirs when, and only when, they inhabit the Eucharist. Since this language is given to them within the Eucharist as the Eucharist, the appropriate preparation for speaking this Eucharistic language, for receiving this gift of language and no other, is silence. When we enter the Eucharist, when we gather within its language, we are not continuing a conversation. We are not here for a discussion, for any linguistic effort to share our views, an occasion for arguing our viewpoint. The Eucharist is not a theological seminar, or any other venue to talk about what we believe, feel, want or think. We do not ask the question: What do I want or need to say here? This is why all such talk, all such linguistic concerns, all other uses of language, are left behind when we enter the Eucharistic place with its own language, for its own purposes.

The silence before the Eucharist, the practice and discipline of silence before the Eucharist begins, is participation in that silence that preceded *creatio ex nihilo*, and the silence of that tomb that first heard the announcement of the resurrection. The Eucharistic gift of language is received by, known as such by, those who enter first the silence of nothing and the silence of the dead. The silence of nothing is the silence that has previously not known silence. There is silence because literally there is nothing to say. This silence marks the beginning of our language. Then there is the silence of the dead whose voices have been muted by the absence of blood in their tongues. Their language died with them. There is the silence that arrives at the end of our lives, and there is the silence that precedes the arrival of the gift of new life with its new language. When we are baptized into the death and resurrection of Jesus, into a death like his, a resurrection like his, we are baptized into a silence like his. Pilate wishes to engage Jesus in a discussion about truth, about being a king or ruler. Pilate presents Jesus with an opportunity to speak in such a way so as to possibly 'save' himself. Maybe, Jesus will demonstrate a heretofore unheard rhetoric that will push back the angry mob, that will placate the religious elders, that might even assuage the political anxieties of the governing establishment. But he does not do any of this; he is opaque to such strategies. Before Pilate, before all political and religious authorities, and before the crowd whose ears itch for another word besides the one they once sought from him, Jesus is silent. This silence of Jesus leads him into another place, the place called Golgotha, when Jesus will know the silence of his Father: 'My God, my God, why have you forsaken me?' (Matt. 27.46b). Finally, Jesus dies, and his silence is final. In our silence before the Eucharist, when we inhabit the silence that the encounter with Eucharistic language demands, we are obedient to the invitation to inhabit the silence of Jesus before the Father and before the world. For it is this silence that can only be broken by the Word of God that creates from nothing, that overthrows all rulers, powers and principalities, and, finally, raises the dead by pouring the shed Blood of Jesus onto their tongues so that they can speak the language of praise and glory, the language of the Eucharist. For the first thing said by tongues lit by the fire of the Holy Spirit, tasting the Blood of Christ, is praise and thanksgiving.

While we are silent before the Eucharist, God is never silent. God the Father is always speaking the Son in the power of the

Holy Spirit, and it is this power that is given to the baptized, and the Spirit dwells within them to lead them into the language that happens in the presence of God. The Holy Spirit is moving within the Body of Christ, and this baptized flesh is learning to speak the Word that God is always speaking to them.

> For the creation waits with eager longing for the revealing of the children of God; for the creation was subjected to futility, not of its own will but by the will of the one who subjected it, in hope that the creation itself will be set free from its bondage to decay and will obtain the freedom of the glory of the children of God. We know that the whole creation has been groaning in labor pains until now; and not only the creation, but we ourselves, who have the first fruits of the Spirit, groan inwardly while we wait for adoption, the redemption of our bodies. For in hope we were saved. Now hope that is seen is not hope. For who hopes for what is seen? But if we hope for what we do not see, we wait for it with patience.
>
> Likewise the Spirit helps us in our weakness; for we do not know how to pray as we ought, but that very Spirit intercedes with sighs too deep for words. And God, who searches the heart, knows what is the mind of the Spirit, because the Spirit intercedes for the saints according to the will of God. (Rom. 8.19-27)

The Holy Spirit gathers us into the Body of Christ; the Holy Spirit realizes this gathering as the Body of Christ. The Holy Spirit takes our creaturely groaning and introduces us to the Word of God; the Holy Spirit gathers us out of the groaning of creation and into the sacrifice of praise and thanksgiving. The Holy Spirit animates us to speak the language within the Eucharist, the language of the Body of Christ.

Analogia Eucharistiae

The economy of the Eucharist is the economy of Eucharistic

language, and therefore, this theological language is not understood as either an *analogia entis* or as an *analogia fidei*. Rather, the language within the Eucharistic works as an *analogia eucharistiae*. When we enter the Eucharist, when we who are the Body of Christ speak, we are not engaging an analogical relationship between creation and Creator. The Holy Spirit draws us out of the depths of our metaphysical speculations into a language that belongs to the baptized; the passage from death to life, from creation into the new creation. Thus, we are not attempting to draw an analogy between our language outside the Eucharist and our language within the Eucharist. We are not relying on our use and understanding of language we would have if we were not baptized, if we were not members of the Body of Christ. Similarly, the *analogia eucharistiae* is not a way to bridge the 'infinite qualitative difference' between the creation and its Creator. Within the Eucharist we do not start from a place of alienation, we are not looking for a theological language that bridges the gap between the landscape of those banished from the Garden of Eden and heaven. The Eucharist is the place where and whereby creation and the Creator depart from the silence of their self-possessed identities and are identified with each other in the mutuality of the Body of Christ: the historical, ecclesial and sacramental Body of Christ. The *analogia eucharistiae* is not an analogical movement from creation to Creator, and it is not an analogical revelation from Creator to creation. For within the Eucharist we do not have a singular nor linear movement of language, we have a *perichoresis* of language flowing from the Father through the Son by the Holy Spirit, and the Holy Spirit moving us into the Son before the Father, all of this language exuding the *koinonia* that we share in, with and as the Body of Christ.

In and as the Eucharist, the Word is made flesh and lives among us as the Body of Christ. Language within the Eucharist is for the realization of the Word of God as the Body of Christ. This realization exists as the three modes of this Body: historical, ecclesial and sacramental. As the historical Body of Christ, we have the mutual identity between Eucharistic language and the words and actions of the historical Jesus. That is, we have within the Eucharist the direct witness to Jesus in the language of the four Gospels. Also, since the language of the Gospels does not stand alone – it is always presented in association with the Hebrew Scriptures – we include the Old Testament as the Word of God that belongs within the Body of Christ. Eucharistic language proper is language that witnesses to this speaking and acting Jesus, language that allows Jesus to speak for himself. The command to 'Do this in remembrance of me' is the command to witness to, to participate in, the theological language of Jesus, the way he spoke of and to the Father, the way that the Holy Spirit animated his life and speech. All Eucharistic language is rooted in this historical language of Jesus for we cannot literally speak as the Body of Christ without the direct speech of Jesus. In a pneumatological sense, the Eucharistically arriving Jesus will hear the echo of what he had to say within his gathered and speaking Body. The Word of God exists as the historical Body of Christ.

Eucharistic language is not confined to the language of Jesus, to the language that belongs within the historical Body of Christ. The Body of Christ is constituted by the Eucharistic gathering of its members; there is an ecclesial Body of Christ. While this ecclesial Body of Christ gathers to hear the language of the historical Body of Christ, this ecclesial Body also has language of its own; it speaks to God as an offering of language to the God who addresses it in the Son by the breath of the Holy Spirit. The Eucharistic language that belongs within the ecclesial Body of Christ exists in a variety of liturgies. Not every Eucharist has the same language. While this recognition of the variety and diversity of Eucharistic language should not be ignored, our focus now is the probity of a proposed *analogia eucharistiae*. Thus, we are exploring the dynamics of Eucharistic language, the movement that this language reflects of the movement of the members of the Body of Christ towards its gifted fulfilment as this Body, the way in which we move into the Body of Christ where we are encountered by the arriving Jesus who gives us his Body and Blood for our consummation. That is, our regard for a theological analogy between God and ourselves, for a language that we share with God so that we have *koinonia* with the God who seeks this *koinonia* with us, leads us to attend to the language of movement, the movement of language. Analogy within the Eucharist is not making a connection between two similar realities however much dissimilarity may characterize their relationship to each other. Rather, analogy within the Eucharist already exists among those who have been baptized into the analogy that is the paschal mystery, the passage from creation, and its inherent fulfilment in death, to the Creator who has sought to create us anew by the resurrection of Jesus. There is an analogy that exists between the historical Jesus and the risen Jesus, and the Holy Spirit realizes this analogy as the act and will of the Father. This is the passage from historical presence to historical absence, and then the move from this absence to the presence that arrives from the eternal presence God enjoys. The resurrection of Jesus is God's gift of God's own presence at the place of our passage from presence to absence, the absence we cannot erase or alter. Again, our silence announces that the Word of God arrives to make us into the Body and Blood of Christ, into the presence that only belongs to this Body. The language that leads from presence to absence, and then the language that moves from absence to the gift of presence, is the *analogia eucharistiae*.

Anamnesis

Language within the Eucharist, the *analogia eucharistiae*, is the movement of language as well as the language of movement that is enacted as anamnesis and as epiclesis. While the whole Eucharist is an act of anamnesis, whose language would not exist without the holding in memory of God's actions and speech on behalf of the world, as the acts and speech that create, choose and call a humanity to live for this God, it is within the Eucharistic prayer proper that we have the distilled concentration of remembering who God is by remembering what God has done and said so that we might be here in this place enacting this memory, that we might be celebrating the Eucharist. The act of remembering God, of remembering the God who speaks and acts this way, provides the content for our Eucharistic prayer; our Eucharistic praying is contingent upon God's prior relationship to us. The enactment of anamnesis is sacrificial because it is dependent upon God's movement towards humanity, God's chosen relationship to the world. That is, anamnesis of this God is the sacrifice of any choice we might make to move towards God, to choose a language appropriate to our self-understanding, to our cultural or historical context. In other words, our anamnesis of this God is our participation in how God remembers us. We remember God because this God has first remembered us. God's remembrance of us is as the people God has created for God, as the people chosen to be witnesses of this God, and primarily as a people who are remembered as the Body of Christ. To put this anamnesis of God in another way, because the Father always 'remembers' the Son,[6] the Father remembers all those who belong within the Son as the Body of Christ, all those whom the Holy Spirit has gathered into this remembering that exists between the Father and the Son. Our Eucharistic anamnesis of God, this language addressed to the Father, in the Son and by the Holy Spirit, is our *koinonia* in and with God's own anamnetic life. Our movement towards God participates in God's prior (anamnesis) and future (epiclesis) movement towards us who are gathered for the arrival of the Logos as sacramental gift. The Eucharistic prayer is a movement from absence to presence, but this absence is not total absence, and this presence is not total presence. That is, this prior absence is shadowed by presence, and this fulfilling and arriving presence is shadowed by absence. We enter into the Eucharistic remembrance of God because God has given us something and someone to remember; we remember a prior presence of God because we desire a renewed presence of God. We begin in a place of the absence of this arrival of Jesus, the arrival of the Logos. We participate in the absence of Jesus from the Father wrought by the Father's crucified silence, the absence of what can be said to abolish this silence. For what can be said to abolish this silence does not arrive from our language, from our ways of speaking about our lives, of speaking to each other. Rather, this Eucharistic silence, this absence of silence-breaking language, is why we enact anamnesis. Eucharistic anamnesis is when the Logos of God arrives from the dead. The Eucharist exists for the arrival of Jesus in our ecclesial midst, an arrival where and whereby Jesus shares his company with us. What do we say to this arriving Jesus? To the Jesus who arrives from the dead, we speak anamnesis. To the Jesus who arrives from the Father we speak epiclesis.

Epiclesis

While Eucharistic anamnesis is the sacrifice of our linguistic past, Eucharistic epiclesis is the sacrifice of our linguistic future. Anamnesis begins in absence and moves into the presence of God as remembered. However, this remembered presence is a renewal of God's absence. That is, our anamnesis brings us to a place where God's presence is now presented as an absence. However, this absence is not a void, a place vacated by what was once there; it is not looking into an empty tomb and remembering how Jesus once was there. That is the language that lives because of the dead, language that looks to the past for its justification. The present that searches for an analogy that once existed. This is not Eucharistic language; this is not the *analogia eucharistiae*. While there is anamnesis because there is the resurrection of the Logos, there is epiclesis because there is the ascension of the Logos. The Eucharist is not a linguistic monument to a dead present or presence. Rather, the Eucharist is the ascent of our language to where the Logos has ascended. The epiclesis, the invocation of the Holy Spirit to realize the presence of the Son among us, the Holy Spirit who gathers the ascended Jesus into our presence, is our invitation for the Word to become our flesh. The language accompanying the arrival of this Word is not the language of now, but of then, not the language of here, but of there. And yet, the epicletic arrival of Jesus is not a vacating of the past; the anamnetic past is not silenced forever: these words that we have offered to God can live. Our anamnesis of God lives because the Holy Spirit washes over it, our past undergoes a death like Jesus so that it can be raised like Jesus. Actually, within the Body of Christ, anamnesis is always shadowed by epiclesis, and epiclesis is always shadowed by anamnesis. In other words, the epiclesis is the invocation for God to move towards us by participating in the way we have moved towards God. God's gift of the future is God's gift of the past, which is always embodied as God's gift of the present.

The Eucharistic movement from absence to presence (anamnesis), and then from an anamnetic absence to an epicletic presence, the movement that will not allow us to reside within a stable present to which our language always refers, is the movement that is the *analogia eucharistiae*. There is an analogy whereby similarity exists between the anamnetic presence and the epicletic presence, and whereby this similarity is always shadowed by the anamnetic absence and the epicletic absence, by God's eternal dissimilarity. In the anamnesis we participate in the similarity God has established with us, a similarity that is known not only through creation but through redemptive history. Residing within this similarity through anamnesis (passing over from death to life), we are brought to a present that calls for God's dissimilarity to arrive in the Son who has, does and will assimilate all our pasts, presents and futures into the Logos that will be all within all human languages. Within the *analogia eucharistiae*, the language within the Eucharist, we are not seeking correspondence; we are seeking communion.

In and as the Eucharist, the Word of God is realized as the sacramental Body and Blood of Christ. The Word of God becomes the gift of the life of this Word, the *telos* of the enfleshed Logos. All the language within the Eucharist takes place in the sphere surrounding these words, this language: 'This is my Body: This is my Blood.' This language is both the centre of gravity shaping all our other theological language and the fulfilment of all such language. These are the words spoken when Jesus speaks for and as himself; these are his words. Jesus announces his own arrival, and by doing so, he proclaims to us the salvation now made real in our midst. In order to appreciate how these words are the proclamation and realization of salvation, which is the gift of his life of communion, let us reflect first on the occasion of their initial utterance. With these words, Jesus identifies himself with bread and wine, which are destined to be consumed by those who hear these words. Words are spoken, an identification takes place, and those who hear them are to receive what has been identified by and as the speaker. Jesus identifies himself with the bread and wine; he identifies himself with what is not who he is. Bread and wine are not associated with him until he says so; he makes this identification. The bread and wine cannot make this association; they do not speak or act. Jesus speaks and acts with these words. Jesus identifies himself with this bread and wine so that those who receive them when they hear his words might be identified with him. Jesus identifies himself with the hearers of his words; he identifies himself with those who take, eat and drink what he speaks as his Body and Blood.[7] While this is known as a Eucharistic act with Eucharistic words, it is the saving act with the saving words. With these words, Jesus not only identifies himself with what can now be received as the gift of life to his hearers, he is revealing to his hearers the reality of his own life. Jesus is who he is because the Father identifies with him in the power of the Holy Spirit: 'This is my Son, the Beloved, with whom I am well pleased' (Matt. 3.17; cf.Mark 1.11; Luke 3.22). Likewise, the resurrection of Jesus is the event when the Father identifies with him by saying to him: 'This is my Body: This is my Blood.' These words spoken by the

Father, spoken by the Son, words shared between them through the voice of the Holy Spirit, always creates life; life from nothing and life from the dead. As such, these words of Jesus spoken within the Eucharist are 'suspended' between Creator and creation, between Redeemer and the redeemed. However, these 'suspended words' are not inert; their meaning is not tethered to the moment when they are spoken, either the moment of the first speaking or to any other liturgical moment. These saving words of Jesus, the words he speaks as himself so that we might have *koinonia* with him, are always the proclamation of fulfilment. 'This is my Body: This is my Blood' are the last words Jesus will ever say to us and to the world.

The consummation of our life as and within the Body of Christ is the absolute identification of Jesus with us, an identification that we cannot create or realize with our speech and actions. This is why salvation always involves offering ourselves to Jesus for his identification. The complete identification of Jesus with us is our salvation. The consummation of our life within the Body of Christ is realized when Jesus says directly to us 'This is my Body: This is my Blood.' There is no longer the mediation of bread and wine; there is no longer the witness of Scripture. All previous theological words are consumed by these last words, which now become the first words of the language of heaven. Speaking these words of Jesus within the Eucharist is the sacramental echo of the language of heaven: 'Therefore we praise you, joining our voices with Angels and Archangels and with all the company of heaven, who for ever sing this hymn to proclaim the glory of your Name: Holy, holy, holy Lord, God of power and might, heaven and earth are full of your glory.'

Notes

1 There is the theological dilemma that the language we have is needed for our understanding of the faith but that this previous language is not fully adequate for this understanding. This is why though the early Christians had 'Scriptures' to draw upon, they produced writings that would become

canonical as well. A crisis of theological language occurred in the fourth century when the church sought to find language for their faith that Jesus was both human and divine, that Jesus is the Son of God. Their understanding of Jesus could not be rendered solely by the language they had already at hand. Fidelity required new language that did not replace the 'old' language. Rowan Williams writes about this moment of 'difficulty' for faith and theology brought about by the Arian controversy in his 'Postscript (Theological)' in *Arius: Heresy and Tradition*, revised edition (Grand Rapids, MI: Eerdmans Publishing, 2002), p. 236. For our purpose in this volume of exploring the Eucharistic nature of theology and of faith, Williams writes of how the church approached the passage from difficulty to confession: 'Hence the quest for an "ecclesiastical" reading of Scripture, one that accords with the confession, the prayer and aspiration of the community in those moments of its life when it sets itself most clearly in the presence and under the judgment of the incarnate Word – baptism and Eucharist, with their public enactment of what is involved in saying that Jesus is Lord or God' (p. 239).

2 This is an intentional reference to the work of Ludwig Wittgenstein, which, even though I am not directly engaging it, I do think has illuminative possibilities for the argument of this chapter. I am arguing for the inseparability of language and living, reality and actions, within the Eucharist. That is, theological language within the Eucharist is neither expressive nor representational. A standard work on the relationship between Wittgenstein and theology is Fergus Kerr, *Theology after Wittgenstein*, second edition (London: SPCK, 1997).

3 The origin of the Eucharist, and therefore the origin of Eucharistic language, was rehearsed in Chapter 1 above.

4 The work of Paul F. Bradshaw provides the background for this claim. See his *Eucharistic Origins* (Oxford: Oxford University Press, 2004) and *The Search for the Origins of Christian Worship: Sources and Methods for the Study of Early Liturgy* (Oxford: Oxford University Press, 1992).

5 The phrase is taken from the Anglican 'Articles of Religion' (1571, 1662) regarding the requirement for vernacular language in the 'public Prayer of the Church'. Of course, after Vatican II the Roman Catholic Church began rendering its liturgies in the vernacular of the various linguistic realms in which it exists. The more contemporary question is not the vernacular as such, but the inculturation of liturgy, the concern for language as culture, or the cultural existence of language.

6 That the command 'Do this is in remembrance of me' can be understood as 'Do this, that God may remember me' is the conclusion reached by Joachim Jeremias, *The Eucharistic Words of Jesus* (New York: Charles Scribner's Sons, 1966). The argument that leads Jeremias to this conclusion begins on p. 237 and is succinctly stated thus: 'Consequently the command of repetition may be understood as: "This do, that God may remember me": *God remembers the Messiah in that he causes the kingdom to break in by the parousia*' (p. 252; his

italics). While I do not think that Jeremias's view ought to replace all other views that 'Do this in remembrance of me' is a command that Christians remember Jesus, I do entertain the notion that the Father's remembering of Jesus is a dynamic of the theological and soteriological economy of the Eucharist.

7 Again, I am not entering into the debate about the nature of the real presence of Jesus in the Eucharist beyond the proclamation and reality of this presence into the sphere how we can understand this presence or not. For my account of this debate, refer to the chapter 'Presence' in *Eucharist: A Guide for the Perplexed* (London: T&T Clark, 2010).

7

Truth

What is truth? This is a question that has been posed either directly or indirectly since we began to ask such questions. As an abiding question of human asking, it has received a variety of answers, many of which would be in conflict with each other if they were compared within the same conceptual framework. Of course, that is the inherent problematic of asking about truth; it is a question that is subject to the shifting tides of intellectual pursuits, to the vagaries of how we as humans have lived in the far-flung regions of culture, history and education. We could even categorize all these historical epochs, cultural contexts and pedagogical endeavours by attending to how each of them treated the question of truth: What was truth for them, for then, and how did they arrive at this claim or conclusion? In this way, we have already encroached upon the neuralgic questions orbiting the question of truth. That is, can truth, which has a universal and absolute reality, be really identified within a plurality, a diversity, of how and why we seek identification of ourselves, our world or, perhaps, even our God? An acute awareness of the reality of the one asking the question of truth begins to take over the question itself so that truth accommodates the prior identification of the questioner. Truth is viewed in terms of the purpose (the power?) of the one who either seeks it, or who pursues the consequences of its existence to one's advantage. Such a recognition of how the proclamation or the pursuit of truth can become hopelessly fragmented by the multiplicity of people and places where this happens, or how the claim to truth can be a way for the powerful and privileged to dominant others, has even led to the abandonment of the question itself. Truth as that which is beyond all possible questioners, as that which exists beyond the diversity of our existences, no longer exists. In a sense, our history of asking the question of truth has gone from Pilate asking Jesus what truth is to the crucifixion of Jesus, to the crucifixion of truth. Is there a resurrection of truth? Notice how we have shifted from asking whether there is truth to asking whether there can be a resurrection of truth: Can truth live again; can it happen? Truth is not then something that is there for us to think about, something that we hope to reach or attain as we climb the ladder of speculation or contemplation. Truth is not something that we can question. Rather, asking about a possible resurrection of truth provides a twofold direction for the future existence of truth among us. First, posing the question of the resurrection of truth permits us to face the prior crucifixion of truth. There once was the claim for truth, and in so many ways this claim for truth is dead among us because it has been crucified by so many rulers, philosophers, intellectuals and even theologians (who might have thrown some dice to claim the cloak of truth for themselves). Also, not only has truth been crucified, but people have been crucified in the name of truth. The true people have sought to impose their truth by rendering others as false. Asking about the resurrection of truth is to remember that truth also has a history of death. Secondly, posing the question of the resurrection of truth is now to speak of the truth as an event, an event that breaks into the way things are, the way things used to be. The question of truth becomes a question that we no longer ask. Rather, the resurrection of the truth places us in question: Who are we in the presence of this truth? The truth has arrived among us, and within the presence of this resurrected truth what are the possibilities for life? We are directed by this arriving truth away from the singular focus on what has been reality towards what now can be realized among us.

Our accounting of the history of truth, at least in this truncated fashion, started with how truth has moved from being taken for granted within philosophy to its exodus from philosophy, and in so doing, we have introduced a blatant theological dynamic by speaking of the death and resurrection of truth. This is a direct signal that we intend to treat the concept or the reality of truth as a saturated theological one. That is, we will not muster whatever philosophical remnants remain of truth and then construct a theory of truth that can be useful to us as we proceed towards saying something theological. Rather, we will take the philosophical, even scientific, 'death of truth' as our point of departure for seeking the place of the arrival of truth, the truth that is no longer wrapped in the rags of a corpse. As the resurrection of truth, the arrival of this truth will seem at first to be unrecognizable to eyes accustomed to locating it within the familiar, within what is already here in the way that it is here. There is not a ready at hand existential place for this arriving truth; it will have to make a home for itself among us, if the truth will live among us, setting us free from the bondage of the familiar, from the prisons we have made for ourselves. The question of truth is the question of God.

The Arrival of Truth

As the question of God, we will seek the truth as something God grants, as a reality provided by God both as something that has been created and as a historical witness. Also, we will seek God's granting of truth as the 'new creation', that which arrives among us with the offer of life. Truth is something that is, and it is something that will be. Furthermore, the 'will be' has a priority of consideration over the 'that is', because any truthful relationship with God always 'will be'. God is more than, other than, who we are and remains so. If we are to abandon our philosophical, existential and at times putative theological ladders to heaven that we climb under our own power and will, and instead, behold where the angels are ascending and descending from heaven, we can be led by the one who leads to all truth, to the place that we now recognize as the gate of heaven, as the place where the truth of God arrives to gather us into this truth. The theological question of truth is not animated by the question of how we make our way to God, but rather, how is God making God's way to us? The priority of movement from God to us instead of us to God ought to become an abiding remembrance that is the 'foundation' on which we proceed to explore God's truth for us. However, this 'foundation' is not a place on which we can now build our theological house; it is a place to invoke the arrival of truth, who will become our place within God.[1]

What is truth? The answer to this question resides within the Eucharist. The Eucharist is the place where and whereby truth arrives as the person of Jesus. The foundation of his arrival is Eucharistic anamnesis, and the condition for his arrival is Eucharistic epiclesis. As the arrival of Jesus, truth arrives both from the dead (the death of truth) and from the Father (the resurrection of the truth). Truth arrives through anamnesis, remembering that there is this God, and truth arrives through epiclesis, calling upon this remembered God to arrive, to realize God's presence in this place. Asking the question of truth is asking the question of theology; it is asking about the nature and purposes of God. The answer to these two questions of truth and theology is the same: the arriving Jesus sent by the Father and realized by the Holy Spirit. Thus, speaking of the resurrection of truth is speaking of the resurrection of theology, or theology as resurrection. The resurrection of Jesus is his arrival to where he once lived before death and his arrival to all those who face death in his presence. He arrives with the offer of his life; he arrives to take us to where he is. The offer of his life is the offer of his truth, and we receive this offer in the way in which it is offered: 'I am the way, and the truth, and the life' (John 14.6). There is an abiding reciprocity, a *perichoresis*, among life, truth and way. Theology will be the exploration of truth in the presence of its arrival in the way in which it arrives. Theology is the passage from death to life; theology must undergo crucifixion so it can become resurrection. That is, all prior places of theology are to be so many cleansed temples;

the demons of self-reference, self-regard and all forms of will to power are to be driven out to make room for the arrival of truth. We cannot receive the resurrection of truth unless we undergo the death of our own truth. So, in order to prepare ourselves to enter into the Eucharist, the place of the resurrection of truth, where Jesus arrives as his truth, his life and his way, let us do some cleansing of the theological temple.

Cleansing the Temple of Truth

The customary temptation residing within our temple of theology is to identify our truth with the truth of God. That is, we do not intend to choose between ourselves and God. We do not consciously reject the presented truth of God in favour of our personal and preferred truth. We think we are still doing theology within our self-constructed temples decorated according to our philosophical, ecclesial and cultural tastes. We will seek then to dislodge the presence of truth from our theological temples where and whereby God is an honoured guest but not the owner. Once truth is dislodged from our temples, we can seek the truth in that place God has prepared for us, the place where truth arrives from the dead and from the Father. Consider then the crucial distinction between these two statements: the truth of my experience and my experience of the truth. In broader theological terms, we have here the contrast between the 'turn to the subject' and the 'turn to the object'.

Before we engage these statements separately, the first thing to observe is that each of them contains the concepts or realities of truth and experience. Thus, the question is not choosing between truth and experience, not opposing subject to object and vice versa. We are not seeking a truth that is so universal, so self-contained or absolute, that it always hovers above the human condition remaining untainted by the vulnerabilities of history. Likewise, we are not striving to give an account of this human existence, which can never be isolated from its history, so that we resign ourselves to either the absence of truth or to its abiding irrelevance. For us, both as humans and as members of the Body of Christ, truth and experience are bonded by the ineluctable desire to know and be our true selves and by striving to locate this true self within a transcendent frame of reference. However, this recognition of both an *a priori* and *a posteriori* relationship between truth and experience will not drive us down the road of religious experience or to some putative religiosity that we somehow assign a theological meaning. The point of contrasting between these two statements on the relationship between truth and experience is to avoid the way of religious experience, or comparative religious experience, so that we are directed singularly to the theological way of truth, the way of my experience of the truth. But, first let us briefly consider that other way, the way that characterizes much of modern theology and that hangs over much of postmodern theology.

The 'truth of my experience' is the proclamation of individual subjectivity. The proposal of truth arises from a prior assessment of a personal experience, indeed, an experience that I am able to claim as a possession, experience that belongs to me. It follows that this possessed experience, governed by the self-asserted pronoun, may or may not be shared with anyone else. If this experience is shared by anyone else, the possibility of this sharing will arise from the other selves who may or may not identify an experience as belonging to them as well. What is primary here is the identification of experience, and hence the possible assertion of its truth, as an act arising from a prior subjective identity. It is possible, and does exist in practice, that a group of subjects will self-identify with each other through the similarities of their physical selves or by the recognition of an undeniable commonality of culture and history. A group of subjects might assert a common truth arising from a common experience that each of them assigns to themselves individually. The 'our' of the group is constituted by the individual 'my' and not vice versa. The obvious thing to note at this point is that there can be and are many truths so asserted by groups and individuals who journey on the way of their own experiences. Truth is there because I or we have put it there. This 'there' is not a temple of truth, the place where we go to enter its presence; it is rather the marketplace where my truth competes with yours, or a place we declare a neutral zone lacking such competition in favour of the gods' respectful co-existence. Eschewing the marketplace of competition for the common ground of co-existence is a preferred way towards allowing some type of individual flourishing, the planting of a new garden for humans to live, move and have their respective individual beings. And this is its appeal for those weary of truths asserted through tyranny, terror and various forms of religious triangulation. Surely, any truth that is imposed on us is not worth the price, not worthy of the sacrifice of our individual and collective subjectivities?

However, the rejection of an exterior truth in favour of one's own asserted truth is not the only option for the truth of my experience. There can be the claim or assumption that there is truth outside the self. Yet, access to this exterior truth is only really available to those who explore the inner self, whether we are speaking of feeling or of thinking. In this way, while truth is maintained as having existence outside the reflective self, it is only through such reflection that we can know, or at least be aware of this truth. Admittedly, this pursuit of truth as an inward journey can be, and has been, accused of the projection of the self, a finite self desiring an infinite horizon of existence. The positive perspective here is that knowing oneself grants the possibility of knowing the truth. A companion to this perspective is the alignment of the potential of the self with the potential for truth. 'Personal growth' becomes the pursuit of truth, so that while there may indeed be truth outside the self, it is always known and constrained by this self. In the history of modern theology, and with its companion of comparative religions, this trajectory from the inner self to the outer truth has led to the designation of generic truths or timeless truths that have had various embodiments and forms of teaching and ritual.[2] The distinctiveness of truth lies with the receptive subject and not with any form or history that may belong to truth itself. There are many ways to this one truth; truth itself is not allowed to have its own way.

My experience of the truth would seem to be a statement arising from this generic truth economy, but this is not necessarily the case. It will be treated here as the acknowledgement that there is an exterior truth, and that this truth can be experienced. The existence of this exterior truth, while it is objective in that it exists over against the experiencing subject, is not absolutely objective in that it would not have any attributes of subjectivity. Thus, what we are not entertaining here is a strict propositional truth adhered to by an individual mind.[3] However, this statement grants a scope to truth that is self-existing and self-determinative; truth may have its own way of being subjective and objective. Truth can have its own way, and to experience this truth might involve yielding to its way. 'My experience' of this truth could then initially be one of alienation or objective difference. In order to recognize this truth, we might have to recognize that we do not have any positive self-asserted way to it. Furthermore, there might not be any neutral zone between ourselves and this truth; there is no place for us to acquaint ourselves with each other, to converse in the pursuit of common interests, to find common ground. In order to know this truth, we might have to go where it is known on its terms, to leave behind our places of self-projection, self-assurance and self-determination, and to enter the place where truth would meet us. The satisfactions of truth are not enjoyed without the sacrifices for truth. This means that to have my experience of the truth is not the endeavour to make my experience the basis for discovering the truth. Rather, I have to permit the truth to give me a distinctive experience. In this way, only the truth is the agent of my experience even though it is still my experience; I am the one experiencing this truth, but I do so because of my encounter with the truth. There is not here a triangulation whereby I take my experience of someone or something and then assign it to the truth. The dynamic proper to experiencing the truth as the truth is always redolent with repentance, humility, discovery, gratitude and celebration.

While we are speaking of the truth as something or someone that we can experience, we need to avoid the temptation of correlating a particular experience with the available existence of the truth. We wish to avoid assigning a particular experience to having encountered the truth. If a distinctive experience becomes a verification, a 'proof' that we have known or met the truth, then we have trespassed the sovereignty of the truth. There is always the temptation to grant a privileged place in our lives for the truth to dwell, thereby avoiding the sacrificial summons to know the truth and to be set free from such domestic places of human existence whether they be cultural, intellectual, historical or experiential.

Eucharist: The Place of Truth

The Eucharist is the primary and paradigmatic place of truth; it is the place where and whereby the truth that is God arrives to grant the true life, to share the true knowledge, and to gather the world into the eschatological celebration of all that is true, good and beautiful. Once again, now regarding the nature and existence of truth (if we are even allowed to make this distinction), the location of theology *within* the Eucharist has abiding consequences for the transformation of theology, for how we understand and live the Christian faith. As such, we are not permitted to dislocate theology from its Eucharistic centre, from its generative place. That is, we are not to isolate a piece of theology and take it somewhere else to dissect it, to analyse it literally to death. We are doing theology *within* the gathered Body of Christ and not *on* a cadaver displayed in our lecture halls or parish halls for our inspection and as an interesting topic for our discussions. Theology is living reality when it is always tethered to the nature and existence of God, when theology lives because God lives among us in the arriving Jesus and the sweeping Spirit. Whether our theological subject is epistemology, language or metaphysics (among many others), we have to remember that *within* the Eucharist, we are there always to receive more than to perceive, to be known more than to know, to commune more than construct, to hear more than to speak and to live into God more than to live from the world.

When theology does consider the world, which here refers to what exists outside the Eucharist,[4] it will not do so as if Jesus has not arrived. The world is a place where Jesus has arrived. This past tense of arrival resonates in all our spheres of location: history, culture and time. Put another way, theology is not first located in a non-Jesus world, a world where Jesus has not been, and then tries to find its way to Jesus from this world. We do not ask how these people know anything, how they understand themselves, what is meaningful for them, and especially not what is their understanding and appreciation of truth, and then strive to find our way to Jesus and/or God from there. Rather, theology is always both preparation for and encounter with the arrival of Jesus, who is the truth God bestows for us to know, the truth towards whom the Holy Spirit leads us ever since we were gathered up into its gale force at our baptism. Therefore, truth is never a mediating concept; it is not a concept that we cook up with some theology here, some philosophy there, while mixing it all together into whatever cultural or social bowl we have at hand. Truth is always derived from, known as, the arriving Jesus and the leading Spirit as they meet us, bring us to the true moment of our lives, when we receive the Body and Blood of Christ. Truth then is a *kairos*, an event, an act, an offering, a gift, both in participation and in consummation, a communion from which we exist, and into which we live.

We have asserted that theology does not operate in a world

or in a church where Jesus is first presumed absent, and then the theological task is to make our way to him according to the accustomed ways of our known location. That is, we do not begin with how we are present to ourselves and then figure out how Jesus might be present to us in this way. We have also paired this background consideration with a foreground perspective; where are we going from where we begin? This is the past, now what is the future? Rather, the argument is that theology begins within the Eucharist and abides there both as it lives from there, and as it turns towards the world. As such, theology is placed within the past that is God-created and towards the future that is God-given and oriented. However, if we really are going to make this argument beyond its assertion, and if we really are going to explore the nature and existence of truth within the Eucharist, we are required to do so the Eucharistic way. What is the nature and existence of truth that is the arrival of Jesus and the reception of his life within the Eucharistic dynamics of anamnesis and epiclesis? Once we have considered truth as Eucharistic anamnesis and as Eucharistic epiclesis, we can then turn our attention to the customary theories of truth as correspondence, coherence and consensus. This turn is a transformative one; these theories are reimagined within what will then be spoken of as the Eucharistic reality. Our consideration of truth within the Eucharist will conclude with a preliminary exposition of the Eucharistic Logos.

Truth is timeless, but we are not. Truth is itself without us, but we are not ourselves without truth. God is timeless, but we exist within time. God is God without us, but we are not who we are created and called to be without God. Jesus is God and human. Jesus is the truth of God and the truth of humanity. The sending of Jesus by God, and the arrival of Jesus among us, is the presence of truth to and for us. Our going to Jesus to receive who he is as what/whom God wills to give us is our moment of truth. This moment is constituted by a particular time, place and action. How does this moment happen? It does not happen without God and without us. So, we can ask, how does God create this moment, and do we 'create' this moment? How is this moment of truth the encounter between God and us such that the truth of God becomes the truth that God gives to us, the truth that sets us free from the world and for God, the truth that is the passage from death to life?

Anamnesis of Truth

The passage of God from God's timelessness to our temporal existence is a twofold movement: from the past to the present, and from the future to the present. We have previously spoken of this passage as Jesus arriving from the dead, and as Jesus arriving from the Father. The passage from the past to the present is Eucharistic anamnesis. The passage from the future to the present is Eucharistic epiclesis. The truth that God offers us in the arrival and reception of Jesus is the passage from anamnesis into epiclesis. What is truth as anamnesis? While God is timeless, God is not without history. While we certainly would uphold the immutability of God, the absoluteness of truth, we do not enter into the moment of truth by speculation on immutability and the absolute. God has already been moving towards us; God has already been entering time along with the historical ramifications and witness of this movement. Jesus arrives as the fulfilment of God's prior history with those whom God has chosen, with whom God has made covenants. Thus, we begin our movement into where God would have us receive God's arriving truth not by the awareness of our minds as such. Rather, we begin our journey to the moment of truth by the remembrance of God's prior movement towards us. We make our way into the moment of truth through Eucharistic anamnesis.

The first act towards receiving the truth is gathering into the presence of God as the Body of Christ. Within the Eucharist and as the Body of Christ, we do not know the truth without moving towards its arrival and without receiving the truth as the gift of life. We will not know the truth without remembering the history of truth, and this remembrance takes place in God's presence. We seek to receive the gift of truth by entering into God's presence through anamnesis. This anamnetic history is not an obstacle to truth, but rather its epiphany. Within and as the Eucharist, history is a gate to heaven and not a tomb of the past. Through anamnesis, through our remembrance of God's history among us, with us and for us, we gain an awareness of the direction and contours of God's truth. We do not begin our 'search for truth' by reflection and analysis on what is as it is. Instead, we deliberately fill our minds with the history of God's search for us. This filling of our minds, this seeking the truth in the mind of Christ, truly begins with our baptism, but it is normatively enacted as and within the Eucharist. As the Eucharist because this is how the members of the Body of Christ, as the Body of Christ, give thanks for what God has done for them and, in this way, give thanks for who God truly is. We do not know who God is without God's history towards and for us. We do not know the truth of God without remembering this history. The Eucharist as a whole is an act of anamnetic thanksgiving, of grateful anamnesis. However, we do move within the Eucharist through the narrative of this history in Scripture towards the distinctive act of anamnesis in the Eucharistic prayer. By this remembrance of God, for the purpose of entering into the moment of truth, we are reminded of who God is, what God wills for us and what truth might really be. The moment of truth that is the reception of the Body and Blood of Christ, the gift of life that is God's life of and as communion, is already a moment within a history; it is a moment created by the forging together of God's past with us and God's future for us. This moment is first composed of our journey there through and from God's way from the past to this present. This is not a past that we have created or enacted; it is a past we gratefully remember as itself a prior gift from God. Eucharistic anamnesis inaugurates the arrival of the truth that frees us from all our other ways of claiming or seeking the truth that would speak our truth, other ways of being who we are. Within the Eucharist, the opposite of truth is not falsehood but death. Having journeyed through God's history with and for us, having remembered what truth really is through this passage from past to present, we are free for the arrival of God's future for us.

Epiclesis of Truth

While Eucharistic anamnesis brings us to the moment of truth, giving form to its potential realization, Eucharistic epiclesis is the enactment of desire to know the truth of God and of ourselves in Christ, to receive the abundant life realized by 'the Lord and giver of life', the one who leads us into all truth. The truth of the Christian faith is not a stable given but is always a renewing gift. The remembrance of God's history with and for us, the being in the presence of God through this memorial relationship to that which has preceded this present moment, should not lull us into a satisfaction that we have all we need now, or especially, that what we do have is available to us for our own interests. Our faithful regard for the past should not bring us to the questions of what we are going to do with this knowledge or awareness, what we are to make of this history or how we are going to navigate the conditions of the contemporary that seemingly demands our attention. That is, how can this remembered past help us to live now? There is the temptation to leave God behind us as we move into *our* present. This temptation is similar to the temptation to consider God so far ahead of us that we strive to figure out how we get to God. How do we make sure that we 'run with perseverance the race that set is before us, looking to Jesus the pioneer and perfecter of our faith' (Heb. 12.1b-2a), crossing the finish line of salvation? Neither the God left behind in the past nor the God of the remote future is absent from the Eucharist. Thus, the truth of Christian faith is not left behind in the past, nor is it waiting for us in a nebulous future. Since we can say that the anamnesis of the past with God is not enough, not *satis-factum*, we say as well that the truth of the Christian faith, the truth that is God, is never a 'foundation' for the present apprehension or achievement of the truth. The truth is not a given that we take for granted; the truth is a gift that we must desire. If we really want to know the truth of God and the truth of who we are in Christ, we will have to ask for it. Anamnesis of the truth gives us what we desire to be given. We remember that truth is not a transcendental and atemporal philosophical concept or theological reality. Truth is the person of Jesus Christ, whom we remember and as whom we are given: the truth sent by the Father and realized, given, by the Holy Spirit. While we have remembered this Jesus, the presence of Jesus in this world is given, Jesus does not arrive where we belong already. Jesus does not show up to meet our religious or spiritual needs. Anamnesis frees us from such a religious and spiritual agenda. To ask for Jesus to arrive is the desire to be with him where he belongs: ' If I go and prepare a place for you, I will come again and will take you to myself so that where I am, there you may be also' (John 14.3). In this way, truth is never domesticated; it is always invoked. When we invoke the Holy Spirit to realize the presence of Jesus among us so that we might receive him, receive his life of communion, we will receive what we are given and not what or for whom we planned. For we remember that Jesus was and was not the Messiah that the people of Israel had expected. While remembered, Jesus remains the epicletic gift of the Father by the Holy Spirit. Knowing the truth of God is to know the arriving of this truth, the truth that frees us from our self-imposed and inherited boundaries of mind, spirit and body. The truth that is the arriving Jesus frees us for our arrival into the mind of Christ, into full membership of the Body of Christ and into the truth shared by the company of heaven.

Body of Christ: Location of Truth

The anamnetic movement towards the arrival of truth and the epicletic invitation for this arrival have thus far been referred to as the moment of truth. This concept of moment involves that which is not contained within our temporal existence and yet arrives within this existence. The moment of truth is the arrival of Jesus, the realization of his presence for us. We arrive in this moment to meet the arriving Jesus, who is the truth of this moment. We do not know this truth unless we have come to Jesus the way he comes to us: anamnesis and epiclesis. Here and now is the truth located within the Body of Christ. Thus, it is more appropriate, more adequate, to speak of the truth of God as embodied rather than embedded. Embedded truth is when it is located within reality, or within our minds. Truth is there, and our task is to go and find it, to develop the skills to uncover it from its prior hidden existence. Or, truth is in our minds as something we have either recognized or conceived as true, depending upon whether our minds are mirrors of reality or makers of reality. Embedded truth is something we must find our way towards and then unveil so it can be seen or known. Embedded truth maintains the dialectic between subject and object and creates a space for a critical distance between the truth and us.

Embodied truth erases this critical distance between subject and object. Within the Body of Christ there is no standing over against each other. The self-autonomy of truth is sacrificed for the sake of the common truth of the Body of Christ. However, each member of the Body embodies this common truth in their distinctive way. To put this in spatial terms, a member of the Body of Christ does not have to find their way to the truth, traversing a distance, critical or otherwise. Rather, each member of the Body of Christ is surrounded by the truth; they cannot separate their existence from the existence of truth. The task of knowing and speaking the truth becomes the formation of the members of the Body of Christ to know and speak the truth that they are and into which they are called. The Body of Christ abides by the arriving movement of Christ and the constituting movement of the Holy Spirit. The truth of God within and as the Eucharist is embodied and not embedded. There is the presence of truth and the absence of meaning. The presence of truth is comprehensive; it surrounds our subjectivity. As baptized into the Body of Christ, we are ontologically swimming in the truth. We do not step out of the baptismal waters, somehow leaving the gift of the Holy Spirit there, and then objectively ask ourselves what this means. The Eucharistic presence of truth requires an ascetic relationship to questions of meaning. We do not stand over against the Eucharist, outside the Body of Christ, and then ask our questions of meaning, which inevitably serve the places where we now stand, outside the temple of truth. Within the Eucharist there is no question of truth, only its presence, and since this presence is the person of Jesus sent by the Father and realized by the Holy Spirit, it is a presence that suffocates the questions we might otherwise ask if we were thinking (and breathing) on our own. If we speak of the hiddenness of truth from us, we place into question our own distance from the truth, rather than the distance of the truth from us. Likewise, this hiddenness is an attribute of presence and not the absence of presence. Hiddenness is a way of presence and not of absence. Meaning resides within the truth and not outside it.

While within the Eucharist as the gathered Body of Christ there is no critical distance between truth and us, there is still the abiding distinction between the truth and us. We who are members of the Body of Christ, gathered within the Eucharist, are not the truth of God. We have stressed that our relationship to the truth of God is embodied rather than embedded; we do not traverse an alien or a neutral ground, foundationalist or otherwise, to get to the truth. We live and move within the presence of truth; and yet, we cannot identify ourselves with the truth by assigning some common attributes to both the truth and us. That is, we do not attempt to circumvent the presence of the truth with and for us. The truth of God has already identified with us, and it is on the basis of this prior, and indeed future, identification that we might understand and live our relationship to this truth. It is within this Eucharistic and embodied sphere or place that we raise the question of a possible correspondence between the truth and ourselves. When raising this question of correspondence, we are aware of the pervasive appeal of the correspondence theory of truth, regarding both the tradition of its dominance and its recent postmodern demise. This theory of truth proposes a correspondence between an object and our perception of it; we understand the object as it truly and really is. This correspondence between our mind and the object has been formulated traditionally as an *adequatio rei et intellectus*, an adequation between a thing and our understanding of it. For this adequation to occur there must be a type of prior commonality between our minds and reality as such. Furthermore, this correspondence or adequation presumes a stability whereby once an adequate truth has been discerned it remains so: What was true is still true and will be true. This presumed ahistorical and atemporal stability has been jettisoned by our acute temporal and historical consciousness and sensitivities. We know and experience time and history as anything but stable. There can be no correspondence, no bridge, between reality and us that will stay built because both sides of this bridge are constantly being changed by the ever-flowing, and at times turbulent, river of time and history. However, our Eucharistic question of correspondence is not rooted in objective minds and stable realities.

Any correspondence between the truth and us within the Eucharist will be one of mutual encounter. The basis of this correspondence is not a presumed stability but an arriving presence. The correspondence between the arriving Jesus and the arriving members of the Body of Christ is the work of the Holy Spirit realizing this Body and leading its members. The Holy Spirit is the corresponding agent between the presence of truth and our presence. Being present here and now within this Eucharist creates the possibility of a correspondence, an adequation between the arriving Jesus and the members of the Body of Christ. Furthermore, within the stable economy of the

Eucharist, this correspondence exists as brought into being, for the sake of communion between Jesus and the members of his Body. Correspondence is a movement towards each other to know each other by a common life shared because it is given so. Correspondence is participation in the life of one given and of the one offered. The stability requisite for this adequation between truth and us is God's Eucharistic fidelity, which we have *koinonia* with when we faithfully enact the Eucharist. Within the Eucharist, the stability of truth is rendered as the fidelity of action. Truth is not located either in the understanding mind or in an objectified reality; actually, truth does not have a location, a stable place identified by the geography of human existence. The place where truth happens is not this kind of location. The place where truth happens is characterized by the correspondence between anamnesis and epiclesis, the adequation between the keeping memory of what God has done for us and the invocation for God to act again as the truth that is the arriving presence of Jesus and into which the Holy Spirit leads and realizes. Only God is adequate to the truth; only the truth is adequate to God, and we participate in this adequation by celebrating the Eucharist. This the truth of God within the Eucharist.

The correspondence theory of truth, the formulation of truth as *adequatio rei et intellectus*, is not developed from, nor accountable to, the celebration of the Eucharist. This correspondence, this adequation, was meant to operate within physical reality as a whole, as a universal human intellectual endeavour. It is a philosophical approach to the nature and existence of truth to which has been added a theological warrant. While we have been reflecting on the nature and existence of the truth of God within the Eucharist, can we, or should we, raise the question of the nature and existence of the truth of God outside the Eucharist? We can and should raise this question of God's truth outside the Eucharist because the Eucharist is celebrated 'for the life of the world'. The Eucharist is not an escape from the world or reality, but the manner and place where and whereby the world is offered back to the God who created it. The truth of the world is located in the presence of God. Before attempting an answer to the question of God's truth outside the Eucharist and in the world, we would do well to set some parameters to this possible answer. Since truth is derived from God – God is the truth, not the truth is God – we cannot allow one truth for the Eucharist and another truth for the world (again, we are considering the nature and existence of truth and not necessarily our knowledge of this truth). God is God whether within the Eucharist or in a relationship to the world. However, while the nature of truth is derived from the nature of God, the existence of the truth can vary. We could entertain the notion that the truth exists within the Eucharist differently, or at least distinctively, from the way it exists in the world. This distinction has already been drawn by the contrast in the previous sentence between existence as *within* and as *to*. Also, we have insisted that existence is not constrained by the contingencies of a particular place or time; the existence of the truth is the presence of truth. So, if there is to be a difference in the truth of God within the Eucharist and to the world, it will be a difference of presence, the difference of being present within and present to. And yet, God cannot have an existence that betrays God's nature; God's existence will be true to God's nature. Thus, there will be a necessary correspondence between the truth of God within the Eucharist and to the world. Since, according to the argument of this book, the Eucharist is the primary and paradigmatic event of God's will for creation, for the world, any correspondence between the truth of God within the Eucharist and to the world will be Eucharistically conceived.[5] There is a Eucharistic horizon to the world's existence according the nature and will of God. The world is called to return to God through the Eucharist, and we as the Body of Christ are to enter into a Eucharistic relationship with the world. The adequation between God and us, between God and the world, and between us and the world, is the Eucharist. The presence of the truth of God to the world will be ordered towards the truth of God within the Eucharist. The Holy Spirit that 'groans within creation' is the same Holy Spirit that leads us into the truth that is the Son sent by the Father. There is a pneumatological correspondence between truth within the Eucharist and to the world. However, this is not a correspondence of mutual identification; it is the correspondence of a movement from origin to *telos*, from creation to the new creation, from the death of truth to the resurrection of the truth.

> For the creation waits with eager longing for the revealing of the children of God; for the creation was subjected to futility, not of its own will but by the will of the one who subjected it, in hope that the creation itself will be set free from its bondage to decay and will obtain the freedom of the glory of the children of God. We know that the whole creation has been groaning in labour pains until now; and not only the creation, but we ourselves, who have the first fruits of the Spirit, groan inwardly while we wait for adoption, the redemption of our bodies. (Rom. 8.19-23)

Creation or the world is in flux; it is unstable. However, the state of the world or creation is not inchoate. Rather, the world is ordered towards a reality that it does not yet have, and furthermore, the world can never have this reality. For this reality is not something that the world can develop from within itself if it is allowed to move freely in its own way. Fundamentally, the world is disordered from its true reality; the world cannot be true as the world. This is another way of saying that the world cannot be its true self without God. The world cannot become the reality of truth without God. The correspondence between God and the world is the potential for the truth of the world to abide or endure, for groaning to become rejoicing. The beginning of the truth for the world is the movement of the Holy Spirit. The brooding of the Spirit brings life out of nothing and from death: creation and the new creation. This pneumatological dynamic of creation, this movement into reality, or the realization of the truth, leads then not to a stable metaphysics of being that we either access or construct with stable minds. The possibility for thinking about the being of the world, or the world of beings, is rendered futile by an appreciation of the suffering, death and turmoil of creation and of the world as whole, the place where humanity lives and dies. There is no innocent metaphysics, no being without history and no creation that is not in labour waiting for the birth of the new creation. There is no world without the Eucharist.

The world has a Eucharistic horizon of truth; the Eucharist is where the one who is the truth arrives to give life for the world. The world is led or driven towards the Eucharistic arrival of Jesus by the movement of the Holy Spirit, which is the potential correspondence between God and the world. We have been relentless in considering the Eucharist as the primary and paradigmatic place of theology; the Eucharist is the place of the arrival of God's truth within the Eucharist as the church and for the world. Therefore, we now need to pose the question: How do we as members of the Body of Christ speak of the world within the Eucharist? Or, how does the world enter the economy of salvation, the realization of the truth that is life itself? The world is placed before the altar of God, transgressing the parameters of death for the boundaries of that 'pleasant land' prepared for it before its foundation, when we intercede on its behalf to Jesus our Great High Priest.[6] The world is brought to the brink of truth through intercessory prayer. The Holy Spirit moves over the world and within us, leading us into our prayer for the world, into the intercession of Jesus for us and for the world before the Father. Perhaps, with this Eucharistic horizon of truth in mind, we could entertain a metaphysics of intercessory prayer. We intercede to Jesus, we enter into his priestly intercession, because the world requires this prayer if it is to become its true self; if the world is to be brought from its creation into the new creation. The correspondence between creation and the new creation, the correspondence animated and realized by the Holy Spirit, is Jesus himself, the truth of God.

Since, then, we have a great high priest who has passed through the heavens, Jesus, the Son of God, let us hold fast to our confession. For we do not have a high priest who is unable to sympathize with our weaknesses, but we have one who in every respect has been tested as we are, yet without sin. Let us therefore approach the throne of grace with boldness, so that we may receive mercy and find grace to help in time of need. (Heb. 4.14-16)

The correspondence that Jesus is between God and the world is a correspondence constituted by being and history; Jesus is God and human, and he has a human history enacted by both divine and human agency. We exercise our Eucharistic agency when we pray for the world, when we intercede for a world suffering under the weight of its falsehood. However, this suffering, this instability of reality, is not an obstacle to truth but the way to it, the way we follow through intercessory prayer. The world arrives to the place of truth through intercession and not by speculation, from embedded graves of thought to embodied prayer before the gate of heaven. While the truth that awaits the world, the one who arrives with his gift of life, is a stranger to the world (he is resurrected), he is not an alien (he is incarnated). The resurrection of the truth will first appear strange to us, but passing through the perspective of intercessory prayer, we will come to see the scars of truth, recognizing the person who arrives from the dead and from the Father, the Alpha and the Omega, the beginning and the end of truth.

The Eucharistic Logos

Jesus is the correspondence between God and the world; Jesus is the truth of God. The arrival of this truth happens within and as the Eucharist. Thus, we understand the truth of God, this Jesus, from a Eucharistic perspective. From within the Eucharist, we perceive the Father as the sender of Jesus to us, we encounter this Jesus when the Holy Spirit realizes his presence among and for us. We know this Jesus as the giver of his life of communion, and in this way we know the truth of God and the truth of ourselves hidden within the Body of the Christ. And when we turn our gaze towards the world from this Eucharistic place of truth, we can recognize what is God's truth in the world and for the world. For the world to inhabit God's truth, for the world to be transformed into the kingdom of God, it must be 'eucharistized', as some of our early sources for the Eucharist spoke of what happens to be the bread and wine. One of the primary ways that Christian theology sought to proclaim Jesus as the Son of God, as the one who is the correspondence between God and the world, is by identifying him as the Logos. Jesus is the historical incarnation of the principle of harmony between Creator and creation; he is the rationale by which everything is connected to God. In Jesus, God spoke the truth to the world, the same world that had been created through this truth.

> In the beginning was the Word, and the Word was with God, and the Word was God. He was in the beginning with God. All things came into being through him, and without him not one thing came into being. What has come into being in him was life, and the life was light of all people.
> And the Word became flesh and lived among us, and we have seen his glory, the glory as of a father's only son, full of grace and truth. (John 1.1-4, 14)

We can now hear these words as a Eucharistic proclamation, introducing us into the mystery of the relationship between God and the world that takes place within the Eucharist, and as such, introduces us to the vision of the fulfilment of God's truth for the world, the dawning of the new creation. This Eucharistic proclamation of the Logos of God is not a 'first principle' of the universe, nor is it an attempt to uphold a rationality on which we can all agree. The Logos is not a principle, but a person with a history of death and resurrection as well as the one through whom creation came into being, and through him creation will be reconciled to its truth. The Logos of God, the truth of God, is the Alpha and the Omega of the world.

The Eucharistic nature and existence of the truth of God for the world inescapably involves the salvation of the world.[7] Truth is life, and we are saved from death by entering this life. Truth is the movement from death to life. Baptism is when we are placed within this life, and the Eucharist is the place where and how we live it. The Eucharistic movement from anamnesis to epiclesis is the movement from protology to eschatology. Here is another text that speaks of the mystery of the Eucharistic Logos:

> He is the image of the invisible God, the firstborn of all crea-tion; for in him all things in heaven and on earth were created, things visible and invisible, whether thrones or dominions or rulers or powers – all things have been created through him and for him. He himself is before all things, and in him all things hold together. He is the head of the body, the church; he is the beginning, the firstborn from the dead, so that he might come to have first place in everything. For in him all the fullness of God was pleased to dwell, and through him God was pleased to reconcile to himself all things, whether on earth or in heaven, by making peace through the blood of his cross. (Col. 1.15-20)

There is no correspondence of truth without reconciliation, no presence of truth without the truth of God's future for us. The Eucharist is the movement from the truth of the past through the truth of the present into the truth of the future. This movement takes places from the Father through the Son and by the Holy Spirit as well as from the Holy Spirit through the Son and towards the Father. Here are four theses regarding the truth of God:

- The truth of God is not a thought; it is a vision.
- The truth of God is not a self-contained idea; it is a relationship.

- The truth of God is not knowledge of an object; it is the presence of a person.
- The truth of God is not a representation of a reality; it is its embodiment.

Therefore, the Eucharistic existence and nature of the truth that is God cannot be rendered by any theory of truth, whether this theory is characterized by correspondence, coherence or consensus. Again, since we do not celebrate the Eucharist in our minds, arrange it so that it is meaningful for us or create it through conversation, any prior or exterior notions of correspondence, coherence or consensus will be left on the other side of the baptismal font, outside the Body of Christ. Within the Eucharist, we seek communion and not correspondence, anamnesis and not coherence, and epiclesis and not consensus.

However, it is not the case that we are unconcerned regarding correspondence, coherence and consensus. Rather, we do seek a correspondence between God's will for us and our understanding and living of that will. We do seek a coherence that exists within the faithful Body of Christ in that each member cannot 'truthfully' say to each other, 'I have no need of you.' We are to cohere in Christ; we are to inhabit the wholeness of God's own catholic truth. As such, we will seek the consensus among us that is this communion and coherence. God's truth re-creates the unity of the Body of Christ, because there really and truly is only one such Body.

Notes

1 A review of the postmodern problematic of 'foundationalism' and the question of truth can be found in Thomas A. Guarino, *Foundations of Systematic Theology* (London: T&T Clark, 2005), especially Chapter 3, 'Christian Doctrine and Truth: Contemporary Challenges'. Overall, this book provides an introduction to the 'state of the question' that is systematic theology.

2 Certainly, I reject the approach to doctrine or truth that Lindbeck characterizes as 'experiential-expressive' as well as any talk of 'mere symbol' whereby the symbol is an expression of our religious or spiritual contemporary state whether than a participatory mediation of God's life to and in us.

3 Hence, I also reject the 'cognitivist-propositional' approach to truth as reviewed by Lindbeck. Of course, he rejects this approach as well for his proposed 'cultural-linguistic' account of doctrine. I will leave aside the debate over whether Lindbeck treats Aquinas's view of truth appropriately, or even if Lindbeck holds any theory of truth that is not mired in any 'ad hoc' constraints.

4 We can also speak of the church as existing outside the Eucharist. The relationship between church and Eucharist will be the theme of the third volume of this Eucharistic systematic theology, while the fifth volume will explore the relationship between the Eucharist and the world.

5 The Eucharist as primary and paradigmatic for theology and faith is explicated further below as the appendix, 'The Holy Eucharist: The Paradigm That Does Not Shift'.

6 While we have spoken of 'cleansing the temple' in order to speak appropriately of the Eucharist as the place of truth, the location of the arrival of Jesus, we have not sought to draw upon the tradition of the temple as a place of God's presence, nor as a possible source for the development of early Christology. Such though is the work of Margaret Barker, *The Great High Priest: The Temple Roots of Christian Liturgy* (London: T&T Clark, 2003).

7 For an exposition of the nature of truth as the communion that is the Triune God, who shares this communion with us as the church and for our salvation, we do well to read repeatedly the chapter 'Truth and Communion' by John D. Zizioulas in *Being As Communion: Studies in Personhood and the Church* (Crestwood, NY: St Vladimir's Seminary Press, 1995).

PART 4

Faith

8

The Eucharistic Faith

What then is the Eucharistic faith? A related question would be, why wait to address this subject at the end of a volume so titled? The answer to both questions lies somewhere in the recesses of the symbiotic relationship between theology and faith. If we take for now the traditional definition of theology bequeathed to us by Anselm – faith seeking understanding – then we can begin to explore the relationship between faith and the operation of theology as seeking understanding of this faith. One pervasive theological approach to understanding the faith is to first propose how this understanding will proceed; or, how is understanding the faith possible for us here and now in the way that we understand ourselves, reality or the world? This contemporary quest for understanding faith can even transform faith itself: How can faith be possible here and now? That is, theology can start within the conceptual or intellectual arena where understanding is thought to take place, and then, having got its cognitive or epistemological bearings, can venture to approach the study of faith. One can note that faith is presumed to be over there, while theologians are here, and theology bridges the critical distance between understanding and faith. Such a mentality or assumption about theology can and does lead to the ludicrous claim that one can be a theologian without faith. Or, if the theologian has faith, they are to set it aside in order to do their theology. The presumption is that theology is an objective exercise and that faith is the object, or that faith is personal to the extent that it cannot be allowed to interfere with the public profile and achievements of theology proper. Of course, the objective study of theology can be completely rejected because faith encapsulates its own understanding. Whatever trajectory might be in play between faith and theology as alluded to thus far, the direction so pursued is inherently individualistic. The individual theologian studies faith; or, the individual has a personal faith that is sheltered from critical regard. Either faith is located outside the individual for the sake of an objective stance, or faith is so deeply located within the individual that it loses any accountable or objective recognition. Is the individual the primary subjective agent of theology? Is faith an objective of individual striving?

We could answer our initial questions by asserting that before one directly addresses faith with the theological task, one must lay the groundwork for this task. Here we are speaking of what is called the *praeambula fidei*, the preambles of faith, which is the province of philosophy an!d so-called natural theology. The task is to say whatever one can about faith, its possibility and sphere of influence, without recourse to revelation. If this has been our theological trajectory, then it makes sense to put the direct question of faith at the end, after we have presented our understanding of theology. Once we understand theology, we are now able to understand faith. Such an explication of the *praeambula fidei* implies that faith is essentially a cognitive act, an act ordered towards understanding. Theology and faith are distinguished not so much by the operation of the mind but by what the mind is engaging. We can engage reality, and then we can engage revelation. The opposing approach to this 'fundamental theology' is the rejection of any *praeambula fidei* or natural theology as inevitably ordered towards the distortion of faith. Instead, the primary claim is that revelation is reality for theology; faith is given to us to understand and is not something that arises from ourselves as we seek to understand God. Thus, in this view, theology does well to stick closely to the faith, and it is a prior definitive faith, so that theology itself will remain faithful. Theology is an exposition of the faith to believers and not a survey of possible common ground between believers and non-believers. Or, to put this in the customary categories, theology is always dogmatic and never apologetic.

Are these two options regarding the relationship between faith and theology the only ones before us? Are we to make a 'foundational' decision whether we will do theology outside categorical or special revelation, perhaps relying on the possibility of general revelation, and then engage revelation directly; or, are we to pursue theology as an unmediated exposition of the substance of faith? It would seem that, since this chapter on the Eucharistic faith is placed at the end of this volume, we have chosen to present our theology, with all its presuppositions and methods, and then turn towards saying something about faith in the style of the theology we have so presented. However, this is precisely what we have not done, and neither have we collapsed theology into faith. A fundamental principle and practice of everything that has been argued and expounded thus far is that we are not trying to establish, or look for, a linear correspondence between a subject and an object, a subject and a subject, a concept and a reality, and this includes any linear correspondence between theology and faith. This is why we have insisted that theology always results in transformation and not translation; it has a corporate existence and not one constructed by correspondence. We are not speaking of a correspondence between our minds and reality, between our words and God's Word, and not between the world's questions and the answers that *our* faith might provide. Furthermore, we have shunned along the way any mapping of a theological territory that relies on the apodictic terms of outer and inner, exterior and interior, expression and experience, or beings and Being. Rather, these terms have undergone a transformation, the transformation of theology that takes place within and as the Eucharist. The Eucharist is an embodied event where and whereby relationships between subjects, or between objects or concepts, are not constructed through strategies of correspondence. All relationships within the Eucharist – and the Eucharist is the relational event *par excellence* – are constituted and realized by participation among each and every one who inhabits this place. The life of communion given and shared within the Eucharist always transforms any and all correspondence between here and there, then and now, and even between God and the world. Hence, within the Eucharist and as the Eucharist we discover the relationship within communion that exists between theology and faith. Nonetheless, there is a distinction between theology and faith, just as there are distinctions within communion. As communion though, these are distinctions without differences of place or purpose. Theology and faith are not separated from each other, somehow kept apart for their mutual benefit. Put another way, within communion, within the Eucharist, distinction does not rely on different spheres of operation or existence. Instead, distinction exists as a relationship that sets its own terms. There is a distinction because there is a participatory relationship already; we do not have to cross a bridge of distinction, which is really a difference rooted in separation, in order to get to the theological or faithful promised land. We inhabit the Eucharist and explore the theology and faith we encounter there because we are within the embodiment of theology and faith: the living Body of Christ.

Eucharist: Theology and Faith

What we are describing as the mutual relationship between, or should we now say *among*, theology and faith within the Eucharist serves as a prescription for theology and for faith. What brought us to this direct engagement with the Eucharistic faith has been not only an exploration but an argument. We have been seeking an understanding of faith that is what it is and what it should be. The nature of this understanding is not analytical or expository; it is imaginative. This volume, through the succession of each of its chapters, is a movement from the Eucharistic theological understanding of faith to the theological reality of the Eucharistic faith. This movement began with the location of the origin of theology within and as the Eucharist where and whereby Christian faith and life seeks to keep company with the risen and ascended Jesus. This origin of theology (Chapter 1) then becomes a generative place, generating theology from within the Eucharist, giving rise to the Eucharistic nature of theology (Chapter 2). Having introduced and outlined how the Eucharist is the proper location and sphere of theology, we then sought to understand this Eucharistic theology by reimagining the basic categories or sources of theology from within the Eucharist. We began this reimagining with the nature and purpose of tradition as a Eucharistic theological reality (Chapter 3). By addressing tradition before the other concepts or sources, we sought to deepen and describe what the Eucharist is, why the Eucharist, and how it serves as the theological place and dynamic. Scripture was taken up after tradition because Scripture is theologically located primarily within and not outside the Eucharist (Chapter 4). Scripture is indeed a source of theology, and it can and should be engaged theologically outside the Eucharist. However, any such engagement is accountable to the place and purpose of Scripture within the Eucharist if it is to share the place and purpose of all sources of theology, of the nature and existence of theology itself. While tradition and Scripture are sources of theology that serve to generate and shape the content of theology, theology is also undertaken and conveyed by working through some basic concepts that constitute 'understanding' (Chapters 5, 6 and 7). Three such concepts were reimagined from within the theological reality that is the Eucharist: knowledge, language and truth. In each of these chapters, and by addressing the subjects of origin, nature, tradition, Scripture, knowledge, language and truth, we were not doing theology so that eventually we could understand faith. Rather, we already were seeking to understand the Eucharistic faith in each of these ways. Each chapter can be viewed as an understanding of the Eucharistic faith through the mode inherent in them. We have already been engaged in understanding the Eucharistic faith, but now we are prepared to speak directly to the nature and existence of this faith.

Eucharist: The Christian Faith

Before we explicate the 'substance' of the Eucharistic faith, we need to state clearly what has been implied and assumed throughout this volume: the Eucharistic faith is the Christian faith and vice versa. While there certainly have been and are various understandings of the Christian faith that are non-Eucharistic, and while they may or may not participate in what is being described and prescribed as the Eucharistic faith, they do not have an equivalence with it. The Eucharistic faith is not proposed here as one version of the Christian faith. Rather, the Eucharistic faith is held to be the normative existence of the Christian faith, the fullness of this faith to which all Christians are called to share, embrace and live by their common risen and ascended Lord. Put another way, the Eucharist is the essence of the Christian faith. While this is a direct assertion, it does not lead necessarily – nor should it – to an oversimplification of the Christian faith, a reduction of the Christian faith to the Eucharist. That is, we are not portraying some sort of competition between various understandings of the Christian faith and the Eucharistic faith (acknowledging again at this point that we have not yet addressed the substance of this Eucharistic faith). Certainly, there are conflicts, mutually exclusive theologies, even doctrines, between an array of understandings of Christian faith (speaking both diachronically and synchronically) and what has been and will be the presentation of the Eucharistic faith found in this volume. There is an argument here of what *should* be the Christian faith as it is essentially and normatively identified as the Eucharistic faith. This identification will not eliminate theological or doctrinal conflict. However, by taking theology into the Eucharist, by seeking to understand the Christian faith as the Eucharistic faith, this conflict is ordered towards transformation. Conflict or disagreement among Christians, and indeed among churches, is to be taken into the Eucharist in order to undergo a transformation. We locate our theological and ecclesial, our perceptions and practices of Christian fidelity, within the

Eucharist so that they might become accountable to the essential and normative scope and depth that is the Eucharistic faith. This move is not one more strategy to appease our conscience for the existence of such conflict, not a postmodern move to arrange the 'fragments' of faith so that they take on the aesthetic of a Eucharistic *bricolage*. No, we take our conflicts and disagreements, again both diachronically and synchronically, into the Eucharist so that they may be sacrificed, removed from the grip of our own minds and wills, our own ecclesial identities and traditions, and offered into the hands of the arriving Jesus and blown into a new creation by the Holy Spirit. The point is not what these conflicts and disagreements look like to us, but what they now look like before the Father as an urgent prayer of the High Priest – that they may all be one as you and I are one – and as they have received the invocation of the Holy Spirit to turn our dry bones of faith into a living body, the Body of Christ. The Christian faith is not embedded in ourselves – we do not celebrate the Eucharist in our minds – but rather, the Christian faith is an embodied existence of ultimate identity and purpose. Faith is a God-given vocation and not a human attitude or attribute.

This brings us to the second consideration of the identification of the Eucharistic faith as the Christian faith and vice versa. To obey the command of Jesus to 'Do this in remembrance of me' constitutes a total and absolute commitment to enter into the life that is the Body of Christ. However, we first need to notice and appreciate that word 'obey' and its correlate 'command'. The act of going to the Eucharist is an act of obedience, and in this way, but not only in this way, it is an act of faith. We go to the Eucharist in order to obey the explicit and direct command of Jesus. That is, the primary reason for going to the Eucharist is not because we feel like it or think it is a good thing to do. We do not go to the Eucharist as a ritual aid to our non-Eucharistic lives and our non-Eucharistic thoughts and beliefs. Rather, we obey this command by handing over our souls, our minds and bodies to whatever happens in the Eucharist, to whatever counts as belief here, to the enveloping life and faith that is only encountered here and in this way. Going to the Eucharist is making a lifelong and total commitment to live, think and speak as a member of the Body of Christ. For here and now, at and as this Eucharist, is the enactment of the Christian faith, the embodiment of the life that is 'in Christ'. We cannot be who we were baptized to be and become unless we are here in this Eucharist. And furthermore, against the tides of modern individualism and postmodern location, the Eucharist is where we are located within the Christian faith and not where 'faith' is located in me. We do not decide or determine what the Eucharist is or what the Eucharistic faith is about; we decide whether we are going to obey a command of Jesus, to commit ourselves to live, speak and know what is going on within this Eucharist, to inhabit the Eucharistic faith.

Obeying the command of Jesus to 'Do this in remembrance of me', to commit to inhabiting the Eucharist and the faith that lives there, is not an ethical decision. This command is not just one of an array of actions that Jesus has bestowed on us that comprise a Christian ethical system or a mission strategy. That is, the teachings or commands of Jesus are not detached from him so that we can locate them within our own lives or worlds. This is not a command to follow his example or his teachings; it is not an injunction regarding our behaviour. The purpose of this command is to enter into the presence of Jesus, to abide in him. The essence of the Christian faith is the presence of Jesus, and the presence of Jesus is the presence of the Father, the presence of the Son and the presence of the Holy Spirit: the presence of Jesus is the presence of God. This presence of Jesus is an embodied (not primarily an embedded) presence. It is an arriving presence, or the presence of arrival, within the particularity of this place that exists for the sake of God's presence and agency. The Eucharist is a particular place for a particular presence; it is not to be collapsed into a general view of worship, liturgy or ritual. The Eucharist must maintain its inherent particularity if we are to inhabit the faith that lives there and not fall into a generic faith in a generic Jesus. The Eucharist is above all the sphere of God's agency. The Eucharist is the place prepared for us; it is God's place for us. Yet, God is present here in a way we are not, and we are present here in a way God is not. Our presence in the Eucharist is called faith. Faith then is not so much an ascent to propositions or ethical demands as it is a habitation of this Eucharistic place because this is where and whereby Jesus arrives to give us his life of communion, which is the essence of the Christian faith. Faith is the why, how and what of our inhabiting this place where Jesus arrives to meet us. The Eucharist is the event where and when Jesus is here for us, and we are here for him. Faith is how we act and believe within the gravitational sphere surrounding the arrival of Jesus, realized by the Holy Spirit. This is faith 'in Christ'; faith is 'in Christ'. Therefore, faith is not a correlation or correspondence between ourselves and Jesus, a correspondence that we draw from ourselves towards Jesus. The Eucharistic faith is the Christian faith because it always places us within the sphere of the presence of Jesus. Within the Eucharist, Jesus is not a distant teacher or example, and faith cannot exist unless it does so within the Body of Christ: the historical Body, the ecclesial Body and the Eucharistic Body.

The Eucharistic Faith

The Eucharistic faith is the faith that happens to exist within and as the Eucharist; it is faith that is the mutuality of faithful action that takes place within the Body of Christ. This mutual action of fidelity is enacted between and among the members of the Body of Christ and the Triune agency of God. Faith is the encounter between members of the Body of Christ and the arriving Jesus, and the content or substance of this faith is constituted as a variety of dimensions of the common life they share in the communion of this Body within and for the communion that is God. The

Eucharistic faith is an array of acts and accompanying beliefs that take place as, and exist within, the Eucharist as place, presence and agency. What then does the Eucharistic faith actually look like, what are these dimensions, and what is this accompanying content? It has been theologically appropriate to speak of the Christian faith in a variety of ways. In his thorough and balanced survey of the history and contemporary theology of Christian faith, Avery Dulles offers a series of 'models' of faith that can be identified. These models are:

- Propositional.
- Transcendental.
- Affective-Experiential.
- Obediential.
- Praxis.
- Personalist.[1]

Certainly, as one goes more deeply into these models one will confront substantial differences in the understanding of faith. These differences can be detected by identifying the primary location and purpose of faith. Faith can be located in the human will by acts of obedience or of liberation, or faith can be located in a human disposition of trust. Faith could be a mental adherence to authoritative statements or an experience of an existence or presence beyond ourselves. The basic and abiding theological distinction employed when seeking to understand faith in its many forms, whether they are in conflict or not, is the distinction between *fides qua creditur* and *fides quae creditor*: faith by which we believe, and faith which is believed. There is the basic distinction between faith as an act and faith as content. Does the distinction between faith by which and faith which, between act and content, apply to what we have been claiming of the Eucharistic faith? Are there various Eucharistic versions of our inherited array of 'models' of faith? The short answer to the first question is yes and no, while the abbreviated answer to the second question is just no.

We have stressed thus far that the Eucharistic faith is located within the Eucharist and has an embodied nature and existence, and not an embedded existence within human thought, will or disposition that somehow is to correspond to a sympathetic revelation. We have noted as well that the Eucharistic faith is constituted by the mutuality of the members of the Body of Christ and the presence of Jesus, which is also the presence of God. Thus, by speaking of mutuality, presence, embodiment and of the location of faith within the Eucharist for the purpose of communion, we have already transcended any prior utility of maintaining *fides qua* and *fides quae* as separate spheres of theological understanding. Within the Eucharist there is only one sphere of theological reality, the gravitational (pneumatological) sphere surrounding the centre of gravity (the presence of the arriving Jesus for communion). However, within this one theological sphere, we can entertain the distinction between *fides qua* and *fides quae* as the mutuality of faithful movement between and among the members of the Body of Christ and the presence of Jesus as the presence of God for and as communion. We can employ this distinction in our exploration of the Eucharistic faith because the Eucharist is a series or set of actions; and furthermore, we can speak of these actions as both human and divine. Thus, the usual pairing of faith and revelation as the pairing of human and divine acts and content is transformed into a set of actions by the members of the Body of Christ (and in this way cannot be deemed 'human' only) and by the presence of the acting God who acts towards these members in the person of Jesus and in the person of the gathering, leading and realizing presence of the Holy Spirit. This dynamic of mutual action 'deconstructs' and transforms any of our prior theological categories of faith and revelation that are first established on their own terms and paired with the other.

The Eucharistic faith is generated, maintained and directed by the mutuality of the active presences of the gathered Body of Christ and the arriving Jesus who is the presence of God. That is, the Eucharistic faith is nurtured in its origin, performed through the warrants of its own fidelity and existing for the ultimate fulfilment of its purpose – communion with God – through a set of actions as *fides qua* that live into and for as *fides quae*. These actions are gathering, listening, confessing, interceding, offering, praising, remembering, invoking and receiving. Each of these actions is a *fides qua* that open us into the *fides quae*, which is the 'substance' of the Eucharistic faith. We will proceed to consider each of these actions as a *fides qua* that brings us into the *fides quae* of the Eucharistic faith, and we will do so by the 'conviction' that each of these actions has dual agencies, human and divine. Also, the *fides quae* exists within and as the Eucharist, which itself is the theological sphere of God's revelation. Faith and revelation are not two separate spheres of theological discussion, but two dimensions of the offered and gifted relationship of communion.

Gathering

The initial act of the Eucharistic faith is the *fides qua* of gathering. Members of the Body of Christ gather for this Eucharist.[2] An act of faith is performed for the sake of faith; the going to the faithful place. One cannot have faith or be faithful while staying put in one's life, one's place in the world. This gathering, as the initial act of faith, signifies that faith is not something to be figured out wherever you are, according to your own lights. Faith is not an attribute of the mind or of experience; we do not get to identify faith on our own with our own frame of reference. Faith is an act whereby we enter into the faith that belongs here and now. We have to decide to go where faith is and not to strive to find a faith that is where we are already. We belong in faith; faith does not belong to us. Furthermore, this initial act of faith is a particular action of gathering with other members of the Body of Christ for the purpose of celebrating this Eucharist. We transgress the boundaries of individualism, autonomy, of thinking for ourselves only, the boundaries that died in Christ so that we can share his life. We gather *into* the Eucharistic faith. The *fides qua* of gathering is the *fides quae* of the gathered. Faith is a corporate existence and an embodied knowledge. We believe what is said and done here, which again, is not subjected to the vagaries of an anxiety that really belongs elsewhere outside the Eucharist. This is not to say that the Eucharist somehow provides us with a certainty of mind and will that can be relied upon once we depart its safe moral and epistemological confines. Rather, such a notion of certainty as an assured stability and course of action regardless of circumstances is not an appropriate category for the Eucharistic faith. We gather into this faith with its own actions and language all directed towards a life of communion, the *telos* of praise and love. There is a body of faith here to be believed, to form us as Eucharistic believers. We might put it this way: because we adhere to Christ in baptism we gather to adhere to the Eucharistic faith and life of Christ, in Christ.[3]

We gather for the Eucharist, and we are gathered for the Eucharist. After the creation of the world, God is the gathering God. God seeks to gather the people whom God has chosen, and this gathering is for the sake of being gathered into the presence of God. The new creation begins as a gathering: 'I, when I am lifted up from the earth, will draw all people to myself' (John 12.32). God is faithful to who God is by seeking to gather God's creation into God's presence. Whatever other actions of God we may be considering, along with the profound questions of God's will and nature, we are addressing either directly or indirectly God's fidelity towards us as gathering. The Holy Spirit is poured out in order to lead, to gather us into the Son. This is the baptismal movement, and hence the Trinitarian movement, that brings God and the world together as the faithful movement of God. The *fides qua* of God is the *fides quae* that is God. Thus, we speak of God's will to redeem, to save or to justify, and we are to understand them as some form of gathering. God is then not a distant or apathetic God, or a God on standby to help us with our problems or needs when called upon. The Eucharist is not only where and whereby we transgress the boundaries of an autonomous humanity; it is also when God transgresses the boundaries that belong uniquely to God. Whatever else comprises the content of faith, the shape of this content is gathering or assembly because this is the shape that life in the presence of God takes. God desires our presence, and the revelation of God provides the substance and direction of this presence. Revelation is God's presence to us, and faith is our presence to God. Gathering is the form that this presence takes as the origin, existence and fulfilment of faith as and for our presence in Christ, realized by the Holy Spirit and belonging before the Father. We gather for the Eucharist so that we can be gathered where our voices are joined 'with angels, archangels, and all of the company of heaven'. Yet, before we reach this *teleological* act of praise, the gathering of our voices with the already gathered, and those voices yet to be heard within this company of heaven, we are gathered to hear the voices of faith that have preceded this gathering, and yet are spoken to us now in the present as echoes of the faithful past because they give voice to the future beckoning Word of God.

Hearing

The Eucharistic faith is the *fides qua* of hearing and the *fides quae* of Scripture. Once again, the Eucharistic faith is constituted by both the act and the content of faith. Within the Eucharist we are not to venture into possibilities, speculations and capacities as the currency of our theological discourse. This admonition is especially viable regarding the act of hearing and the content of Scripture. Faith is not something that arises from our human capacity or willingness to hear; we are not seeking to identify and argue for an innate attribute of the human condition that is hearing. That is, we are not laying the groundwork for saying now that we know what it means for us to be hearers, what is there to hear? Or, in stark theological terms, now that we have identified faith as hearing, what revelation is there to be heard? Within the Eucharist, we are considering directly the act of hearing a particular content; the hearing that is faith is the actual hearing of something.[4] We become hearers of the Word when we are hearing the Word: 'So faith comes from what is heard, and what is heard comes through the word of Christ' (Rom. 10.17). However, before we move to the role of this Word within the Eucharistic faith, we can enquire about the act of hearing as a Eucharistic act, an act performed by the gathered Body of Christ. Having gathered, and having been gathered, the members of the Body of Christ progress passively towards the purpose and fulfilment of this gathering, this Eucharist. All further acts are for the sake of being acted upon. All further words spoken are for the sake of hearing another speak. We enter into the disposition before the presence of God that is hearing from God and receiving from God. Thus, we can say that this gathering is for the sake of hearing the Word *from* God and receiving the Word *from* God. There is the faith that claims both that we need to hear from God and that God has a Word for us. Faith is not the capacity to hear but the willingness to hear from God, and faith is adherence in advance (the adhesion to Christ in baptism) to what is going to be heard.

The Eucharist is where and how the Word of God is heard, the *fides quae* that is Scripture. The Body of Christ gathers for the Eucharist and to hear Scripture. Texts from Scripture are read aloud, and these texts come from the writings of the Old Testament, the New Testament and from the Gospels, in that order. The texts that are read are given to this gathering from the outside; they are already chosen as part of the Eucharistic lectionary, the assignment of scriptural texts to all the Sundays and major feasts of the liturgical year. The important point for faith is not how the lectionary is constituted but that there is a lectionary. The texts read are not chosen from within the congregation or at the homiletical whim of the presider. Rather, the texts are given to them to read and hear for themselves and not how a particular text may or may not be 'needed' right now, whether a text is assigned the attribute of relevancy in advance. Questions of what we need to hear now, or what we are interested in, any questions that arise from within the concerns of the hearers, are not criteria for what Scripture will be heard. Regardless of any prior presumed hierarchy of applicability or utility of any text, Scripture will be heard as itself, and not as it might be for me or for us. We will hear Scripture; we will not gather to decide whether we will hear Scripture, and if so, what have we chosen to hear this time, why? Faith is the continual hearing of Scripture without any mediation of need, interest, relevance or evaluation. This does not remove any further act of interpretation or applicability, but it does not allow such acts to be placed between Scripture and its Eucharistic hearers. Scripture is heard for and as itself; it is not another 'ancient text' or 'sacred text'. That is, Scripture has to do with God because of God's speaking and acting agency within it. Scripture is the Word of God because hearing this Word invites us into the presence of God. Scripture is not heard to learn more about ourselves and the world; it is heard to be formed more into who we are, what the world might become, when we hear this Word and offer ourselves into the life so narrated. God is always on the horizon of our engagement with Scripture. The Eucharistic faith is the hearing of Scripture in the hope and expectation that such hearing leads us more deeply into our formation as the Body of Christ and towards the arrival of the Word as the gift of the new creation. This formation and this gift takes place when Scripture is heard as and for the Word of God.

We do not go to the Father without going through Jesus, and we do not go through Jesus without going through Scripture. We cannot separate the arrival of Jesus, either historically or Eucharistically, from Scripture. Likewise, we cannot separate God from Scripture or Scripture from God. We do not approach Scripture as if it is not the Word of God, and we do not approach

God as one who does not already have this Word. Thus, we do not look behind or beyond Scripture, we look through Scripture to see God, 'to give the light of the knowledge of the glory of God in the face of Jesus Christ' (2 Cor. 4.6). The Eucharistic faith is both our act of hearing Scripture and our passage through it towards the presence of God. The Eucharistic faith is also God's fidelity to Scripture, God's passage through Scripture to be in our presence. God is faithful to what we hear from Scripture, and God is the God so heard. God addresses us through the narrative of God's ongoing fidelity to gather a people into God's presence, to be their God. God's presence in history is God's presence here and now. Hearing Scripture forms our faith because Scripture witnesses to God's prior, present and future fidelity to us.

Confessing

The Eucharistic faith includes the act of *confessing* the faith and *the faith* so confessed. While this confession is certainly identified when the Nicene Creed, or one of the other creeds, is recited in the Eucharist, we can regard the Eucharist as a whole as an act of confessing the Christian faith. The Eucharist exists because there is the Eucharistic faith to confess; the celebration of the Eucharist itself is confession of the Eucharistic faith. There was the practice in the early church of teaching the catechumens the basics of the Christian faith 'by handing on the Creed'. The bishop gave them the Apostles' Creed line by line. You were baptized into this faith, the particularities of this faith, and to confess it faithfully for life. If anyone was martyred for confessing the faith before being baptized, they were considered baptized due to this ultimate confession. The Eucharist is never then a *lex orandi* in search of a *lex credendi*. Here, we can speak of how the *fides quae* requires an appropriate *fides qua*. This confession of faith, this content of faith, cannot be forgotten during the various acts of *fides qua*. That is, while the recitation of the Nicene Creed is a direct act of confession, all the texts of a Eucharistic liturgy are to reflect, be accountable to, the content of the Eucharistic faith. In this way, every prayer, and this primarily holds for the Eucharistic prayer, is an act of confessing *the faith*. Again, it has to be stressed, the Christian faith is not an act of self-expression or a way of trying to make sense of the world, and it is certainly not a way to project an agenda for a life and world that we would prefer. The Eucharist is a gathering in Christ where and whereby we inhabit the Eucharistic faith; it is not an aggregate of opinions. We do not go to the Eucharist to share our stories; we go there to confess a common faith.

However, we would misunderstand the confession of a common faith if we presumed this was the same act of faith as assent to propositions. While language is held accountable to what has been given to us as the Christian faith, this language, as Eucharistic language, is an act of witness and prayer, the sacrifice of praise and thanksgiving. The language is how we express what is given to us as faith, and it is language that allows us to recognize that we are still speaking of this faith and not something else. Furthermore, this faithful language as such is not just a witness of our fidelity to God, but is a sign of God's fidelity to us. God has not ceased to be the God addressed by, spoken of, in the Nicene Creed or in the rich and expansive Eucharistic prayers emerging from the fourth and fifth centuries. Confessing the common faith in and as the Eucharist does not mean we always get our language right about God. Rather, it means that through this language, as the confession of this faith, we are addressing the right God; we are seeking the right relationship with this God that is the arrival of Jesus by the power of the Holy Spirit.[5] Confessing the faith does not mean getting the faith right; it means being formed rightly in the faith. Thus, the act of celebrating the Eucharist, while it presumes the prior existence and normativity of the Eucharistic faith, is still how this faith is realized. We do not just sit around and talk about the Eucharistic faith; we confess it in and as our celebration of the Eucharist. The purpose of the Eucharistic faith is not to have something to believe; it is life in Christ, communion with and as the Body of Christ. The substance of faith is for a faithful relationship, but there is no faithful relationship without the substance of faith.

Intercessory Prayer

While indeed there is the Christian or Eucharistic faith, *the faith* to be gathered into, heard and confessed, there is a sense in which this faith remains unfinished or unfulfilled. Since the essential nature and purpose of this faith is inhabiting the place God has prepared for us, to receive the life that God gives us, to find ourselves enveloped by the presence of God, faith is always the movement into this place, life and presence. And when we are there, faith ceases; faith and hope subside, love abides. We remind ourselves at this point that faith is a movement towards and into the life, place and presence God has prepared for us and gives us from God's future, because this is the proper perspective for all the acts and content of the Eucharistic faith that follow gathering, hearing and confessing. If we stopped with gathering, hearing and confessing, our understanding of the Christian faith could easily become overly objective and absolute. We might consider 'the faith that was once for all entrusted to the saints' (Jude 3) as a closed system that we are to guard or protect from any alien intrusion. We can become the God-chosen sentinels keeping watch lest someone trespasses into this faith, someone who does not belong there. That is, if we concluded our understanding of the faith with the acts of gathering or assembly, hearing and confessing, we would be tempted to believe that the place, life and presence of faith is already here where we are now. Fidelity becomes staying within the boundaries of this place established by our gathering, our hearing and our confession. However, within the Eucharist, we do not stop with confessing the faith, we do not enclose where we are and proclaim, 'it is finished'. Instead, we begin to intercede before God on behalf of ourselves, the church and the world; we enter into the prayer of the unfinished and unfulfilled faith.

Every Eucharist includes, in some form or fashion, intercessory prayer, the 'prayers of the people', or the ministry of intercession by the priesthood of all believers. Having heard Scripture, while still confessing the faith, we are called to intercede for others, for church and world, because God's own fidelity towards us is not yet finished or fulfilled. The *fides qua* is the act of praying for others, the act of interceding before God for lives other than one's own, and the *fides quae* is the belief that God is receptive to this intercession and that there is more to God's fidelity 'than we can ask or imagine' (Eph. 3.20). The act of intercessory prayer, as well as the action of the Eucharist as a whole, is a dispossession of the primacy of our own agency, even of our own faith. We no longer regard the world as the arena for our actions or projects, and we no longer have 'faith in ourselves'. The Eucharist is an *askesis* of a *fides qua* and a *fides quae* that would rely on our own actions and substance.

Offering

The Christian faith is not striving for a better or happier life; it is the desire for another life that only God can grant. While this other life is created solely by God's agency, we do not abandon our life in order to receive it. Just as we do not forget the world outside the Eucharist, but remember it in the act of intercessory prayer, we do not leave our life behind when we enter the Eucharist. Instead, we offer our lives to God so that our lives may be lived and known in the presence of God, in Christ, as the Body of Christ. The movement into communion with God and with each other in Christ is the movement of offering. While there is the distinct act of offering within the Eucharistic economy, the offertory of money, bread and wine, the entire Eucharist is an offering to God. The language of offering is one of the primary idioms of the Eucharist. The *fides qua* of offering ourselves to God leads to the *fides quae* of what God does with this offering. The act of faith that is our offering of ourselves is in the hope that God performs an act of faith on what is offered. There is the mutuality of agencies, of fidelities; we offer ourselves to God and God offers us the life of the Body and Blood of Christ.

The faithful act of offering, or offering as the faithful act, is the fulcrum point of the Eucharistic economy. It is the definitive turning away from the 'turn to the subject' towards the turn to God. After this act of offering, all that we are, have been and will be belong to God, and we cannot look back to the more familiar and assuring confines of our own subjectivity. We have given up being the narrator of our own lives. For this offering to be proportional to the offering that we receive from God, it will be a total offering. An appropriate 'offertory sentence' for the Eucharist could be, 'into your hands I commend my spirit'. Faith is baptismal and Eucharistic; it is being buried into the paschal mystery so that this mystery is the life we are raised into, and we offer ourselves without remainder so that we would receive the gift of life from God. Nothing is held back; the gift is abundant life. Our speaking of faith as offering and of God's fidelity of receiving and transforming this total offering of self, allows us to speak of faith in two traditional ways: trust and obedience. Faith is trust in God, but this is not a formless trust within the Eucharist. Faith within and as the Eucharist is not a blind trust, or a trust for trust's sake. The act of offering is trust in God, but it is a trust that emerges from gathering as the Body of Christ, hearing the Word of God and confessing a common faith. And while these acts of faith are not themselves a radical act of trust, the total offering of self, they do provide a background, a context, even a rationale for such an act of trust. While the background of this act of trust provides the context for this act, the foreground of trust is not formless either. Trust in God has a direction and an expectation of what follows. Offering as trust is also obedience to the promising and commanding God; trust and obedience exists as our faithful response to 'Do this in remembrance of me'. Our act of trust is an act of obedience, and this act is not left adrift without the content that is the act of God on and towards us. Offering, trust and obedience have the horizon of the resurrection of Jesus; these acts of faith take place within the sphere surrounding the arrival of Jesus not only from the dead, but from the Father as realized by the Holy Spirit. The closer we get to this centre of gravity that has shaped this sphere of Eucharistic fidelity, the more this place becomes the presence of God for us, the more we rely upon and turn towards God's agency. Offering, trust and obedience is the turn away from the transcendental self to the transformative self, the turn beyond our faithful agency towards the primacy of God's faithful agency. This is the transformative transition from our giving and receiving to God's receiving and giving.

Praising

Arriving into the presence of God having offered our self-referential presence, we undergo the transformation that takes place here and now. The transformation begins with language. We give voice to the sacrifice of praise and thanksgiving. Praise of God is the language that exists solely for the sake of God's presence; there is no linguistic agenda. We sacrifice using language to advance ourselves, to produce meaning, to explain, to control or to express ourselves in any form or fashion. Any language that makes sense elsewhere, any language that seems to still follow the contours of describing reality, that belongs within our contained systems of logic, is cut loose and destabilized in the presence of God. Consider how God is named in the great Eucharistic prayers of the fourth and fifth centuries where we find an awareness of names spoken as if to say God is all these names and yet none of them. The language of praise is the sacrifice of description; it is the acknowledgement of the futility of drawing correspondences between our words and concepts to the presence of God. All such correspondences, analogies or metaphors break down under the weight of the glory of God. This is why, if we broaden our scope of faith beyond the Eucharist, we learn that, within the Christian tradition of prayer and language, praise of God is companioned by silence before God. Our language in the presence of God is just that; it is not language that will get us somewhere or get us something. We are already here. Language in the presence of God is both worship and worthless. The presence of God is the 'content' or reference for our language, which is to say, that praise has no content or reference other than the presence of God. As the 'object' of this language, the presence of God cannot provide a satisfaction or resolution for the speaking of such language. Praise of God does not fulfil itself; it has no terminus; at no point would this language exhaust itself, or would we deem ourselves satisfied that we have said enough. The presence of God is what animates this language and not our attempts to describe this presence.

Thanksgiving

However, arriving into the presence of God through the sacrifice of praise is not a place devoid of content; it is not a *fides qua* without a *fides quae*. This is the sacrifice of praise and *thanksgiving*; there is a substance for which to give thanks. This content is remembering God's fidelity towards the world, towards creation, but especially God's fidelity in choosing a people and seeking to be their God. We remember God's faithful relationship to us, how God has sought this covenanted relationship through history and finally and fully in the sending of the Son in Jesus. Our *fides qua* of remembering, thanksgiving as anamnesis, has the *fides quae* of God's faithful history. We do not remember how we got to this Eucharistic moment. We remember how God got to this Eucharistic moment, and this anamnesis of God's fidelity becomes our anamnetic fidelity. We remember *why* we are at this Eucharistic moment, and this remembrance leads us into a profound trust, Eucharistic fidelity as epiclesis.

Invoking

Whenever we speak of the Holy Spirit, there is the temptation to leave behind the normativity of language and tradition. Faith can become 'led by the Holy Spirit' into new language, new actions, even a new type of faith. The Holy Spirit leads us away from where we used to be, how we were acting and how we understood ourselves as Christians and as church. There is an abiding arrogance to this perspective of 'led by the Holy Spirit' in that there is the presumption that the Holy Spirit is an agent of our own agenda, our own sense of expediency and urgency. This is a Spirit unhinged from history; a Spirit that 'frees' us from the past. However, this open-ended view of the Spirit, this emphasis on freeing us from the past, from the accountability of tradition, and in some cases, a freedom from prior restrictions on our actions and beliefs that have been rooted in Scripture, is not Eucharistic fidelity as epiclesis.

We invoke the Holy Spirit, we ask the Father to send the Holy Spirit over our offering of bread and wine, over the gathered members of Christ's Body, *within* the saving and faithful economy of the Eucharist. We invoke the Holy Spirit from where our thankful remembrance of God's agency has placed us, and the Holy Spirit will not free us from this place, but rather sanctify this place by realizing the deeper presence of God here in the arrival of Jesus, in the giving of the life that only God gives. The epiclesis of the Holy Spirit within the Eucharist is not the movement of leading so much as it is the movement of giving. There is a history of the agency of the Holy Spirit, and while the Eucharist is a thanksgiving and remembrance of this history, the Eucharist is also the event of this agency, an agency that arrives from God's future for us. The realization of God's future for us by the outpouring of the Holy Spirit on us does not remove us from the anamnetic past, the Spirit-driven history that we share with God and with each other in Christ. For our Eucharistic past, present and future are in Christ; we have passed over into the remembered past, the offered present and the invoked future that is life in Christ, that is the life of Christ. And this is the clear purpose of invoking the Holy Spirit within the Eucharist, the fulfilment of Eucharistic fidelity, to live in Christ.

Christ's own fidelity to the Father, the fidelity animated and directed by the Holy Spirit, was and is the living into of the relationship between the Father and the Son. The Holy Spirit drove Jesus into the desert to undergo temptation so that Jesus could realize for himself, and to witness and proclaim, who he is as the Son of God. That is, there is the recognition that 'Son of God' is not self-evident, that there could be various versions of what this Sonship was about, of who God really is. Temptation in the wilderness allowed a clarity and purpose, a vocation and mission, to emerge as to who Jesus is as this Son of God. He is and will be the Son *of God*, the Son *of his Father*. This is not an open-ended and amorphous vocation and mission; it is one ordered both towards us as the one who knows the Father, who speaks for the Father, and as one who is on his way to the Father. The Father is the beginning and end of Jesus. Jesus is faithful to the Father in his coming and going, in his Spirit-origin and in his Spirit-destiny. Our faith in Christ begins with the resurrection, the arrival of Jesus from the dead, and the origin of our faith in Christ is the ascension. It is the ascended Christ who arrives from the Father, who is 'led' to us by the Holy Spirit in the Eucharistic epiclesis, in whom, through whom and by whom we receive the gift of his life of communion. The Eucharistic faith is becoming the Body and Blood of Christ.

Faith and Revelation

Eucharistic fidelity is participating in the fidelity of Jesus to the Father, the fidelity that is the Holy Spirit. Thus, our faith is not our own. We are baptized into the faith in Christ, the faith of Christ.

The *fides qua* and the *fides quae* that we designate as our faithful acts, along with the content of this faith that we confess, participate in the faith of Christ, his faithful acts towards us and towards the Father, his faith in the Father. 'Do this remembrance of me' can be rendered as Jesus commanding us to participate in, to receive, his *fides qua* and *fides quae* before the Father, constituted and directed by the Holy Spirit. This mutuality between, this *koinonia* among, the faith of the members of the Body of Christ and Christ himself is the Christian faith as the Eucharistic faith. Theology serves this Eucharistic faith, and it does so by not allowing self-enclosed categories of theology to become the template for tearing asunder what God has bound together. The categories of 'faith' and 'revelation' are not to be undertaken either as self-referential – faith refers to humanity towards God, and revelation refers to God towards humanity – or as modern or postmodern problems. There is neither the assumption that the content of each category can be explicated in a given and straightforward way, or that we can no longer do so because of outside forces of culture, politics or philosophy. From the perspective of the Eucharistic nature of theology, and thus from the exclusive focus on understanding the Eucharistic faith, there is no self-referential humanity or divinity, and there is no series of theological categories or subjects that must be discussed and arranged if we are indeed to construct a theology. The Eucharistic economy of theology and of faith yields its own concepts, which often go by the names of our customary theological subjects. While this is the case with 'faith' and 'revelation', these two theological realities are not understood here from their respective locations with humanity and with God. Faith and revelation within the Eucharist is a *koinonia* between the gathering members of the Body of Christ and the arrival of Jesus, which are both Spirit animated and directed. Another reason why we cannot allow faith and revelation to be overtly distinctive theological categories, in addition to their expository transformation within the Eucharistic economy, is because we have not yet addressed the theological background and foreground of their existence. We have not yet systematically engaged the questions, what is the Eucharistic life and who is this Eucharistic God? However, while we faithfully avoid doing theology as the construction and arrangement of categories, concepts and subjects that are distinguished from each other, that may or may not rely on their own methodology, theory and sources, we can identify various themes that have emerged thus far in our theological understanding of the Eucharistic faith.

Theological Themes of the Eucharistic Faith

The primary and paradigmatic theme of our exposition of the Eucharistic faith, and therefore, the inherent theme of this faith, is movement. We have portrayed the Eucharist as 'a place prepared for us' by God, as a place that is the normative location of where and whereby we are with God and God is with us, where we are in Christ as the Body of Christ and where the arrival of Jesus takes place. We as the baptized move into this place, and in so doing, we participate in the economy of the Eucharist that is the mutual movement of the Body of Christ with the arriving Jesus, who himself is the movement to us and from the Father. We understand this mutual movement of the Body of Christ among its members and with Jesus, to and from the Father, as the operation of the Holy Spirit. We move into the Eucharist when we gather for, when we are gathered for, its enactment, which is the movement to become the Body and Blood of Christ, the gift of the life of communion shared with the company of heaven. The Eucharistic faith is the movement from the non-Eucharistic exterior of the world into the Eucharistic interior of the Body of Christ. The first movement from this exterior to this interior is the transformation of human subjectivity that is baptism. The second movement is when the baptized gather, and are gathered by the Holy Spirit, for the Eucharist. Having entered into this normative place for faith and for its understanding, the baptized move towards the arrival of Jesus through hearing the Word, confessing this faith, confessing sin, receiving forgiveness and praying for others; it is a movement through Scripture, tradition, conversion of life and prayer.

Once we have moved into this place prepared for us, we can begin to identify the nature of this place, what takes place here, how and why; we can identify the thematic movements of the Eucharist. Along with place, we have been guided by the theological and faithful reality of presence, our presence to God and God's presence to us. However, this presence is not reduced to a presence to each other. That is, we have recognized the theological impoverishment, if not distortion, of speaking and thinking in terms of linear encounters or progressions. Thus, a theme of our exploration and exposition of the Eucharistic faith is to speak of faith and theology as embodied rather than embedded. The Eucharist is the place where there is an embodied presence and not the possible encounter of two embedded presences towards each other. We do not locate our theological point of departure in an understanding of human subjectivity exterior to the Body of Christ. We are not to search for an embedded presence of a disposition towards the possible presence of God, or our possible presence to God. Also, we do not set forth on our theological journey by scouring the world – physical, philosophical, moral or religious – looking for signs of the existence of God embedded there. Rather, we are in the Body of Christ moving towards the arrival of Jesus, towards the gate of heaven. We are moving towards God and not towards the world or towards a better understanding of ourselves located outside the Eucharist. The embodied faith leads us to speak of the revelation of God, the presence of God, as a presence that surrounds us. Within the Eucharist we are enveloped by the movement of God towards and with us, by the movement of God itself. This is why we understand the Eucharist as a place and presence that co-exist as a sphere that takes shape around the centre of gravity that is the arrival of Jesus sent from the Father and realized by the Holy Spirit. This embodied movement is not characterized by addition but by participation, not by possibilities but by potentialities. This sphere that takes place around the arrival of Jesus, this embodied faithful existence, is always a prepared place for us and not a place we construct for ourselves. Put another way, our theological perspicacity is not the goal; the Eucharistic faith and theology abides before the horizon of God.

The theme of embodied faith and theology rather than an embedded one, the theme of sphere instead of linear progression, has led us as well to speak of communion over correspondence. Our understanding of the Eucharistic faith is the imaginative exercise of being in communion as the Body of Christ, and any effort to speak of two persons, subjects or realities will be pursued within communion and not be strategies of how to bring these two entities together. Rather, they are already together within the Eucharist. This is why we have spoken of an *analogia eucharistiae* and of truth as communion and not correspondence. This is also why any theology that remains Eucharistically faithful will not engage in any method of correlation between exterior questions and interior answers. Theological language as Eucharistic language is not the effort to express what is already there, nor is it the effort to speak of a disembodied truth. Theological language is the language the Body of Christ speaks in the presence of God, language that witnesses to God's fidelity towards us and language that is the faithful movement of us towards the arrival of Jesus, who is capable of speaking for himself as himself.

We inhabit the Eucharistic faith; we do not invent it. The primary characteristic of the Eucharistic faith and theology is transformation and not innovation. As such, themes that have emerged for us have been the priority of the concrete over the abstract, the particular over the generic, participation over producing, potential over possible, contemplation over speculation and the present as the arrival of the future rather than a residue of the past. As a life bestowed, as the 'taste and see' of the new creation, the Eucharistic faith is a gift from

God and never a human, nor ecclesial, possession. Faith is not a state of being, nor is it only a disposition towards; faith is expectant, receptive and celebratory. The Eucharistic faith is that movement from anamnesis to epiclesis, from thankful remembrance of what God has done for us to the invocation of what, really who, God will give us now, which is the future prepared for us. The abiding movement that is the Eucharist is moving into the abundant understanding that takes place before the Father, in the Son and animated by the Holy Spirit. It is the movement from:

> So if you have been raised with Christ, seek the things that are above, where Christ is, seated at the right hand of God. Set your minds on things that are above, not on things that are on earth, for you have died, and your life is hidden with Christ in God. When Christ who is your life is revealed, then you also will be revealed with him in glory. (Col. 3.1-4)

To:

> The one who testifies to these things says, 'Surely I am coming soon.'
> Amen. Come, Lord Jesus!
> The grace of the Lord Jesus be with all the saints. Amen. (Rev. 22.20-21)

Notes

1 Avery Dulles, *The Assurance of Things Hoped For: A Theology of Christian Faith* (Oxford: Oxford University Press, 1997).

2 The following reflection of the basic actions of the Eucharist regarding Christian faith parallels the reflection on them in Chapter 2 on the Eucharistic nature of theology.

3 This speaking of 'adhering' refers to the act in the early rites of baptism whereby the candidate for baptism turns away from the world and turns to Christ; they pledge their loyalty to Christ, and thus, there is an adhesion between Christ and them.

4 Thus, I am not following the trajectory of first considering how we are possible 'hearers of the Word' before directly engaging this Word. Here it is clear that this project of a Eucharistic faith differs significantly from the work of Karl Rahner. See Rahner's *Hearer of the Word: Laying the Foundation for a Philosophy of Religion* (London: Continuum, 1994). One could make the fundamental distinction that for Rahner we are *hearers* of the Word, and for Karl Barth, we are hearers of the *Word*. I am closer to Barth here than to Rahner; however, contra Barth, I locate the Word and its hearing with the formative dynamic that is the economy of the Eucharist.

5 Regarding how this relates to the question of 'inclusive' or 'expansive' language in liturgy, see my 'Keeping the Memory of Jesus in our Eucharistic Prayers' in *How Shall We Pray? Liturgical Studies Two*, edited by Ruth Meyers (New York: Church Publishing, 2000).

Epilogue

Going Where We Are Already

Where are we? We have entered the Eucharist; we are within the Eucharist. It is here that we have sought to understand the faith that resides here, the faith that brought us here. Inhabiting the Eucharist, the exercise of our baptismal Eucharistic fidelity, we have begun to be theologically renewed in the ways that we seek to understand this Eucharistic faith through tradition and from Scripture. Our understanding of this Eucharistic faith has transformed how we regard knowledge, language and truth in the presence of God. That is, while we are within the Eucharist, we are aware of the presence of an Other; we are not the only ones here. Furthermore, this presence that is not ours is not a benign or strictly objective presence. Rather, this presence comes upon us, moves within us, has something to say to us, arrives among us, breathes on us and offers us a gift that only happens in the presence of this Other. So, while we have begun to understand our own presence within the Eucharist, we still have not sought to understand the presence of this Other.

The second volume of this Eucharistic systematic theology is *The Eucharistic God*. We have spoken already of this God; we have presumed a theological reality that is this God and no other. We have done so not by speculating about how God might exist, or by offering tentative conjectures about God's nature and will. That is, we have not tried to speak of this God outside the Eucharist. Instead, we have come into the presence of this God because of the arrival of Jesus among us, and because the Holy Spirit has gathered us into this presence and realizes the life we have called the Body of Christ. Therefore, we will seek to understand the God who is present in and as the Eucharist, the Eucharistic God. However, we are not claiming that this Eucharistic God is one way to speak of and understand God. Remember, we are arguing for, we are claiming theologically, that the Christian faith is the Eucharistic faith and vice versa. There is no other God besides this Eucharistic God, while God is not reduced to the Eucharist. We can state this another way by rendering Rahner's axiom about the Trinity for our purpose: The immanent Trinity is the Eucharistic Trinity and vice versa. We will begin to seek our understanding of the Eucharistic God in whom this God arrives to give us the life of communion. That is, the second volume will begin with the quest for the Eucharistic Jesus.

The Eucharist is not an aggregate of individuals coming together to do the same thing, even if they have their own 'personal' reasons for doing so. The Eucharist is the gathering and realization of the Body of Christ, where and whereby each member is joined together into a common life, even if each member shares this life distinctively. God gathers a people; being fully in the presence of God is to belong to the company of heaven. The third volume of this systematic theology is *The Eucharistic Church*. While we will be aware of all the customary subjects of any adequate ecclesiology, we will perceive them within and as the economy of the Eucharist. We will take up de Lubac's ecclesiological gauntlet that 'the Eucharist makes the church', and we will see where this will take us in our understanding of the appropriate life of the church. We will not be offering any Eucharistic rationale or justification for any existing church, any ecclesial institution. Rather, we will seek what the true Eucharistic church looks like, how this church would really and truly live. We will not locate the Eucharist within the church; we will locate the church within the Eucharist. We will see then and there what kind of transformation is called for if we are to become the Eucharistic church worthy of the Eucharistic God.

A word that has been regularly employed throughout

this volume is 'life'. We have sought to remind ourselves, to remember Eucharistically, that the Christian faith is a life. It is not just a way of thinking, believing or doing; it is a life given and inhabited. It is the life of communion, the life that is communion. The fourth volume of this systematic theology is *The Eucharistic Life*. Again, while we will be aware of the usual subjects of theology pertaining to an understanding of life, or Christian living, we will do so from within the Eucharist. What is the life that takes place here? What is the life that does not belong here? What does a faithful Eucharistic life look like? How does the Body of Christ behave? Thus, such theological subjects as anthropology, nature and grace, sacraments and personal morality will undergo a Eucharistic transformation as we seek to understand and to live the Eucharistic life.

What about life outside the Eucharist? What about the world? These are concerns that we cannot ignore if we are indeed faithful to the arrival of the Eucharistic Jesus, to the nature and will of the Eucharistic God. The Eucharistic arrival of Jesus is 'for the life of the world'. The fifth and final volume of this Eucharistic systematic theology is *The Eucharistic World*. We will not strive to give a Eucharistic account of the world as it is; there is no 'anonymous' Eucharistic world. We will ask how the world might be different if it were located within the Eucharist; if there were indeed a Eucharistic world. This is our way of posing the question of the salvation of the world, of the transformation of creation into the new creation. By world, we mean the whole world. What would our political and economic life become within a Eucharistic world? What would our common life look like – we would then have a common life – if gift and reconciliation were at the heart of this life? If we shared the peace of Christ among us and not fought over what the world calls peace?

We have entered the Eucharist; we are inhabiting the Eucharistic faith. Now, let us go and meet the arriving Jesus who offers us his life of communion. Let this life be ours as the one, holy, catholic, and apostolic church, and let us be formed as those who seek only to live the life that is the Body of Christ. And let us never forget that this arriving Jesus comes not just for us but for the life of the world.

Appendix

The Holy Eucharist: The Paradigm That Does Not Shift

The purpose of this paper is both ambitious and modest. The ambition is to present the Eucharist as the central and formative place for theology and for the church. Furthermore, I will argue that the Eucharist is the generative event of the accountable relationship between theology and church, the place where and whereby the ecclesia has a theological life and theology inhabits its ecclesial existence. This is a modest effort because, while I hope to give a sense of this Eucharistic centrality, and of some crucial directions it would take for both academy and church, I am not presenting a full or complete programme or picture of what theology and church would look like if they fully embodied and expressed the centrality of the Eucharist. Of course, we already have such an image or embodiment, the celebration of the Holy Eucharist itself. That is, I am not proposing some startling innovation or dazzling creative manoeuvre; I am engaging where we are already, but also where we are called to be and what we are called to become. In this way, I am speaking of a Eucharistic renewal of theology and church. I will proceed in three phases: the shift to paradigm shift; the Eucharist as paradigm; and the Eucharist as the paradigm that does not shift.

The Shift to Paradigm Shift

In the world of consultants, workshops and webinars, there is a phrase that is probably second in the frequency of its use, following somewhere behind the phrase 'thinking outside the box': the phrase 'paradigm shift'. This phrase is employed as an argument that one cannot believe, think or act the way one has to this point. Things have changed, and depending on the gathering, what has changed is the world, society, culture or some popular rendition of philosophy. And since what surrounds us has changed, the presenters of this argument will exhort the gathering towards changing themselves, and that is why these people are listening, so that they enact the change the presenter will convey. There has been a paradigm shift, and we must shift too. The invocation of the paradigm shift frequently occurs within the church. It becomes the rationale for whatever 'creative' or 'innovative' strategy the presenter wishes to impart that will get the church headed in the right direction, to adapt the church to the exigencies of the times and cultures in which we live. The world has changed, and the church cannot engage in 'business as usual'. Regularly, the presenter, consultant or expert will invoke paradigm shift by appealing to the book *The Structure of Scientific Revolutions* by Thomas Kuhn. This book, which I will consider more substantively later, is credited with the concept of paradigm shift and its significance for our appreciation of how knowledge changes or develops. Briefly, knowledge of something, and in Kuhn's case this would be the scientific knowledge of nature, does not so much progress by increments along a linear path but by 'revolutions' or new ways to perceive nature. That is, our understanding of nature cannot be charted solely on a pure epistemological grid; we have to consider the historical situations by which, and through which, scientists themselves are formed as questioners of nature. Epistemology is historical and communal. As such, discontinuities occur in our perception of what nature is, and these discontinuities lead us, or force us, to form and adopt new ways of perceiving. How we have understood nature is no longer adequate to what we now know about nature. Of course, nature has not changed, but those who study nature have changed. Nevertheless, a change of epistemological models, or a shift in paradigms, does happen.

We might ask, why is it that a somewhat technical study

of the stages of development in the natural sciences comes to play a leading role in a good bit of our church-talk? (Paradigm shift is also a concept employed in academic theology, and the bulk of what I wish to say will operate within this sphere.) The answer to this question is twofold: one, the world is changing around us, and the church is undergoing change of all sorts. Some churches define themselves by these changes, and other churches define themselves by their resistance to change, and ironically, this resistance is changing them. Secondly, we lack the theological substance and facility to respond faithfully to this change. Our ecclesial heritage is one of either ignoring theology or dabbling in some of its more popular renditions. For the moment, what I mean by 'theology' is focused and sustained cognitive and behavioural attentiveness to the things of God. This is not to say that we as the church should try to create and maintain a ratiocinative refuge from all other intellectual adventures. Grace perfects nature and does not destroy it. Rather, I am pointing to the theological void that exists within the discourse of the church, and like all voids, it gets filled by the overflowing pressures surrounding it. If we do not talk of and about God, we will talk of and about other things. We might say something about God along the way, but we tend to do so in the way we have now learned to talk. We have not been formed in proper God-talk, and then talk about the world or the church in that way. Thus we look around for appealing assessments and strategies for what will 'help' us, or what will fix the problem. However, by not being formed in the rhetoric of God, by speaking mostly about the world and the church (and occasionally about God), we have lost the capacity to perceive theologically what is going on, and what fidelity would look like here and now. That is, we can misname our problems as well as our solutions. Above all, the task is not to identify a theological solution to a worldly problem, or to find some God-stuff to plug a leaking ecclesial dam holding the world back, the task is living and thinking and believing from within the proper theological imagination, an imagination that includes the life of the world. Before addressing directly this theological imagination and the concept of paradigm, I would like to outline how change or paradigm shift is an operative dynamic within theology itself.

Theology has a history, and one dominant approach to narrating this history is the delineation of various ages or periods of theology, that is, the pre-modern, modern, late modern or postmodern ones. Note that the appellation of these periods does not belong solely to theology but to all continuous intellectual endeavours, for example philosophy or science. We tell the story by giving it chapters; we narrate history as epochal developments. Furthermore, we have advanced in our naming of history by no longer waiting for a period to give way to another before naming it, and thereby attributing its inherent qualities. Such is the case with postmodernism. Note as well that the naming of these historical periods is due to their proximity to, and difference from, the modern period. For this was the time when we thought we could transcend history or at least shape its course to our will. Thus, we have the perhaps inchoate categories of pre-modern, modern and postmodern theology or theologies. My point is neither laudatory nor pejorative; I am rehearsing some of the basic ways that theology assesses change. Another way that we assign change or paradigm shifts is by identifying various accompaniments to the theological task. In this regard, there is Platonism, Neoplatonism, Aristotelianism or process thought. We can identify a constellation of thinkers or a singular figure who shape much of the theology of a given period. Theological change is wrought by the changing of the intellectual guard. Why this change takes place is inherent within the perception of the basic task of theology. If one views the theological task as the exposition of Scripture, then one's theology is shaped by how Scripture is studied or primarily engaged. If the theological task is making the Christian faith intelligible to others as well as to contemporary Christians, then theology develops along the lines of current modes of intelligibility, how we understand things now. Or, theology could be the exercise of mediation between the Christian faith and its surrounding culture or context. Theology is contextualized; theology and culture mutually influence each other. The theological task can be compartmentalized according to different ecclesial arenas of activity; we can speak of doctrinal theology, pastoral theology, biblical theology, ascetical theology or liturgical theology. Theology is directed towards an area of the church's life, or it can be directed towards an area of the church's encounter with the world, that is, political or liberation theology. Changes in theology, or theological paradigm shifts, can be located within prior assumptions of what theology is and what it should be doing. And the more theology is directed towards that which undergoes significant change, the more extensive the change in theology. Hence, the story of theology is one of many chapters written by several authors each belonging to different times and places. The history of theology is told by those who occupy this history. Where does the theologian belong, what shapes or forms their theology, their paradigm, to where are they primarily directed, and what is considered normative or faithful change? Is there, or could we identify, a normative theological paradigm, a paradigm that endures dynamically, and whose tradition provides the shape of theological creativity?

The Eucharist as Paradigm

In order to speak of the Eucharist as a theological paradigm, or as *the* paradigm of theology, we will need to have a more definitive understanding of paradigm, and then of the Eucharist. In the 'Postscript' of the third edition of *Structure* (1969), Kuhn relates two senses in which the term 'paradigm' is used: 'the entire constellation of beliefs, values, techniques, and so on shared by the members of a given community'; and 'denotes one sort of element in that constellation, the concrete puzzle solutions which, employed as models or examples, can replace explicit rules as a basis for the solution of the remaining puzzles of normal science' (p. 175). Paradigm can refer to a constellation, an aggregate, of shared beliefs, practices and priorities of a particular community. A paradigm is the designated corporate identity in which to locate a community's self-understanding of what it says and how it acts. Is the Eucharist this kind of paradigm for the church? Perhaps a prior question would be whether the church, or churches, is capable of such a paradigm? And if a church were capable of having this type of paradigm, would it want it? The operative word here is 'shared'. What do Christians, what do members of a given church, share? Now 'share' can exist as both content and commitment. Members of the church can have many things in common; there is an identifiable sameness about them, a descriptive sharing. Then there is this type of sharing: 'All who believed were together and had all things in common; they would sell their possessions and goods and distribute the proceeds to all, as any had need. Day by day, as they spent much time together in the temple, they broke bread at home and ate their food with glad and generous hearts, praising God and having the goodwill of all the people' (Acts 2.44-47a). This is sacrificial sharing, the commitment to a shared life. What is common among a group of Christians is not an identifiable sameness residing in thought, attitude or cultural attributes. Rather, what is common among them is the willingness to do what it takes to be bound with each other within the confines of a normative gathering. There is no separation between one's personal identity and this gathering. Sharing is an act of the will, a normative form of faithful living.

Turning to the Eucharist as a paradigm in this sense, we can observe that several churches share the celebration of the Eucharist. That is, several churches have the Eucharist as a regular ecclesial act. While this kind of sharing is certainly the case, can we speak of the other type of sharing, the common commitment to sacrificial living with and for each other. The disunity among the churches would testify otherwise. Even though we have numerous agreed statements on various aspects of Eucharistic theology, we do not have a common Eucharistic life, a life whose principal manifestation would be a regular ecclesial encounter within the confines of the celebration of the Eucharist. (Note that I am not referring to a common Eucharistic rite.) It seems that the Eucharist exists within the boundaries of distinct churches, for how each church defines itself; it bolsters the self-identity of this or that church. This phenomenon can exist at the local level, the parish or congregation, and it can exist on the national and international levels, such as among the provinces of the Anglican Communion or among churches. We can adopt other ways of relating with other Christians, other churches, than the ways of a Eucharistic paradigm. If the Eucharist were a paradigm shared by all Christians, all churches, then we would do what it takes to share a common Eucharistic life. We gain a keener appreciation of this challenge or paradox posed by the Eucharist as paradigm by exploring some of the implications of Kuhn's second version of paradigm.

While Kuhn's first sense of paradigm considered the 'entire constellation of beliefs, values, techniques, and so on shared by the members of a given community', his second sense 'denotes one sort of element in that constellation'. This element is constituted by the 'models or examples' a community will use to investigate remaining questions; they are basic perspectives by which members of the community will identify what the remaining questions are and how to answer them. Put in more familiar words, a paradigm is another way of speaking of what is deemed the nature and method of theology by a church or group of theologians. As theologians, what should have our attention? How do we do theology? What will be the model that shapes and directs this attention and performance? Of course, there are manifold answers to these questions all across the theological landscape. The question I am posing is this: Is the Eucharist such a theological paradigm, and if not, should it be? As the theological paradigm, the Eucharist would provide the model and example for faithful work. Theology would be essentially and inherently a Eucharistic reality. Theology would be the regular exposition and exploration of, the engagement with, the theological implications and consequences of celebrating the Eucharist. By 'theological implications and consequences', I do not mean just those topics customarily found in the texts on Eucharistic theology, for example Eucharistic sacrifice or real presence. Rather, I am referring to all the major subjects of theological investigation, such as God the Trinity, the person and work of Christ, Christian anthropology and eschatology. The parameters and direction of theology are identified within the Eucharist. This does not mean that every possible theological topic or discussion has to be fitted into a Eucharistic mould or jettisoned altogether. Rather, that whatever falls within the purview of theological consideration will be approached from a Eucharistic perspective or with regard to its Eucharistic implications or consequences. The Eucharist becomes the grammar of our theological language, the paradigm of our discourse.

The grammar of the Eucharist is the economy of its enactment, what happens and why when the Eucharist is celebrated. (I will not address the vexed question of how.) The Eucharist is a set of normative actions, and these actions constitute the Eucharist as such. Put another way, the Eucharist is recognized as, or identified by, these actions. They are: gathering, praise, listening to Scripture, proclamation, confession, absolution, sharing, offering, thanksgiving, remembering, invoking, giving and going. Admittedly, each of these actions is realized textually; they display a narrative movement. What varies among the Eucharistic enactments of the churches are the words but not really the actions, and yet these words can still be recognized as Eucharistic texts. Taking the first sense of paradigm, we can say the Eucharist does exhibit a 'constellation' of beliefs, values, and practices that a community, or local church, shares.

However, the Eucharist is not a grouping of texts, beliefs and actions that a community has established for convenience, or because it makes sense for now. It is not a constellation or compilation bound by time and place; it is always already given to the community to perform. The Eucharist is the possibility for a community to enter into the life it presents and offers. I say 'possibility' not because our subjectivity determines the Eucharist's objectivity, but rather because a community can ignore the Eucharistic economy in all aspects of its life outside its Eucharistic enactment. As the paradigm of a community's life and faith, the Eucharist must be appropriated paradigmatically for the whole of this life and faith. This appropriation never reaches any definitive conclusion because what is happening theologically is the community's participation in the life of communion. The Eucharist is the theological economy whereby Jesus offers his life of communion, a life realized by the Holy Spirit and directed towards the Father. If we accept this offer, we will do so only as the Body of Christ; our acceptance is not a reception of something into *our* life previously determined. We are accepted into the life of the Body of Christ, a life we do not create or control. The paradigm of sacrificial sharing begins with offering ourselves into a life that bestows its own proper shape and direction. We yield to this paradigm and no other. The Eucharist is the paradigm of God's life of communion with us, and consequently, it is the paradigm for our life of communion with each other. Are our relationships with each other, within our local churches and among the churches, Eucharistic ones? Do we manifest and witness to the Body of Christ given for the life of world?

Regarding the nature of theology and the first sense of a paradigm as a 'constellation' that is 'shared', the Eucharist provides the economy in which we identify the sources of theology. What is found within the Eucharist and as the Eucharist becomes the basic material and concepts for theological exposition and study. Furthermore, the relationships among the sources within the

Eucharist can guide theological consideration of them outside the direct arena of the Eucharistic economy. The Eucharist has the communal context of the gathering of the baptized, there is the reading of Scripture, intercessory prayer, remembrance centred on Jesus, invoking the Holy Spirit to realize the presence of Jesus through sanctifying the bread and wine and the gathered people, there is the confession of sin and its absolution, the sharing of the peace of Christ, and the reception of what is deemed the Body and Blood of Christ. That is, we can identify the theological subjects of revelation, Christology, pneumatology, soteriology, ecclesiology, anthropology, ascetical theology and even political theology. The Eucharist presents us with a theological curriculum. While the first sense of paradigm is what we study, the second sense of paradigm is how we study these subjects.

As the second sense of paradigm, the model for continued understanding and investigation, the Eucharist exhibits relationships between the various subjects of theology; the Eucharistic economy is the theological economy; how theology works and how we work as theologians. How we approach such fundamental questions as the relationship between Scripture and tradition, or between Christology and pneumatology, would be construed within a Eucharistic perspective. That is, we would pursue a discussion of Scripture in such a way that our discussion originates from the place of Scripture within the Eucharist and is directed towards the horizon of Eucharistic accountability. Certainly, there would be, and is, much to say and to study that does not fall within the bounds of transparent Eucharistic discourse. The principle here is what is our point of departure and where is our destination? As the paradigm for theology, the Eucharist is the answer to both of these questions.

Thus far, I have argued for an appreciation of the Eucharist as a paradigm for the church and for theology. I have done so by drawing on the two senses of paradigm given by Kuhn: as a shared constellation and as a model for understanding. However, this argument is not ontologically or epistemologically absolute.

The Eucharist is not truly and really a paradigm; the Eucharist is the Eucharist. Paradigm is a concept or analytical tool to assist our effort to describe, understand and to reason about something. Something is a paradigm because it is designated and treated as such. While it is appropriate to speak of the Eucharist in this way, to designate and to treat it as the paradigm for church and for theology, we should not yield to the temptation of mastery or comprehension. The Eucharist is not confined or defined by our intellectual pursuits. The proper theological orientation towards the Eucharist is a cognitive *kenosis*, an offering for the sake of discovering and realizing an identity, an openness and response to our vocation, as the Body of Christ. To be the Body of Christ is to inhabit this Body. The Eucharist is never a self-referential exercise in expressing who we are, or would like to be, outside the Eucharistic performance. The primary agent of the Eucharistic performance is the Triune God. The Eucharist is habitation of the mystery of God, and this mystery is not a euphemism for confusion, ambiguity or even the *via negativa*; mystery is the inexhaustibility of knowing. The mystery of God's presence and activity, which cannot be separated, has a faithful shape and direction; to know this 'paradigm', we are called to enter into it, to abide within the contours of formation. Our enactment of the Eucharist is also an act of existential and intellectual displacement. Whatever we take with us into the Eucharist is there to be offered, to be a sacrifice, and consequently, whatever we take with us from the Eucharist is a gift to be shared. God is not contained or defined by the structures of our minds and of our lives, but God does provide the substance and activity of thought and the possibility of life shaped by and for the purposes of God. The Eucharist is God's provision for thought (theology) and for life (church). Our fidelity to this provision, which is greater than anything we can postulate or project as provided, will have a continuous shape, narrative and direction. In other words, the Eucharist is the paradigm that does not shift.

The Eucharist: The Paradigm That Does Not Shift

The theological reality of change is what happens to us and to the world due to God's activity (ongoing) and God's act (singular, although perhaps a regular event). For God's act that changes us to be recognized as such, something will change in our life, a difference between then and now will take place. However, God is not the only possible agent of change or the arbiter of difference. A lot of things change for several different reasons. So, how do we recognize a change that can be attributed directly to God's agency? Recognition is possible within an abiding framework for petition and faithful performance, within a context that is always already one of God's agency; that is why we are here. We can say that the recognition of God's agency, and its consequential change, takes place within the paradigm that does not shift, and thereby not obscuring or distorting the attribution of these acts to God. The construction or adoption of our own paradigm distorts the attribution of agency; we can come to believe that what really and truly matters is what we think and do. Change is not eliminated or avoided, neither is it embraced as a necessary or inevitable result of 'progress' or 'development'. The appreciation of authentic theological change takes place within the Eucharistic economy. This is the economy of communion: God's communion offered to us in the life of Jesus, a communion we inhabit only as the Body of Christ. Practising this change should alert us to the temptations of self-referential subjectivity that lie close at hand when we speak of progress and development. Contemporaneity can be the idol of this kind of self-presence: the human now that must be served.

The movement of the Eucharistic economy is participatory and not progressive or developmental. The Eucharist is the enactment of the movement from non-communion to communion, the movement from *kenosis* to *koinonia*. Our primary and paradigmatic theological concern is not changing times but the time given us to be changed. Temporality allows for the habitual return to God's redemptive act and presence, time to inhabit the contours of transformation, the framework in which change is sought, practised and perceived. The Eucharist is the paradigm that does not shift; and as such, it is where and how theological change takes place. This is where we consume God's change for us and for the life of the world. This is where we are shifted from the fragility of the present to the tradition of eternity.

Index of Bible References

Index of Names and Subjects